I will without reservation, recommend this book to others who ache desperately for a child.
　　　　　　　　—Carole Gift Page, multi-published author

I know of no other book that covers the subject of infertility in such a thorough way.... I'm most thankful for the author's willingness to step out and address the ethical questions couples face in trying to decide, "How far do we go in our desire to conceive a child?"
　　　　　　　—Janet Malcolm, former Coeditor, Stepping Stones newsletter

The first edition of Aching for a Child *sat on my shelf as a trusted resource for couples facing the marital, emotional, ethical, financial, physical, and spiritual crisis of infertility. The second edition of this great guide includes both important updates and an improved reference book for couples as they seek to manage their own treatment. Those who hold a high view of human life as created in God's image from the moment of fertilization will especially appreciate the author's understanding of infertility's spiritual and ethical issues and treatment options that align with their faith. Gruelle leaves readers feeling "We are not alone."*

—*Dr. Sandra Glahn, seminary professor and multi-published author of books that include* When Empty Arms Become a Heavy Burden *(Kregel) and* The Infertility Guidebook *(Zondervan/Christian Medical Association)*

God sees your pain just as he saw mine. He will use this book to speak his love for you. I pray Aching for a Child *will restore your heart in the same way it restored mine.*

—*Jennifer Saake, Author of Hannah's Hope, Director Emeritus, Hannah's Prayer Ministries*

Deb Gruelle delves into the issues of infertility, making the journey easier for those who are walking through the maze. Aching for a Child *is an inspired, thorough, great work in which she shares reliable information, answers, and personal experiences.*

The author approaches the medical and ethical issues from a biblical perspective. She shows what those involved need to consider to make their personal decisions. She highlights the pain of those going through many difficult decisions in attempting to move toward an awaited baby. This book not only explains and informs readers about infertility and assisted reproduction but introduces the idea of adoption, shares practical advice, and gives insights from those who've experienced infertility. It also shows the kind of situations or statements that can cause pain and hurt and how we can stand by those experiencing grief.

I recommend this book for those for whom creating a family does not come easily, for my doctor colleagues who deal with infertility, for pastors and Christian leaders who want to make people feel part of their community, and for those who are seeking God on their hard journey, because they will find questions and answers that will bring them closer to him.

—*Tolnay Lajos, MD, Obstetrics and Gynecology Specialist*

[Deb] shares deeply and candidly from her own experiences about the cycle of hope and grief, and the sorrow of pregnancy loss. To anyone living with the daily ache of infertility, Deb offers encouragement in going through the grief process and coping with the stress.

Aching for a Child also explains various solutions from medical interventions [from] using fertility drugs, to artificial insemination, and adoption. Deb not only introduces them but also examines them from a biblical perspective: What moral dilemmas arise in these decisions? Are solutions possible for couples who don't want to give up their strongly-held convictions? What does the Bible say? And where is God when it hurts so much?

This is a book about pain and lost dreams often carried in silence when we experience a baby's death during pregnancy too. It touches our hearts while sharing the emotional rollercoaster that infertile couples ride and guides us through the labyrinth of medical tests and offered solutions. Its empathic tone makes us feel understood and gives us hope and trust in the love and care of God.

—*Tapolyai Emoke, Psychologist*

With exquisite care and warmth, Deb gives the reader ample opportunity to personalize their journey by answering questions at the end of each chapter and journaling their own rocky passage toward parenthood. As a mother who experienced the loss of my newborn daughter,

Aching for a Child

EMOTIONAL, SPIRITUAL, AND ETHICAL
INSIGHTS FOR WOMEN STRUGGLING WITH
INFERTILITY OR MISCARRIAGE

DEB GRUELLE

Unless otherwise noted, Scripture quotations are from *The Living Bible*, ©1971, Tyndale House Publishers, Wheaton, IL 60189. Used by permission. Quotations marked NASB are from the *New American Standard Bible*. © 1960, 1962, 1963, 1968, 1971, 1972, 1973, 1975, 1977, The Lockman Foundation. Quotations marked NIV are from the *Holy Bible: New International Version*®. Copyright © 1973, 1978, 1984, International Bible Society. Used by permission of Zondervan Publishing House. All rights reserved. Quotations marked PH are from *J.B. Phillips: The New Testament in Modern English*, Revised Edition, © 1958, 1960, 1972, J.B. Phillips. Used by permission of Macmillan Publishing Co. and Collins Publishers. Quotations marked TPT are from The Passion Translation®, © 2017 by Passion & Fire Ministries, Inc. Quotations marked MSG are from The Message, © 1993, 2002, 2018, NavPress. All rights reserved. Quotations marked VOICE are from The Voice Bible, © 2012, Thomas Nelson.

Copyediting: Afton Rorvik, Matthew Bridwell
Cover Design: Klára Karcagi, Harmat Publishers
Cover Photo/Illustration: istockphoto.com

Published in association with Books & Such Literary Management, 52 Mission Circle, Suite 122, PMB 170, Santa Rosa, CA 95409-5370 booksandsuch.com.

Library of Congress Cataloging-in-Publication Data
Gruelle, Deb.
Aching for a child/by Deb Gruelle.
p. cm.
Originally published in 1994 as The Ache for a Child.

Includes bibliographical references.
ISBN 978-1-7365646-0-8
Childlessness—United States—Psychological aspects.
Infertility-United States-Psychological aspects. I. Title.
HQ536.B75 1994
306.87—dc20   03-48902

© 2021 by Deb Gruelle, 2nd Edition, TurquoiseSea Press, Sacramento, CA
© 1994 by SP Publications, Inc., Wheaton, Illinois: Victor Books, David C. Cook
All rights reserved.

The purpose of copyright is to encourage writers and artists to produce works that enrich our culture. Scanning, uploading, or distributing this book without permission is a theft of the author's intellectual property. If you would like permission to use material from this book (other than for review purposes), please contact permissions@achingforachild.com.
Thank you for your support of the author's rights.

Printed in the United States of America.
99 00 01 02 03 Printing/Year 10 9 8 7 6 5 4 3 2 1

2nd Edition
Copyrighted Material

EDICATION

To
Justin, a bloom in the desert,
Nicole, a treasure from afar,
Matthew, a funny, endearing gift
and my "geriatric pregnancy."
And the seven precious buds who never had
a chance to bloom here on earth—what a reunion we will have.

Also, to the Hungarian women
who passed the first edition of this book around,
adding translations between the lines and in the margins,
and called it a lifeline.

And to God, who at a time when my world felt small,
lifted life's curtain to give me a rare glimpse of miraculous things
he was still doing with my little offering of lunch
loaves and fishes.

CONTENTS

Foreword by Jennifer Saake ························ xi
Preface ·· xv
Acknowledgments ································ xvii
Introduction ····································· xix

Part I: Is This Infertility? ························ 1
Chapter 1: Naïve Excitement Becoming Anxious Uncertainty ·· 3
Chapter 2: Longing for a Family ······················ 11

Part II: Can Medical Experts Help? ················ 21
Chapter 3: Deciding to See a Doctor ·················· 23
Chapter 4: Expecting Tests and Treatments ············· 33
Chapter 5: Seeking Biblical Guidelines for Assisted
  Reproductive Technology (ART) ················ 56
Chapter 6: Facing Ethical Issues within Assisted
  Reproductive Technology (ART) ················ 67
Chapter 7: Facing Ethical Issues with Embryos ·········· 95

Part III: Why Do We Ache This Deeply? ············ 125
Chapter 8: Feeling Broken ·························· 127
Chapter 9: Desperately Questioning God ·············· 148

Part IV: Does Anyone Understand? ·73
Chapter 10: Learning to Cope—Self · · · · · · · · · · · · · · · · · · · 175
Chapter 11: Sharing Support—Spouse · · · · · · · · · · · · · · · · · · 192
Chapter 12: Finding Support—Friends, Family, and Church· ·212

Part V: Will We Ever Be Parents? ·241
Chapter 13: Anxiously Hoping—The Apprehensive
    Joy of a Pregnancy · 243
Chapter 14: Grieving the Empty Cradle—Miscarriage
    and Stillbirth ·252
Chapter 15: Adopting—A New Path · · · · · · · · · · · · · · · · · · ·273
Chapter 16: Parenting after Infertility or Miscarriage · · · · · · · ·297
Chapter 17: Living In-Between—Secondary Infertility · · · · · 306

Part VI: Is There Life Beyond Infertility? · · · · · · · · · · · · · · ·327
Chapter 18: Using Infertility to Benefit Our Lives · · · · · · · · · ·329
Chapter 19: Embracing a Family of
    Two –Choosing to Lay Down the Burden · · · · · · · · · · · · 342

Epilogue· ·353
Glossary ·357
Endnotes ·365

FOREWORD

Aching for a Child is a must-read for couples facing the pain of infertility, miscarriage, or stillbirth. I know this because I found it on a day I desperately needed it.

It was after I, a woman who loves the Lord with all her heart, had thrown my Bible across the room, raged in agony, shook my fist at God, and sobbed until I had no more tears to heave. I felt rejected in the area that mattered most to me, both by God (through infertility) and by the news that a single mother chose a different family to adopt her children instead of us. We didn't make the cut. What was wrong with me, with us? I started to seriously and regularly entertain fantasies about accidentally steering my car into oncoming traffic.

Then Mother's Day arrived. I went to church in hope of comfort. Instead, I was blindsided by the celebration of all I was not. My husband spent way too much money trying to show me that he still valued me that Sunday afternoon. He feared that his bride was slipping away before his eyes.

His fears were grounded. I slipped into bed and didn't get up for days except to crawl the few feet to the bathroom. No showers. No care for teeth or hair. Suicidal thoughts.

Then by God's grace, my husband, who managed a Christian bookstore, had a buyer's meeting with a publishing rep. As the rep spread out samples of upcoming new books for Rick to consider buying for the bookstore shelves, one book—this book you're holding in your hands—caught his eye. The very day the book arrived for his store, right at this crucial time of my despair, Rick brought home this book and placed it into my hands. Isn't God good to see our pain and do things like this?

Initially, I couldn't even gather enough interest to read it. Then I scanned the first few paragraphs. Soon my life began to change.

A few weeks later, my copy was already tattered and covered in almost more highlighter marks and tear stains than the original print. The change in me was remarkable. An energized, showered woman now stood before my husband. I read this book many times during the next few months. God astounded me with the similarities between Deb's story and my own. In this book, I found some real tools for surviving the emotional roller coaster and cycles of anticipation and grief.

More important, God was beginning to answer many of my deepest questions, the ones infertility had spotlighted, about what I believed about him. God used Deb's words to start gently showing me that being someone's mom was a God-given desire, that my pain over this unfulfilled longing was rightly profound, yet God never intended motherhood as my primary design. My value was found in being his beloved creation, his daughter. The underlying message of these pages was that I wasn't the only one experiencing this suffering and that God was walking this journey with me.

Six months later, after much healing between us, I mentioned the idea of starting a support group to Rick. We moved forward to start a small monthly group of three or four couples, like the groups Deb had described. My introverted husband wasn't overly eager to bare his heart nor fill our home with strangers, but he was willing.

Jen and Brad were the first couple to respond to the support group notice hung in our bookstore—the same day Jen found her own copy of this book. Jen, a veteran of both infertility and miscarriage, read passage after passage of Deb's words of comfort to me when our first pregnancy miscarried days before we started our monthly meetings. Losing our baby added a whole new layer to our grief, along with a heightened appreciation for Deb's words of wisdom in yet another area of heartache. We decided to call our group Hannah's Prayer (HP).

Shortly after our HP meetings launched, I reached out to the only other Christian infertility newsletter resource I'd found (where I was delighted to find Deb was a regularly contributing author). I sent in an announcement of monthly meetings to be listed alongside other local groups that God was forming around the country. By a divine mistake, our group was announced to their mailing list of thousands as a new *national* Christian infertility network. We started receiving letters from around the world. We started printing and mailing a quarterly newsletter. Soon, we were emailing almost six thousand copies per quarter, many to international addresses. (Our growth skyrocketed when Deb became a regular contributor.)

I had the delight to host our first HP board of directors' weekend. Deb was there, serving on the board to support us. There's no question that Deb's words were integral to God's healing my heart, so I could help others.

I'm so glad this book is updated and available again, because it's been my number one book to share with those with hurting hearts. I eventually went on to write a Bible study book about infertility that focuses on Hannah in the Bible, *Hannah's Hope*, to further this message.

It is with overflowing joy that I recommend this book to you.

I pray *Aching for a Child* will restore your heart in the same way it restored mine as Deb faithfully leads you to the Word of God. God sees your pain like he saw mine and will use this book to speak his love for you through it. Please share with us and others if God uses it to change your life.

—Jennifer Saake, Author of *Hannah's Hope*, Director Emeritus, Hannah's Prayer Ministries.
JenniferSaake.com

Preface

Advances in medical technology have provided many changes in infertility treatments since I first wrote about infertility and miscarriage. The deep hurt though, as well as many of the same questions and issues, remain for those struggling to have a child or experiencing grief over losing a baby during pregnancy.

Thank you to those who requested the 2nd edition of this book and for those who helped with the process.

I've prayed often for those of you reading this new edition, who are struggling to create a family. I've prayed for comfort, hope, wisdom, and that you will see God working for good in your lives while you travel this difficult path. I've met so many amazing people who love God deeply while on this journey. I hope you meet some of these wonderful fellow-travelers too. I pray that ultimately, you will be blessed beyond measure.

Acknowledgments

I'm so grateful to the following people for both the original and this second edition:

Linda Holland for acquiring and Victor Books/David C. Cook for publishing the first edition.

Wendy Lawton, Literary Agent Extraordinaire—thank you for welcoming me into the amazing Books & Such Literary Agency, for your godly example, and for championing my writing. It means the world to me. And to Virginia Smith, fellow Bookie, for her assistance with this 2nd Edition.

Anna Bayer, Editor at HARMAT Publishing—thank you for tracking me down to request that a 2nd Edition of this book be translated for Hungarian readers. Only God.

Those who contributed their time, medical expertise, and experience to this book:

Tolnay Lajos, MD, Obstetrics and Gynecology Specialist, and Tapolyai Emoke, Psychologist, for assistance in updating medical and other portions of this book.

David Adamson, MD, Director of the Fertility and Reproductive Health Institute of Northern California, and Clinical Professor at Stanford University School of Medicine; William Brown, MD, past Chairman of OB/GYN at The Good Samaritan Hospital of Santa Clara Valley, California; Patricia Rogers, MD, Mountain View, California; and Marianne Carter, RN, MFT, San Jose, California.

Those who contributed theological and ethical assistance:

Brian Morgan, Pastor, Peninsula Bible Church, Cupertino; Gary Vanderet, former Pastor, Willow Glen Bible Church, San Jose; Dr. Vernon Grounds, former Chancellor, Denver Seminary; Dr. Alan McNickle, former Professor of Theology, Moody Bible Institute, Chicago; and Steve Zeisler, former Pastor, Peninsula Bible Church, Palo Alto.

For editing: Afton Rorvick, first edition.

Beta readers: Rebecca, Jan, Susan, Valerie, Kathleen, Elaine, and Matthew. Your encouragement kept me going.

For those who shared their pain, dreams, and frustrations in the hope that others would find healing: my WE CARE infertility and loss community of support, those at Bethany Christian Services, and several RESOLVE members.

INTRODUCTION

My intense desire to be a mother made infertility heartbreaking for me. During my struggle, I've identified with the deep distress of Rachel in the Old Testament when she cried to her husband, "Give me children or I'll die!" Genesis 30:1. During the earliest part of my infertility, years ago, I felt so isolated and wished I knew just one person who had experienced the same thing.

I wrote *Aching for a Child* for those of you unable to conceive and for those who are grieving the loss of an irreplaceable baby during pregnancy or at birth. If you're struggling with infertility or if you've lost a baby, know you're not alone. Because many of the feelings and even medical treatments overlap, for the sake of simplicity I often use the general term *infertility* within this book to refer both to technical infertility and the loss of a baby. (I also address the issue of pregnancy loss specifically in chapter 14.)

As you read through this book, I encourage you to record your feelings in a journal to help you analyze and face them. If you're honest, what you write may embarrass, depress, or even scare you, but you should write even when you're at your worst. Later when you look back at what you have written, you'll realize how far you've come. To assist you in getting started, I've included questions at the end of each chapter in a section called "Your Personal Journey." These questions can also be used as discussion starters for a support group. For information on starting or joining a support group, go to: AchingforaChild.com.

I wish there was a way to bypass the grief process that accompanies infertility. There isn't. But in this book I've shared parts of my journey and the experiences of others who have struggled to have children in the hope that you will find encouragement while you work through your own struggles and grief.

Although at times I've felt uneasy about sharing so openly about the most private areas of my life (my infertility and my spirituality), I've chosen to do this in the hope that my words will help those of you traveling the same path. I also hope that this book will guide you to a place of emotional and spiritual strength, where you will grow in the knowledge that God does love you and that he longs to give you strength and wisdom for today as well as hope for your future.

Some of you may be reading this book to learn more about infertility and pregnancy loss to support those who are struggling. Your concern will go a long way in comforting them in their struggle and lessening their sense of isolation.

Some names and personal details in this book have been modified to ensure the privacy of individuals. I have also alternated using masculine and feminine articles (he and she) to avoid awkwardness. For help in defining some of the terms used in infertility, see the glossary at the back of this book.

Part I

Is This Infertility?

1

Naïve Excitement Becoming Anxious Uncertainty

We can make our plans,
but the final outcome is in God's hands.
—Proverbs 16:1

Lord, when doubts fill my mind,
when my heart is in turmoil,
quiet me and give me renewed hope and cheer.
—Psalm 94:19

Two of our dearest friends, Denise and Eric, turned toward the door as my husband, Mike, and I walked in. The cozy floral wallpaper, comfortable easy chair by the bed, and lack of visible medical instruments or antiseptic smell in the cozy hospital room surprised me. Then I focused on Denise, who looked exhausted but smiled with the glow of someone who has just succeeded in accomplishing an enormous task. Eric looked like a man in love as he gently held his brand-new daughter.

Seeing their newborn infant, I recognized for the first time what a miracle a baby is. Before that, I hadn't stopped to wonder at the process. I'd taken for granted that new babies were born all the time. I'd been involved in the day-to-day progress of Denise's pregnancy though and felt privileged, even awed, to be included in the first hours of this amazing new human being's life. She pulled at my heart instantly.

This birth also had special significance for us because of the timing of her birth. We felt an undercurrent of excitement as we held this hours-old baby. You see, we had started trying to conceive two months before and were sure that we would be announcing that a new member of our family was on its way any day. Little did we know then of the years of heartache we would face as we sought that dream.

Mike and I had thought a great deal about starting our family. Though we were young, we'd waited two years after marrying and finally felt the time was right. We wanted to share our love and lives with a baby of our own and thought that raising a child would be wonderful. Our well-discussed plan was to have two biological children and then adopt a child. We were so excited to stop waiting and start creating our family—to finally hold our own baby.

We were so excited to stop waiting and start creating our family—to finally hold our own baby.

We also planned for Mike to go to seminary, and though we knew it would be difficult financially, would there ever be a perfect time to have a baby? In August, we packed up and drove a moving van to Colorado—away from all of our family and friends in California—for Mike to start grad school. I missed everyone deeply, but I consoled myself with the idea that a new baby would soon fill some of that loneliness.

Going about our daily tasks took on a new dimension. It was as if we shared a joyous secret. To others, it looked as if we were going through the normal motions of life, but we knew that we were also working on creating a new life!

We began to plan. "If we get pregnant this month, then…" So many decisions hinged on getting pregnant—my job, the number of classes Mike would take, the size of the apartment we should rent, even the type of insurance we should get. We hoped I would be pregnant by Christmas when we would fly back home and announce the tremendous news to our families.

Instead, although the visit home eased some of our homesickness, it was a difficult Christmas. My sister-in-law was now six months pregnant, but I still wasn't. (They'd started trying to conceive a few months after we had and were successful on their first attempt.) Much of the holiday talk revolved around the imminent arrival of their baby. Meanwhile, we began to feel a growing concern about our ability to have children. We'd so wanted to celebrate and join the club of parenthood with my brother and sister-in-law. I wondered why having a baby had been so easy for others. Why had God chosen to answer friends' and family members' desires quickly but not ours?

I wondered why having a baby had been so easy for others.

One of the presents Mike bought for me that Christmas was a beautiful navy-blue maternity dress with a white collar. As we walked through malls, I had taken to stopping to look in the windows of maternity shops, sometimes gazing longingly and sometimes appalled at the things pregnant women were expected to wear. He said he'd passed a maternity shop window and thought I would be needing a dress like this soon, so he bought it for me. I tried it on for him with a pillow underneath and dreamed of the time when I could wear it. I hung it carefully in the back of our closet to await the time I would need it.

We emptied the linens from my wedding hope chest and began to fill it with tiny socks and soft baby clothes. We bought books on what to expect during pregnancy. I changed my eating habits to ensure a healthy baby—more fruits and vegetables, less junk food. I stopped taking medicine unless it was approved for pregnant women. I eliminated caffeine and began to take vitamins. We adjusted our budget. We began to focus our lives on preparing to include our baby-to-be.

We knew that we might have a slightly harder time having a baby than some of our friends because I had irregular periods. After stopping birth control pills, I had gone for as long as six months without a period, but my cycles were usually every five to seven weeks. After a couple of months with no success, I picked up some basal body temperature charts from my gynecologist to help us determine my fertile time.

We certainly didn't want our lovemaking to become just an attempt to make a baby, so we made a conscious effort to always take time to be loving and romantic in our lovemaking. The doctor said to have sex "every day or every other day around ovulation." We began to chart my time of ovulation and focus on great, romantic sex every day or at least every other day around that time.

If we were at a friend's house during this "I might be ovulating" time, we would yawn at 8:00 or 8:30 p.m. and say, "Sorry we have to leave early, but we need to be going now." We didn't want to tell them we were trying for a baby—we wanted to wait and tell them we were expecting. We knew our friends would understand when we would be able to tell them our happy news.

Living this way was wonderful for a while. People often joke to infertile couples, "Well, at least you have the fun of practicing!" To begin with, putting our physical and romantic relationship as a top priority over other things was wonderful. We could be spontaneous without worrying about using birth control. We felt close and had the added knowledge that we were doing something very important—making love to connect physically, emotionally, spiritually, and create a new life. When we'd have an intimate time of lovemaking, we would share our hope that this would be the moment of conception and that our baby would be born from this expression of love.

The problem was that my temperature was as irregular as my cycles. It was supposed to hover below 98.0° for the first two weeks, dip about four-tenths to six-tenths of a degree right before I was to ovulate, then rise about a degree and remain higher for two weeks until my period came. What my temp did was go up and down constantly by four-tenths to six-tenths of a degree during the weeks before I would ovulate. So, we tried to make sex a priority all the time since we never knew when I might ovulate. (Thankfully, now ovulation predictor tests are much better at verifying hormonal changes that indicate imminent ovulation.)

For four to eight weeks each cycle, we would wonder whether I was about to ovulate, and then I finally would. Then I could spend the next two weeks waiting and hoping that every twinge of nausea might mean I was pregnant. But each time we discovered I wasn't pregnant, the sadness came, and we tried to turn our hope to maybe next time. As the months went by, though, it was harder and harder to carve the hours out of every day. We had other deadlines. I was working full-time. Mike was in seminary and working a part-time graveyard shift before heading off to class. In addition, we volunteered with the high school youth group at church.

Stress began to creep in when my temperature dropped (meaning I might be about to ovulate), but we would have other things scheduled.

As time went on, it seemed we would almost always have something imperative happening during the time. I would have the flu. Mike would be stressed over a midterm or final that required all-night cramming with a study group. Or an overnight activity was planned with the high-school students. To miss the time of ovulation, though, when it might not happen again for a couple of months could be so depressing. (Years later we learned that we were given some false information because typical sperm can live up to seventy-two hours. Having sex every two to three days around ovulation allows sperm to be constantly available to fertilize any egg that appears. But we were doing the best we could with the information we knew at the time.)

As the months dragged by, we started to withdraw from our friends. Who had time for them? Besides, one by one they started announcing that their baby was on the way while we were still having trouble.

We began to fit sex in between our other priorities and plan less time for it out of necessity. At times our focus turned to getting the job done. When pressure was on in other areas, sex began to feel like a pressure also. The sadness began to grow with each passing month that we failed to conceive. We began to worry we might have a problem having children.

Well, I *began to worry.*

Until about a year into this stage, we'd been united in purpose, united in our idea of timing for children, and united in our plan. Now a distinct difference was beginning to emerge. Mike still thought of having a baby as an important but secondary event in our lives that would eventually happen while we were pursuing other things. He didn't see anything to worry about and wanted to give it more time without looking into potential medical issues. I wanted to go to the doctor. I knew that people who had trouble conceiving were called infertile, and I began to realize that we were in that group. For me, it altered my primary life course.

The forcefulness of my feelings amazed me. I know infertility was harder on me than some others. There were many layers of reasons why.

Some infertile couples are able to pivot and say, "Okay, that road is closed, what other alternatives do we have?" They just move on.

For the majority, though, the realization of infertility becomes a deep frustration. If it continues, it also involves a grieving process.

For me, having a baby became a driving force in my life. I began to feel desperate, the desire almost overwhelming me. Seeing my blue maternity dress hanging in the back of the closet began to hurt too much. I also worried that people might see it and bring up the subject. I folded it gently and placed it in our hope chest with the baby clothes, where it would be out of sight.

Daring to Voice the Question

For some couples, the realization of infertility can be signaled by a drastic event, such as a hysterectomy or a semen analysis that shows no sperm. These couples are suddenly forced to confront the issue head-on.

But for most couples, the problem of infertility dawns on them slowly because infertility is diagnosed only by something that isn't happening over a period of time. In the back of our minds, the question forms, *why is it taking us so long to conceive?*

As the months go by, the realization creeps in that something is wrong.

About 9% of men and 11% of women of reproductive age in the United States[1] deal with the crisis of infertility. *Infertility* is generally defined as the inability to conceive after a year of unprotected intercourse (using no birth control) or the inability to carry a baby to live birth.[2] The statistics describe the number of people, but not the emotions and tears behind the numbers.

Deciding to have a baby—to bring a new life into the world—can be a time of dreaming about the future and the changes a child will bring to our life. Even if the decision is made with some apprehension about what some of those changes might be, there is a sense of excitement, of moving ahead in life. When the wanted baby doesn't come through, our feelings of excitement can quickly change to confusion and sadness.

Your Personal Journey

1. How did you feel when you first decided to try for a baby? (Ambivalent? Excited? Nervous?)
2. When did you begin to realize something was wrong? Was there a time when you finally began to identify yourself as infertile? How did you feel?
3. How did others react to your difficulty conceiving? (Your spouse? Your family? Your friends?)

2
Longing for a Family

God made each precious baby
so delicate and small....
And of his many blessings,
babies are the greatest gift of all![5]
—*Greeting Card*

Then God said, "Let us make human beings
in our image and likeness...."
—*Genesis 1:2 NCV*

When you give them your breath,
life is created...
—*Psalm 104:30 NLT*

In our premarital counseling session, our pastor asked my husband-to-be and me the important question, "Have you discussed having children?" He didn't ask the question out of idle curiosity, but because he knew the issue of having children was central to a couple's values, goals, dreams, and view of the world. We were proud when we could answer that we'd thoroughly discussed the matter and agreed that we both wanted three children.

It seemed reasonable at the time but later I wondered why during premarital counseling we weren't also asked to consider, "What would you do if you found out you couldn't have children?"

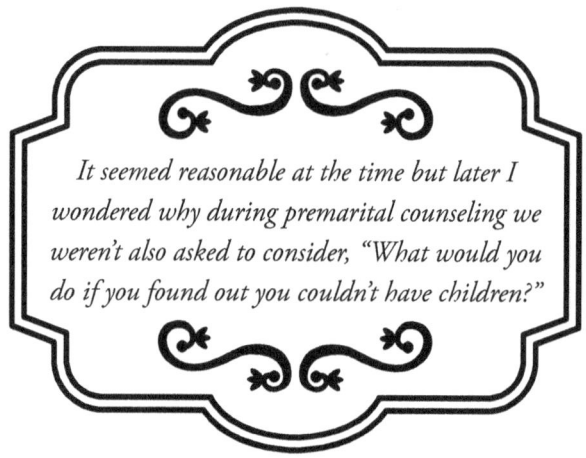

Reasons for Wanting to Have Children

Many positive (and negative) factors influence our desire for children.

As my husband and I became more certain of our infertility, we needed to invest more time, money, and effort into trying to have a baby. We naturally began to reexamine our purpose in wanting children. Our motives were complex. While some were meaningful and realistic, others were laughable. One of my laughable motives was the picture I envisioned as to how my life would change if I had a baby.

I hated the cold, and each winter morning as I shivered while scraping ice and snow off my car at 6:00 before heading to my terrible job in Denver that I hated, I longingly thought of someday in the future when I would be able to stay home with my baby. I dreamed that when that finally happened, I would open the curtains in the morning to see it was snowing, then decide to stay in that day. I would cancel whatever plans I'd made and spend the day rocking my baby and playing with him or her. Maybe I would invite another neighborhood mom over for warm cinnamon rolls and let the babies play together.

In these unrealistic dreams, I hoped that having a baby would help me escape difficult circumstances, unlock better life choices, or give me the excuse I needed to make important decisions to change my future.

Because there are so many reasons for wanting a baby, we benefit from thinking about the underlying reasons for our desire to have a child. How superficial or deep are they? Which ones are based on curiosity? Do any arise from feelings of inferiority? Which ones are part of a lifelong goal in us that motivates us to action? If we're aware of and understand these influences, we can better cope with the dilemma infertility brings. In facing the reasons, we can separate those that are superficial and downright silly from those that have essential worth to us.

This is especially important if we should choose at a later date to follow the path of adoption. Adoption fulfills the deep desire to connect with and raise a child. And Adoption is such a resounding symbol of how God longs to adopt us into his own family. But we often still need to leave room to grieve the loss that our dysfunctional body couldn't carry a biological child. Knowing the reasons behind our desire for a child will help us determine what future action or path to take.

Adoption is such a resounding symbol of how God longs to adopt us into his own family.

We all have multi-faceted reasons for wanting to have children. It's good to explore our motivations. Some might be:

Expectations Within Ourselves or From Society

- A baby would bring a new dimension into my life and make me and others feel that I've become a full-fledged adult. I'm ready to settle down and take my place in society. Starting a family is part of making that statement to the world.
- Like always a bridesmaid, never a bride, I'm tired of being always a shower attendee, never the mom-to-be. I feel like I'm missing out on a big growth part of life.
- A baby would be the needed catalyst for change and growth in our lives. I want to be motivated to grow as a person or couple, to be inspired to new heights by the trust that my own child would place in me. (Or I'm tired of a stressful job and want the freedom to make a change and stay home with a child for a while.)
- I want to fully experience the part of my body that was created for having a child. I would feel more fully a woman (or man) when I have given birth to (or helped conceive) a child.
- I want to have someone to carry on my family name. I feel an especially strong expectation or pressure in my family or culture.
- It's the thing to do. I've always assumed I would have kids. My parents, friends, and society expect it. I might be seen as selfish if I don't have children.
- God intended us to have children in marriage. I consider children to be a blessing from God.
- I feel pressure from my family, culture, or church community to have a child to show we've arrived at a new level of

maturity. There's an expectation that only through marriage and having children can we ultimately please God. I've even heard some churches teach that the salvation of women comes through childbearing. (Like some of these other expectations, this one carries the suggestion that we would be more valuable to others and God if we have children.)

Fulfillment of Belonging to a Child

- I want to share and learn from the spontaneity, rediscovery, and simplicity of a child. They're cute, fun, and inspirational. Children haven't yet built up walls to their hearts. Their emotions are all out in the open. Kisses heal all hurts. They find the joy of life in everything—at least one wonderful thing can be found on any walk or even in the discovery of their toes.
- If I didn't have a child, I'd feel as if I were missing out on something people say is amazing. There's a certain mystique about having a child, similar to the mystique about sex. I want to experience it to see if it is truly as great as everyone says. Comments like "I didn't know what the word *joy* meant until I had my child," make me wonder if there's a level of joy that I've never experienced.
- Having a child is the closest relationship. I want the permanent, secure relationship and tie with future generations that having a child would bring.
- A baby would create a greater bond between me and my spouse. A child would seal our union and be the ultimate symbol of our love. Or, we need a baby as a last-ditch hope to save our troubled marriage.
- I'd enjoy the companionship and friendship a child would bring. Or, I don't want to be alone in my old age.

Transmission of Values

- I want to do something meaningful with my life.
- I want to make the world a better place to live by raising a child with my values. I want to leave something worthwhile in this world when I'm gone (for example, someone who loves God and is compassionate to others).
- I can think of no job more important than nurturing eternal souls.
- I want to nurture, teach, and raise a child. I enjoy caring for others.
- I had a great childhood, so I want to share that example with a child. Or, I had a horrible childhood, so I want to give a child the good I didn't experience growing up.
- I think my husband and I have some good physical, intellectual, creative, or emotional traits that we'd like to pass on to a child.

Unique Influences

Of course, the reasons for having children are as diverse as the individuals wanting them. Unique experiences in our lives can also contribute to our desire to have children. Rich, for instance, longed for a relationship that he missed as a child, "One of the reasons I had always hoped to be a daddy is because I never knew mine."

In Kayla's situation, her previous abortion created an intense desire to have another child within her marriage to help heal her pain and guilt. She said:

> My suffering started with my abortion, so I was obsessed with having a baby. In my mind, that would make things right. I was so relieved and excited when we decided to start trying. I thought it would take away the pain.

Added to these can be the time-frame pressure of a biological clock saying it's now or never.

Created with the Desire to Create

The intensity of the desire to have children varies among and even within couples, but most couples desire to have children. The reasons listed above account for some of the drive to have a child but they still don't seem to account for the depth of loss that infertility can cause. For these people, the desire to procreate is so tied to their values and self-concept that when their ability to have children is thwarted, they still find it inconceivable to see their lives without children. For them, the word *infertility* is devastating. Why is their desire so deeply rooted? Is there something in the basic desire for children that's petty, selfish, or unwholesome?

I felt confused about this when others didn't seem to understand my grief. Like many infertile individuals who chose to share their struggle with others, when I got up the courage to mention our problem to a few people, I sometimes received a blank look that implied that talking about infertility was indiscreet and shouldn't be mentioned in polite society because it was linked to sex or female problems. Another category of response I received was that the problem was incomprehensible to the listener, "What's the big deal? Do something else with your life." When I heard these types of reactions, I began to feel shame that my strong desire for children was inappropriate.

I continued to question why I wanted children so strongly until I studied Genesis one year with my women's Bible study group. When I read the verse, "Then God said, 'Let us make human beings in our image, to be like us'" Genesis 1:26 NLT, I saw it with a fresh perspective. I saw that God had the desire to create new life, and he wanted to create it in his own image. If he, being perfect and complete, had this desire to create, how could it be selfish or wrong?

Since God created us in his image, it makes sense that we also have an innate desire to create life. And because he created us in his image with many of his attributes, it should come as no surprise that we share his desire to create.

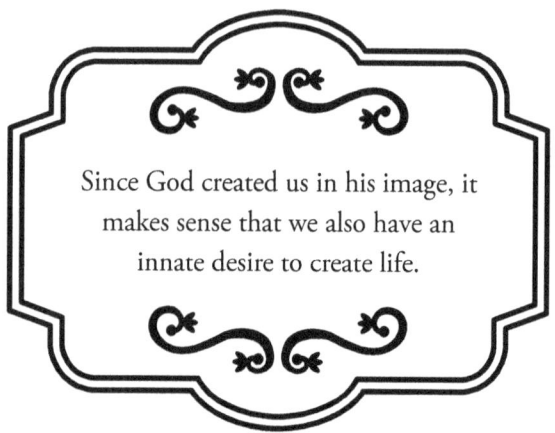

If we yearn to take part in the miracle of creating a new life in our image with attributes like our own and want the intimacy of nurturing our child to maturity, that's only natural. This yearning is God-given and a part of how we're created. It's no wonder that we can feel jarred and confused when we aren't able to fulfill it.

I felt a piece of the puzzle fall into place once I understood this basic reason for my drive. I still struggled with why I wasn't able to have children and how to respond correctly to this obstacle in my life, but I no longer felt guilty for my innate desire to have children.

Some couples choose not to have children. For couples who desire to create new life, infertility can be heartbreaking. If children don't come to us easily, we can choose to go through extraordinary measures to have a child because we have a right to have a child and deserve to have one, or we can work toward the goal of building our family because we believe children are a blessing in God's original purpose for humans. After going to God for direction about our particular situation, we can believe he wants us to pursue having a child.

Are our motives always pure? Of course not. Infertility gives us the chance to lean in though, and look at our many diverse motives for wanting children. We can learn more about ourselves in this process. And just because having children isn't coming easily doesn't mean the longing is wrong.

For me, as the excitement of trying turned into the frustration of no results, I began to search for answers. I prayed constantly for God to purify our motives and keep our hearts seeking him first. And then we started medical testing.

Your Personal Journey

1. What are some of your reasons for wanting children? (Meaningful or silly, positive or negative.)
2. What or who has influenced you to want children? Would you feel any guilt if you didn't have children? (Consider your values, marital relationship, family, society, church culture, friends, self-image, and view of God.)

Part II

Can Medical Experts Help?

3
Deciding to See a Doctor

*I thought that something was wrong when I didn't get
pregnant after six months.
Darius thought I was being obsessive.
Finally, after three years, he agreed to see a doctor.*
—Kayla

Without consultation and wise advice, plans are frustrated.
—Proverbs 15:22 AMP

After six months of charting my resting temperature, the jagged lines made it increasingly obvious that I couldn't predict my ovulation. My resting temperature charts looked nothing like the templates, so I guessed that I wasn't ovulating regularly. I went back to my gynecologist. The decision to seek medical help was easier for me than some because of this obvious physical symptom.

The gynecologist prescribed the fertility pill, Clomid, to stimulate ovulation. Hope sprang anew.

But I was also more emotional as a side effect of this medicine. As months went by, each time I learned I wasn't pregnant, I felt deeper confusion, sadness, and even despair.

Still, we held out hope that a doctor would find the root of the problem and eventually solve it.

Do I Have the Right to Tinker with the Body God Gave Me?

When a baby doesn't come, couples begin to wonder if there is something medically wrong. But because fertility involves mysteries and miracles of life such as sex and procreation, some couples feel or are told that they shouldn't seek medical help.

Another barrier to deciding to get medical help can be the carrot of hope, *maybe if we wait until next month, the problem will fix itself.*

If we begin to delve into possible solutions offered by science, we may begin to wonder, *is infertility a spiritual problem or a medical problem?*

Sara had to deal with this question in her family. She said, "My mom feels that if I was truly spiritual I'd just accept my infertility. But my sister tells me the opposite—that if my faith is strong enough, God will heal me so I'll become pregnant."

Some churches have specific teachings regarding procreative practices (or regarding medical treatment in general), limiting them to a natural process. But generally, most Christian theologians and communities believe that medicine is a gift and grace of God, and we're free to gratefully use medicine to help make our lives better unless using that medicine contradicts any higher guiding principles for our lives that are found in the Bible.

I finally understood that the reasons for infertility were the same as for any other health problem. Someone once gave me the example that infertility is similar to developing cataracts, a condition in which a person gradually loses their eyesight. Medical treatment for cataracts isn't necessary for survival, but if the cataracts aren't removed, the person will eventually go blind and lose a valuable part of life. Infertility isn't life-threatening either, but it does involve important organs in a person's body not functioning correctly. Infertility is a dysfunction of the body that reduces the quality of a person's life.

I finally understood that the reasons for infertility were the same as for any other health problem.

As with any struggle in life, infertility can open us up to God, drawing us closer to him. That doesn't mean that infertile couples are dishonoring God if they seek medical treatment to fix their problem. We are responsible, though, for using extreme care when considering treatments that play a role in creating new life. (For ethical and biblical issues related to medical treatments for infertility, see chapters 5 to 7.)

A well-meaning church member once told me, "If children don't come easily to a couple, they shouldn't go to great lengths to pursue medical treatment but should just adopt because so many children need a family." Well-meaning people are often unaware of the details and intricacies of infertility and adoption, so they may be unaware of the obstacles such as cost, health issues, or the high ratio of couples waiting to adopt compared to available babies in the United States. Also, although it's good during any trials (even infertility) to stop and seek God's guidance, the Bible makes no distinction between infertile or fertile couples in the command to care for orphans (James 1:27).

So, we can listen to wise counsel but not let others make our major life decisions for us. We're responsible for looking at Scripture and listening to God for specific direction about our own life path.

Listen to God first. Ask him to let you only hear his voice through what is being told to you by others.

Getting Started at Home

Some of the most basic steps to investigating the causes of infertility can be done without medical help. You can start investigating through temperature charting, mucus testing, and ovulation predictor test kits. These simple tools focus on finding a woman's most fertile time each month. Knowing for certain that you're having intercourse during your fertile time and presenting your doctor with records showing this over a few months can also speed up the doctor's investigation process later on if needed.

Using Ovulation Predictor Kits

Reasonably priced ovulation predictor test kits can be purchased at pharmacies or online stores. These tests measure the production of the luteinizing hormone (LH) in a woman's urine that triggers ovulation. On the day of the month that this test shows positive, it indicates that ovulation will occur in the next day or two. Ovulation predictor tests may be used over several days until the strip shows positive results. Be sure to use them at the same time each day. This will help to time intercourse for when ovulation occurs.[4]

Charting Resting Body Temperature

Tracking your basal body temperature (BBT) or resting temperature is one of the least expensive ways to track when and if you're ovulating. In a typical woman's menstrual cycle, she has a relatively lower body temperature during the (approximately two) weeks from the onset of her period through the time of ovulation. Then her temperature often quickly drops right before ovulation. After ovulation, the release of progesterone causes her temperature to rise a few tenths of a degree for the (approximately two) weeks until her next period starts.

To track your BBT, take your temperature with a regular or BBT thermometer each morning after you've been asleep for at least four to five hours, and before you move, eat, or talk. Record it in an app or on a graph template. If you ovulate during your cycle, your chart will show two phases. In the phase before you ovulate, your resting temperature should be a few tenths of a degree lower than after you ovulate. Tracking your BBT can help determine when and if ovulation is occurring in your cycle.[5] You can download phone apps or several web templates for this purpose (Search *basal fertility chart* or *basal fertility app* for sample charts or apps to track your BBT.).

When It's Time to See a Doctor

Several factors go into deciding when to see a doctor. After a year of trying to conceive, the odds of conceiving spontaneously show a dramatic decrease. If you are over age thirty-five, have experienced multiple miscarriages, or have reason to suspect a problem, consulting a doctor makes sense after trying for six months. If medical tests for infertility show blocked fallopian tubes or a lack of viable sperm, these tests may save years of wondering if pregnancy is possible and the resulting frustration each month.

In the overwhelming majority of cases, infertility can be traced to a specific medical problem. Professionals can't determine a specific biological cause of infertility in about 15-20% of cases, leading to a diagnosis of unexplained or idiopathic infertility.[6]

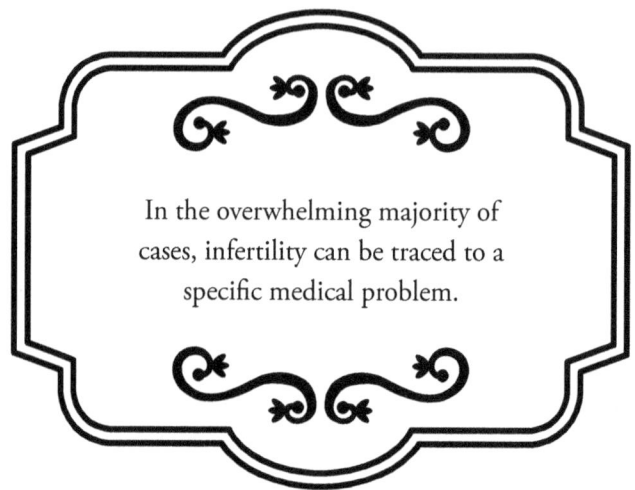

In the overwhelming majority of cases, infertility can be traced to a specific medical problem.

Going to a doctor can be difficult because with that first appointment, we're admitting there's a problem. Other hurdles we may need to overcome are the invasion of our physical and emotional privacy, as well as the sacrifice of money, time, and energy. These are real parts of the infertility investigation, and we need to face them and discuss them with our partners. Remember, we can decide the amount of medical testing and treatment we're comfortable with one step at a time.

Many couples start the medical portion of their infertility journey at the woman's gynecologist for a medical history and physical exam. Because most women of childbearing age may already have a relationship with a gynecologist, this can be an easier way to start.

However, if your gynecologist doesn't usually treat infertility patients, you might choose to see a gynecologist with a specialty in infertility, who is a doctor with additional training to diagnose or treat infertility. Your husband would be referred to a urologist or andrologist for male reproductive testing.

If your infertility problem is more complex, you might go to the next level up—a reproductive endocrinologist, who is a doctor trained to treat more difficult cases of infertility.

What to Look for in a Fertility Doctor

If you have a choice of doctors, look for:

- someone with strong medical credentials and specific training in infertility, who is board certified
- someone who offers a specific plan for testing and treatment, including a total time frame
- someone compassionate about the stress infertility causes
- someone whose manner or personality makes you feel comfortable enough to ask questions
- and someone who will take the time to fully answer your questions

Through interviews or consultations with doctors (on the phone or in person), you should be able to find answers to many of these questions.

If you need help locating a doctor in the United States, RESOLVE is a national infertility organization that maintains a database of fertility physicians.[7]

Questions to ask when deciding on a doctor
Some specific questions to ask a doctor's office staff during a phone interview or to ask the doctor during a consultation appointment include:

- What are the doctor's medical credentials and experience in treating infertility?
- Who performs the actual tests or treatments?

- What percentage of their patients are infertility patients? (This can be an indicator of the amount of time doctors are able to spend keeping up with the latest advances in treating infertility.) If a doctor treats both pregnant women and infertile patients, ask if they schedule infertility patients during specific hours, so you won't need to sit in a waiting room full of pregnant women.

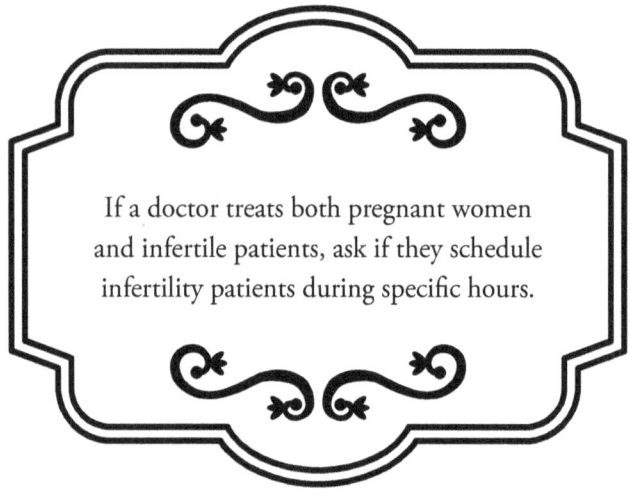

If a doctor treats both pregnant women and infertile patients, ask if they schedule infertility patients during specific hours.

- What range of services does the practice provide? Do they offer an itemized plan with a timetable for tests and treatments?
- What is their price schedule for the costs of routine tests and treatments? (Which insurance plans do they accept? Feel free to ask for any medical procedure codes you might need to verify the coverage amount with your insurance company.)
- How many infertility surgeries (such as laparoscopies or varicocele surgeries) do they perform per year? If you know a type of procedure or surgery you are anticipating needing, ask specifically about their track record for this type of surgery.

- Do they feel comfortable honoring a patient's moral or religious views concerning testing and treatment?
- How available will they be for tests or treatments that require critical timing? Do they have backup coverage? This becomes more important with injectable treatments and inseminations, where close monitoring and timing are critical.

This is also a good time to check with your health insurance to ask.

- Does your medical insurance plan cover infertility tests and procedures with the doctors you're investigating?
- What percentages will insurance cover?
- Are there any limits or exclusions on your coverage? (Coverage for infertility treatment varies widely and may even be excluded.)

Changing Doctors When Needed

At some point, you may feel the need to change doctors. You may find this change difficult because you've built trust in your current medical staff or you fear hurting their feelings. However, good doctors acknowledge their limits. No one can be an expert in every medical area. The best doctors will happily refer you to a specialist when needed.

You may also feel that you need to change due to specific problems with your doctor. Carole, for instance, decided to change doctors after a particularly problematic dilation and curettage (D&C) following her miscarriage. She found that her doctor didn't have the bedside manner and skills she needed to best care for her as she dealt with her body's physical trauma from her miscarriage.

And Vicky found she needed to change doctors because of relational issues. She said:

Our first doctor was terrible. I can't believe we stayed with him for a year. I think he didn't like or respect women. He talked to me like I was a little girl but to my husband like an adult. When I asked about the side effects of a certain drug, he said, "If I tell you, you'll just imagine you have them." He was also rude and rough with the nurses. My second doctor, though, was wonderful and understanding.

Don't feel you have to continue seeing a doctor who won't answer your questions or with whom you're unable to resolve concerns after discussing them. Seeking another opinion from a new specialist might be just what you need. Infertility is stressful enough, so a supportive and knowledgeable doctor is crucial in this journey.

Your Personal Journey

1. Have you spent time alone with God asking him to lead you in your decisions? To what extent have you prayed about your infertility?
2. In what ways do you and your husband agree on pursuing medical treatments? In what ways do you differ? Do either of you have reservations about testing or treatment?
3. What qualities are important to you in a fertility doctor?

4
Expecting Tests and Treatments

The medical procedures for infertility are hard on one's self-esteem.
They're a little easier to bear if your doctor is someone you
trust and respect.
—Dana

I wish we had gone to the best doctor we could earlier than we did.
We basically wasted the first two years.
—Mick

A time to search...
—Ecclesiastes 3:6 NIV

After six months of taking the fertility medicine, Clomid, with continued basal temperature charting, I still wasn't pregnant. The gynecologist asked Mike to see a urologist, who ordered a sperm analysis. When the sperm analysis turned out fine, my doctor prescribed stronger doses of Clomid to make me ovulate more regularly.

About six months later we moved back to California. I started over with a new gynecologist. He told us to continue the now-irritating task of temperature taking, and he began infertility testing on me that included blood work, a hysterosalpingogram, and a diagnostic laparoscopy. During these tests, he prescribed six more months of Clomid. By this time, I began experiencing extreme emotional ups and downs with fatigue as side effects from the Clomid.

From the laparoscopy, the doctor found I had endometriosis, but he said he would be uncomfortable doing the surgery to remove it. So instead, he suggested trying Clomid again. Emotionally, I couldn't handle more Clomid—the side effects seemed to increase the longer I took it.

About that time, I heard of a reproductive endocrinologist who was skilled at and often did the surgery I needed, using newer technology. Since our insurance would cover seeing this new doctor, I decided it was time to switch doctors before the surgery.

When we first visited the reproductive endocrinologist, we felt that we'd finally found someone who understood our struggle and had the expertise to investigate the problem well. We felt he would get to the bottom of the issue, so at least we'd have a more definitive answer, no matter what the outcome. This new doctor was familiar with the latest infertility technology and found that there were some tests we'd missed.

During the consultation, he listened, looked at our records, then outlined twelve steps of tests and treatments we could still do. He then told us that we should know within a year and a half what our chances were of having a biological child. That sounded great. We were tired of the ups and downs of the infertility merry-go-round that just seemed to go on and on. I wanted any issues found to be with me because I didn't think Mike would handle it well if the medical problem lay with him.

The additional tests showed I had a high prolactin level and Mike had a mycoplasma organism. Both my hormone level and Mike's microorganism could be corrected with medicine. The doctor did laparoscopic laser surgery to remove my endometriosis and also open up my right fallopian tube (that had been blocked since birth, but the blockage hadn't shown up on the hysterosalpingogram test).

After a break, I ended up taking a few more cycles of Clomid, and eventually also tried eight cycles of injectable fertility medicines. The whole ordeal of medical testing for infertility frustrated us, wore us out, and took as many hours as a part-time job. But we felt compelled to find out if there was a medical answer.

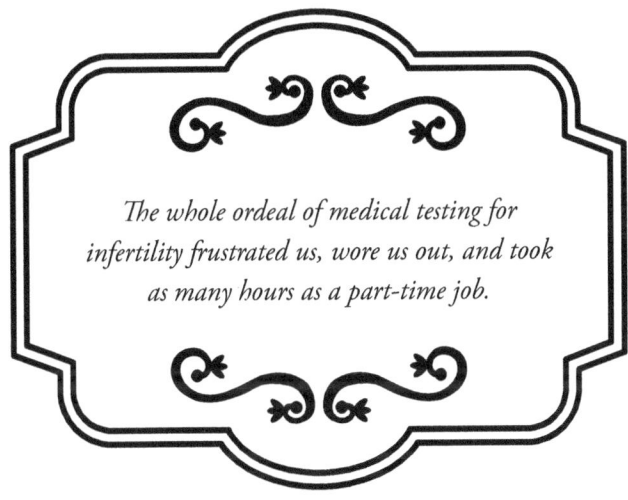

The whole ordeal of medical testing for infertility frustrated us, wore us out, and took as many hours as a part-time job.

Medical Disclaimer

The purpose of the next few medical chapters is to introduce you to the medical side of the fertility process. I share them as a fellow patient, not a medical professional, so they're not meant to be used as medical advice, as a basis for treatment, or to replace consulting with an expert medical professional for any decisions regarding your fertility treatment. I wanted to share these because I often got stuck when introduced to infertility's new five-syllable-word vocabulary. I'd get stuck figuring out and processing the new words or wondering what a new treatment would involve. Often, by the time I'd caught up again to listen to the conversation, the doctor had moved on to another topic. With this introduction, I hope you'll become a savvy communicator earlier than I did.

Some tests or treatments may raise ethical issues for those coming from a Christian viewpoint. See chapters 5 to 7 for further information regarding biblical and ethical issues.

Testing and Treatments

So many factors need to go right for a baby to be created, it's truly a miracle when the process works! Think about it. In a typical conception, the man needs to develop enough sperm with the proper shape, structure, and ability to move. Then the sperm must be released from the testicles through the penis and into the female vagina during ejaculation. In the woman, a mature egg needs to develop and be released from the ovary, then the fimbriae on the end of the fallopian tube need to catch the egg and transport it down the tube.

The sperm must pass through the cervix and swim up to meet the egg. If a sperm succeeds in penetrating the egg, a new life begins. Finally, the fertilized egg still needs to attach and embed in the wall of the uterus. Typically there is a 30 percent chance a fertilized egg will implant. Then a healthy placenta needs to differentiate and grow to nourish the developing baby. The uterus needs to hold the growing baby, and the cervix needs to stay closed until the baby can live on his or her own.

You may have difficulty with infertility if there are any problems with any of the following:

- egg or sperm production
- egg or sperm maturing
- egg or sperm's ability to travel to meet each other
- egg and sperm joining
- fertilized cells dividing correctly
- fertilized egg implanting in the uterine wall

- multiplying cells differentiating (an extremely fascinating mystery—how do some cells know they're supposed to become a nose and others a toenail?)
- or the baby staying put long enough to grow to term and develop well.

Any of these steps can go wrong and can contribute to infertility.

Common Tests for Both Women and Men

The tests for infertility focus on determining where the breakdown occurs in the reproductive process.

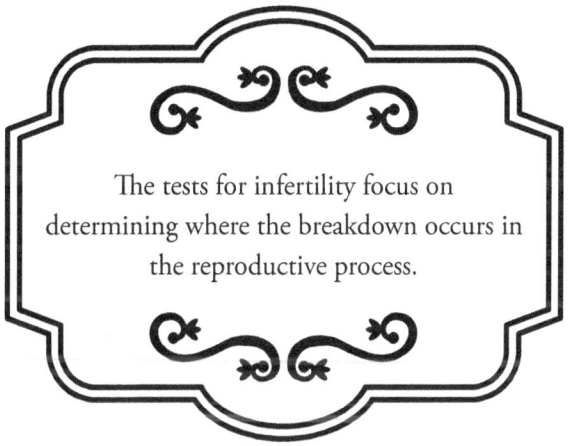

History Evaluation

For a more comprehensive understanding of your specific infertility issues, the doctor will thoroughly question both your and your spouse's medical history. They'll ask about your current health, any symptoms you're experiencing, previous injuries and surgeries, prior exposure to toxins, and previous illnesses and diseases (including those that are sexually transmitted). They'll ask about the use of regular medications, alcohol or tobacco use, and even the health of your extended family members. They'll also be interested in your age, and if you've experienced sudden weight changes, any gynecological screening results, and any prior pregnancies (normal, tubal, or ectopic pregnancies, and any that ended in miscarriage or stillbirth).

After a thorough consultation, history evaluation, and general physical, your doctor should offer a plan for the most important tests or recommended treatments, along with an estimate of how long it will take to complete them.

Fertility problems are divided fairly evenly between men and women. An abnormality can be detected in the woman about 40 percent of the time and in the man about 40 percent of the time. There may be multiple factors involved in a couple's infertility. Doctors recommend that both husband and wife begin testing at the same time.

Note about your comfort during testing: As with any medical tests, feel free to ask about any discomfort that might be associated with any of the suggested tests. (What doctors often describe as discomfort, patients may call pain.) Pain often depends on factors such as the patient's sensitivity, the doctor's expertise, and the use of numbing agents. If you are anxious about pain for any test or know you have a low pain threshold, feel free to discuss these concerns with your doctor before any tests or procedures.

Blood Tests

Blood samples from both husband and wife can reveal a wide variety of viruses and infections that may affect fertility. Further blood work can test the base level of hormones that control maturing of the eggs and sperm, and it looks for any antibodies that might adversely affect the sperm. In addition, blood samples are often tested on specific days of the woman's cycle to check for necessary hormone levels during that time of her cycle.

Tests for Women

Ultrasound/ Sonogram
An ultrasound uses sound waves to create a two-dimensional picture. An *abdominal ultrasound* slides a wand over the woman's abdomen, and a *vaginal ultrasound* uses a wand inside the vagina to create a sonogram image showing the physical characteristics of her ovaries, fallopian tubes, and uterus.

Hysterosalpingogram (HSG)/Hystero Contrast Sonography (HyCoSy)
A hysterosalpingogram or HyCoSy is used to evaluate if the fallopian tubes are open and get a more accurate picture of the shape of the uterus as well. In this procedure, radio-opaque dye is transferred through the vagina and cervix into the uterus. If the fallopian tubes are open, the dye travels up the tubes and spills out the ends at the top, and the test—if an egg can pass through each fallopian tube)—is passed. X-rays are taken during this procedure (in the HSG) or ultrasounds are done (in the HyCoSy) to watch the progress of the dye.

Hysteroscopy
A hysteroscopy looks at the inside of the uterus to obtain information about the shape, inner surface, and mucus membranes of the uterus by an optic scope inserted through the vagina and cervix. This test can also find fibroids, tumors, polyps, adhesions, lesions, or tubal damage.

Laparoscopy
A laparoscopy is an outpatient surgery that's done under general anesthesia. The doctor makes one or more small incisions in the woman's abdomen and inserts a small scope to examine the outside of the uterus, abdomen, and fallopian tubes. During this procedure,

the doctor fills the abdomen with gas to better separate and view each reproductive organ. Minor surgical repairs such as removing cysts, fibroid tumors, scar tissue, endometriosis, or opening blocked fallopian tubes may be done during a laparoscopy. (It can sometimes take between two days and a week to recover from this test. Some women may experience pain in their shoulders from the gas spreading to their shoulders from their abdomen before it dissipates—lying flat can help with this.)

Post Coital Test (PCT) or Hüner Test

This test is less common and requires the wife to visit the doctor within a few hours after sexual intercourse. At this time, the doctor takes a sample of the wife's cervical mucus to find out whether the sperm deposited there are still alive and check on how they're behaving. If the sperm have become paralyzed or very few moving sperm are found, this may identify an incompatibility with destructive cells potentially interfering with vaginal secretions. This may need to be addressed.

Endometrial Biopsy

A small piece of the uterine lining is removed in the doctor's office and then evaluated under a microscope. This tests to see if hormone levels are enabling adequate development of the uterine lining to support a fertilized egg implanting.

Tests for Men

Semen Analysis

This evaluation of the man's sperm is usually one of the first tests a doctor orders in the infertility workup. The semen sample is usually obtained by masturbation (after three-to-four-days of abstinence) in a separate room at the fertility center. Since the quality doesn't remain constant, this test will likely need to be repeated a few times. (See chapter 6 for concerns about pornography use in fertility clinics.)

If collection by masturbation poses a problem or sperm parameters test low, another collection option—using a sterile condom during intercourse—is available. (See chapter 6 for information about seminal collection condoms.)

In a semen analysis, three properties are first analyzed: number, shape, and movement.

- **Number**: The number of sperm counted in 1 ml. of ejaculate. This number can be affected by the time of prior abstinence and other factors, so check with your doctor on these.
- **Morphology**: The shape of the sperm. Healthy sperm are characterized by an oval head, a long tail, and no abnormalities or disproportions.
- **Movement (motility)**: The ability of the sperm to move. Typically, healthy sperm move forward in a straight line or circle.

The WHO (World Health Organization) defines fertile semen values as having:

- a volume of 2–5 ml.,
- a count of male sperm cells of over 20 million per ml.,
- a proportion of well-moving and normal cells as 60 percent, and
- is slightly alkaline (pH 7.4).

Sperm parameters can vary for individuals and regions, so feel free to ask for a urology or andrology consultation to interpret any results found through a semen analysis.[8] If the sperm analysis shows a low sperm count, poor motility, or abnormal morphology, the andrologist or urologist will investigate the issue further.

Other Male Tests
An andrologist or urologist may also perform a physical check of the testicles and epididymis for damage and may perform a rectal prostate exam. If necessary, an ultrasound exam of the penis may check for anatomical differences in the penis, arteries, veins, or changes in the testes. Further tests may be needed to exclude infections, inflammations, or genetic disorders.

Treatments for Women

There's a wide range of treatments for infertility depending on the cause. Here are some highlights of a few of the most common treatments for women.

Fertility Medications
Fertility medications are often prescribed to assist in inducing, timing, or regulating ovulation. These medicines will not help a woman with issues such as blocked fallopian tubes or uterine abnormalities. They can also have strong physical and emotional side effects.

Clomiphene citrate (Clomid or Serophene) is a synthetic hormone pill that is taken to induce and regulate ovulation. Some of the more common side effects of Clomid include mood swings, fatigue, hot flashes, vaginal secretion fluctuation, increase in painful menstruation, reduced cervical mucus quality, thinning of the endometrial lining.[9] Clomid also increases the chances of a multiple pregnancy by about 10 percent, mostly with twins.

Human menopausal gonadotropin (hMG), Follicle Stimulating Hormone (FSH), and Luteinizing Hormone (LH) are injectable medications used to stimulate the ovaries directly. Pergonal (hMG) contains both FSH and LH. Metrodin contains FSH alone. These medications are usually prescribed after a lack of results from oral ovulation stimulating medicines. They require several days of injections that can be given at home by the husband, a friend, or can be self-administered. Medical checkups and regular monitoring of the ovarian follicles are required while taking these medicines. These injectable medicines are pricey, often well over $1,000 per cycle. Possible side effects of Pergonal and Metrodin include mood swings, breast tenderness, and inflammation. A rare but dangerous complication of these medicines can result from overstimulating the ovaries, which can cause abdominal pain, bloating, and in rare cases require hospitalization. These medicines increase the risk of a multiple pregnancy, most of which are twins.[10]

Chorionic gonadotropin (hCG), is a hormone that assists the egg to mature and release from the ovary when it's ready for fertilization. This injection is given when an ultrasound shows the eggs have grown large enough to be mature and is administered before artificial insemination, sexual intercourse, or other fertilization.

Natural Progesterone is often referred to as *the pregnancy hormone* and can be prescribed as a vaginal gel, a suppository, or as an injectable medicine to supplement a woman's own progesterone hormone production. Progesterone aids in preparing the uterine lining and placenta to assist a fertilized egg to implant properly.[11] This medicine is taken after ovulation or during early pregnancy. Some of the more common side effects of progesterone include breast tenderness, nausea, lethargy, vaginal dryness or irritation, and breakthrough bleeding (vaginal bleeding other than at the time of your period).

Bromocriptine (Parlodel) is a pill that regulates excessive prolactin hormone levels. Prolactin is the protein that triggers the start of milk production in nursing mothers. Women with high prolactin levels can show reduced fertility. Possible side effects of Parlodel include nausea, dizziness, headaches, and decreased blood pressure.[12]

Metformin is a pill used to treat insulin resistance by reducing and regulating glucose levels. Insulin resistance is linked with Polycystic Ovarian Syndrome (PCOS) and infertility (as well as diabetes).

Safety of Medicines

Researchers continue to study fertility medicines to ensure safety for the children created with medical assistance. So far, there has been no conclusive evidence that fertility treatments increase risks for future problems for these children later in life.[13] Long-term effects on the mother or child haven't yet been studied because these medicines are still relatively new.

Read any literature that comes with fertility medicines you plan to take so you'll be informed. Search vetted medical sites for the latest studies on a medicine before you take it. You can ask your doctor to refer you to some of the relevant or latest research on the medicine you're considering.

The injectable medicines listed above in particular increase the risk of multiple pregnancies. The more embryos that develop together, the greater the chance of premature labor and embryos developing abnormalities. Multiple pregnancies also raise serious ethical issues, as your doctor may recommend removing one or more of the growing babies. See chapter 7 to be able to identify and think through related ethical issues you may encounter.

Surgery

Besides an operative laparoscopy (mentioned earlier in this chapter) the following surgeries may be suggested.

- A *laparotomy* is major abdominal surgery in which problems with the ovaries, fallopian tubes, or uterus can be surgically corrected under fiber-optic-aided vision.
- *Tubal surgery* involves removing scar tissue or correcting congenital deformities in the fallopian tubes. Because the fallopian tubes are so delicate, the pregnancy rate following tubal surgery is lower than that following surgery on other parts of a woman's reproductive system. This surgery also increases the risk of ectopic (tubal) pregnancies.

- A *balloon tuboplasty* can sometimes open a blockage in the fallopian tube. This is an outpatient procedure in which a deflated balloon is inserted into the fallopian tube to the place where the blockage occurs. Then it's inflated, resulting in reopening the tube.

Treatments for Men

Here are highlights of some of the most common treatments for men.

Lowering Scrotal Temperature

Doctors often instruct men on how to lower their scrotal temperature for better sperm production. This includes avoiding tight underwear and outerwear that is too restricting, saunas, Jacuzzis, and hot baths.

Sperm Washing or Processing

Sperm washing or processing concentrates the healthiest sperm together and reduces detrimental substances in semen (ex., sperm antibodies, that can inhibit sperm from fertilizing an egg). The washed or processed sperm are used with intrauterine insemination (IUI) or other Assisted Reproductive Technology (ART).

Fertility Medicines

Clomiphene citrate (Clomid or Serophene) is sometimes prescribed for men if the underlying cause of maldeveloped sperm is hormonally based. Studies regarding its effectiveness have been divided.

Antibiotics, while not unique to fertility medicine, can assist in curing infections that may interfere with fertility. For instance, gastrointestinal infections can be cured by powerful antibiotic treatments.

If the fertility issue is due to a genetic disorder, medicinal solutions will likely not be available.

Surgery

Laparoscopic varicocele procedure
If the doctor finds a varicose vein in the scrotum, it could raise the scrotal temperature sufficiently to affect hormone production. A higher scrotal temperature can severely damage the sperm being formed. This can often be fixed with a laparoscopic varicocele procedure that takes only ten to fifteen minutes. In this procedure, a small incision is made in the scrotum and the varicose vein is tied off. Two days after the surgery, the patient can return to daily activities.

This procedure can also be done without surgery using embolization, in which a soft catheter is fed into one of the gonadal veins where small coils or balloons can be placed to block off the blood flow of the varicose vein.[14]

Testicular Sperm Extraction (TESE) and Microsurgical Epididymal Sperm Hypersecretion (MESA)
If the sperm tube is completely blocked, not allowing sperm to be released during ejaculation, this procedure, done with local anesthesia and usually without pain, takes the sperm directly from the testicles (TESE) or epididymis (MESA). The sperm is then frozen to use in future IVF cycles.

A Brief Overview of Common ART Procedures

Assisted Reproductive Technology (ART) procedures are the big guns of medical fertility assistance and can raise some complex moral questions. ART procedures need to be treated with more care in decision-making because they're not as simple as other medical procedures. For instance, having a broken leg set doesn't involve many ethical choices. But because ART techniques involve the beginning of human life and the most intimate part of a marriage relationship, they require more consideration.

Some would say that because moral questions need to be addressed, we should condemn all forms of assistive reproduction. This view lacks compassion for those struggling with infertility. I haven't yet found an infertile couple who prefers to go through any non-natural process involving others if they have a choice.

At this time, medical research seems to have invested much more into the development of reproductive technologies that bypass reproductive problems. These solutions manipulate eggs, sperm, and embryos outside of the body rather than solving the root causes of the issues. So, these techniques place reproductive control in others' hands. I continue to hope for more studies and development of technologies that focus on repairing fertility such as tubal repair, hormone balancing, and methods to raise sperm motility.

Even though we may feel assured that God has led us to pursue medical treatment to assist us in trying to have a child, we may face the offer of Assisted Reproductive Technology. So, we'll need to consider the ethical dilemmas they raise.

I've listed several procedures here to think through some of their ethical considerations. This isn't meant to imply that everyone will come to the same conclusions. My goal is for these thoughts and questions to help spark meaningful discussions between you, your spouse, and your doctors.

Intrauterine Insemination (IUI)

An IUI procedure is often used when the cause of infertility is related to low sperm volume or reduced mobility of sperm due to a cervical mucus issue. The husband's sperm is placed in a culture medium, spun in a centrifuge, and the purified concentrate is then inserted into the woman's uterus at ovulation time.

The woman is usually treated with fertility medication along with this procedure to induce and time ovulation (described in the previous chapter). IUI is usually less expensive than In vitro fertilization (IVF).

In Vitro Fertilization (IVF)

During IVF, the woman's ovulation is stimulated by medication, usually injections, for several days. When her egg(s) is/are mature (monitored by ultrasound tests), she receives another hormone injection. The next day under twilight or local anesthesia, a specialist performs an egg (or oocyte) retrieval guided by ultrasound, using a needle through the vagina to suction out (aspirate) each mature egg.

Sperm obtained on the same day are combined in a lab dish with the retrieved eggs. Eggs that fertilize and properly divide into embryos are placed back into the uterus (embryo transfer) within five days using a thin catheter.

With the typical method of IVF, the eggs and sperm are not manipulated once they're placed in the dish, but are left together for spontaneous fertilization to happen. In this procedure, the goal is often to create multiple embryos with the available sperm and eggs.

Expect that you'll need to make decisions about the embryos you may create but don't use in each IVF cycle. You may need to decide whether to freeze, donate, transfer all, or discard/destroy them. See chapter 7 for more on making decisions with embryos.

Other Options within IVF

Intra-cytoplasmic Sperm Injection (ICSI)
ICSI (pronounced "ick-see") may be offered during an IVF procedure to assist fertilization when the number of available sperm is low. The embryologist injects a single sperm directly into an egg.

Assisted Hatching (AHA)
With AHA the embryologist makes a small opening in the embryo's membrane before transferring it back into the woman's uter-

us to assist the embryo to attach to the uterine wall. This is because an embryo that is unable to break through its outer protective membrane may have difficulty attaching to the uterine wall after transfer.

Further Treatments for Both Men and Women

Lifestyle Changes

I hesitate to put this section in the book because studies on lifestyle changes remain mixed. Many couples with extremely unhealthy lifestyles become pregnant quite easily. I also know those experiencing these struggles don't need any additional guilt related to their infertility. I'll add that if common sense or the desire to be around for possible future children motivates us to take better care of ourselves, it's good to lean into that goal during this time.

Medical professionals often recommend making lifestyle changes to eliminate harmful habits, such as recreational drugs, smoking, and excessive caffeine or alcohol. These types of lifestyle changes won't unblock a blocked fallopian tube though.

So simply give yourself permission to be kind to yourself. Allow yourself to prioritize taking care of your body as well as your emotional health through this stressful time. Care for your whole self while you're pursuing fertility by exercising moderately, eating a balanced diet, and finding healthy ways to relieve stress.

Alternative Treatments

Some couples also choose to explore alternative methods for treating infertility. Many other alternative treatments from the mundane to the exotic have been offered to cure infertility since ancient days. A partial list of what I've heard suggested to help infertility includes herbal teas, special fertility diets, acupuncture, homeopathic medicine, chiropractic procedures, relaxation therapy, mega-nutritional supplements, aromatherapy, etc. We can do our own research. We don't need to feel guilty if acquaintances suggest an expensive alternative that we don't want to try.

We need to be especially careful to listen to see if the benefits of a treatment are anecdotal. We can be much more cautious in attempting a treatment that's worked for only one or two individuals and doesn't yet have any double-blind studies supporting it.[15]

Counseling

While infertility is in no way our fault as a couple, we shouldn't hesitate to see a counselor or pastor to help us through this tough time. Seeking support from a counselor can help us address added stress, anxiety, or depression that may come to light during this trying time. Working through these issues can develop a stronger emotional base for the future as well as help us deal with any relational issues between us as a couple.

As in all other pursuits, taking care of ourselves on all levels is important. Becoming aware of the stress we may be feeling and asking to see a licensed marriage and family therapist (LMFT), psychologist, church counselor, grief counselor, or pastor may be helpful. It's worth looking for someone with experience counseling infertile couples who shares our faith to help us feel secure that our faith values are understood and supported. Joining a support group while pursuing medical treatment may also help us deal with the added stress.

Making a careful decision to invite a professional to walk on the sacred ground of our mind and soul includes ensuring that we feel comfortable with their credentials, process, and world view too. Feel free to find a different counselor if you don't feel your counselor is a good fit.

Those who have struggled with anxiety, depression, or other mental health issues before infertility may have already developed the gift of a relationship with a trusted counselor.

If we humble ourselves to ask for help, particularly during infertility's weighty life and identity questions, we'll come out ahead. Wise counsel can help us make good decisions that impact our future and becomes an investment in our relationships.

No—stress doesn't cause infertility.

Yes—infertility can certainly cause stress.

We need to give ourselves permission to take good care of our physical, emotional, and spiritual health during this journey.

Decision Making within Tests and Treatments

Searching for medical solutions on the one hand can renew our hopes, but it can also bring a stab of anxiety because we're stepping into a strange new world. Most couples are diagnosed and treated without the need for the heavy guns of assisted reproduction. Even so, we must consider our moral boundaries and pray about our decisions, asking God for guidance as we navigate the medical issues that infertility thrusts on us.

Infertility testing and treatment is difficult because we need to be informed, confident in our knowledge, and assertive about our choices during a time when we can feel so vulnerable. Information can help us make knowledgeable decisions. If we've asked our doctor about a treatment and don't feel we've received a complete answer yet, we can ask again before moving forward with the treatment. Or, if necessary, we can consult another specialist.

For instance, I was once told that our insurance wouldn't cover intrauterine insemination (IUI), so I asked the nurse again how much this procedure would help our specific situation. I remembered the doctor referring to it previously as *helping a small percentage of couples*. The nurse came back the second time and said it would help our particular problem maybe 1–2 percent. I was amazed. I had guessed that *a small percentage* meant around 35 percent. Knowing this new and much more accurate information, specific to our situation, made it easier for us to weigh the drawbacks against the true benefits. We decided not to go forward with that treatment.

I believe the majority of medical professionals assisting infertile patients chose this field because they genuinely want to help a couple have a baby. But doctors are only people. They may naturally lean toward suggesting their specialty because they know it so well. If the doctor is a surgeon, she may recommend surgery more often than another doctor. We need to be careful consumers and deliberately involve ourselves in the decision-making process.

New medical research is being conducted around the world daily, bringing us new information and possibilities through published studies. Talk with your doctor and check credible internet sites for respected articles and large medical studies (ex., GoogleScholar). Most medical libraries allow access to the public to research medical issues. Some medical libraries have research librarians who can often search the medical literature for you (sometimes for a fee), then send the information to you. (Some of my favorite people are the Stanford Hospital librarians who so kindly helped me research my many medical questions.)

What Financial Challenges are We Facing?

In making financial decisions about medical choices, we can investigate financial issues such as:

- Will medical insurance cover part or all of the test or treatment?
- Is this where God would have us spend our financial resources at this time?

The cost of treatment is a major consideration because the cost can range from a hundred dollars to hundreds of thousands of dollars, depending on the doctors, clinics, and treatments. This is a great time to ask God to guide us in our financial matters as well.

What Physical Challenges are We Facing?
The further we get into fertility treatment, the more our bodies are taxed. Take time before and during treatment to ask:

- How am I feeling physically this month?
- Am I worn out?
- Am I taking care of my body?
- Will these procedures harm my health?

It can be exciting to participate in the cutting-edge technology that reproductive medicine offers. It's also worth noting though, that because the field of reproductive medicine is still fairly new, much is still unknown about the possible long-term detrimental effects of certain treatments (for both adult patients and babies). Until these children grow up and participate in some longitudinal studies, we won't know for sure about long-term effects. If we do our due diligence to learn about each procedure, we can at least rest assured that we've made the best-informed decision we could with the information we had available at the time.

What Emotional Challenges are We Facing?
The emotional roller coaster of infertility can make even the most even-keeled person feel as though the ground is shifting beneath them. And that's before introducing the side-effects of fertility medicines. Infertility often interferes with our life's equilibrium. Before and during treatment, we can check in with our emotions to ask ourselves questions such as:

- Have we been putting enough emotional energy into caring for our marriage?
- Are we strong enough as individuals to handle the grief this month if the hoped-for procedure doesn't work?

- Is our relationship strong enough to handle the grief of a possible failure next month?
- Do we need some more emotional support through this next part of the process?

Questions to Ask Your Doctor about Tests or Treatments

In a stressful situation, we can easily forget the questions we wanted to ask the doctor during our appointment. Many infertility patients find it useful to make a list of questions or items we want to clarify with our doctor before each consultation, test, or treatment. Some questions we might want to ask our medical professional:

- Are there any side effects from this test or treatment? What should I watch for?

  Once a doctor opened up a sample box of new medication, took out the papers inside the box, and threw them away. Then he handed me the pills. When I asked what he'd thrown away, he said, "Oh, those are just alarmist warnings. You don't need them." I silently added, *and don't you worry your head, little lady, I know what's best for you.* I realized then that there had been several red flags with this doctor that indicated I wasn't considered an adult participant in my own treatment. I soon chose to change doctors.
- What will this new test tell us?
- Will the results of this test suggest a new treatment?

  Some tests may be suggested to help find a conclusive reason for infertility, but if we ask this question, we can also consider other factors in our decision such as whether the test is particularly costly. If the answer is that the test result won't change our options regarding treatment, we may choose to skip that test.
- How many patients in your practice are currently undergoing this treatment?

- How many have my particular infertility problem?
- Has this treatment been shown to improve pregnancy rates for other couples in our situation? What percentage has it helped?
  We may or may not want to be one of the first patients to try a new procedure.
- How many live births have happened as a result of this treatment?
  This is such an important, definitive question.
- Where can I find reliable, accurate, and unbiased literature to more fully explain the new tests and treatments you're suggesting?
- If your spouse can't attend an appointment, ask if you can record your appointment to help you communicate with your spouse. For key appointments, try to attend together with your spouse.

Your Personal Journey

1. How far are you and your spouse willing to go to pursue medical solutions mentioned in this chapter before pursuing other options?
2. Is either of you making any sacrifices to become pregnant for which you currently don't have a sense of peace? Will either of you resent your current treatment if your outcome isn't what you hope for? Write these issues down to ask God for guidance on them.
3. Can each of you identify another support person or prayer partner (besides each other) who might be willing to walk alongside you and pray for you as you begin or walk through the medical process? Identify one person each and take the step to ask for their support.

5
Seeking Biblical Guidelines for Assisted Reproductive Technology (ART)

*Give me discernment
that I may understand your statutes.*
—*Psalm 119:125*

*He that always gives way to others
will end in having no principles of his own.*
—*Aesop*

When we first started trying for children, I believed this goal was a God-honoring pursuit. I hoped the children we created would honor God too. Stepping into the world of Assisted Reproductive Technology, we faced new and tricky ethical questions at several points. It was a learning process to work out our desire to honor God within this new process.

I love the stories about how Johann Sebastian Bach longed to honor God in his process of creating. I admire that Bach prayed before writing each piece of music. He prayed, "Jesus, help me show your glory through the music I write. May it bring you joy even as it brings joy to your people." Bach wrote Jesu Juva, Latin for, Jesus, help! at the top of his pages before he started writing his music. When he felt the song was complete, he wrote the letters SDG at the bottom of the page for Soli Deo Gloria—for the Glory of God Alone.[16]

I felt the same way about wanting to honor God through each step of this adventure to try to create life. If Bach could ask for this kind of help in creating music, surely we could ask for the same kind of help in attempting to create life. As we embarked on this new leg of our infertility journey toward Assisted Reproductive Technology, I was drawn to look more deeply at scriptural principles for creating life. I knew I wanted to be praying for God's help in each decision we'd need to make.

Where Do We Find Help?

Since medical help for infertility wasn't available when the Bible was written, could it offer us any help in making decisions about our options for treating infertility?

There's a major difference between theoretical discussions about assisted reproductive techniques versus the ethical choices we as infertile couples need to make as we walk through medical treatments. Our choices can directly affect our futures. Our dilemmas don't revolve around growing a baby in a cow's stomach or creating a super race, but as Christians, we want to know if it's within our moral bounds to use medical technology to help us have a baby.

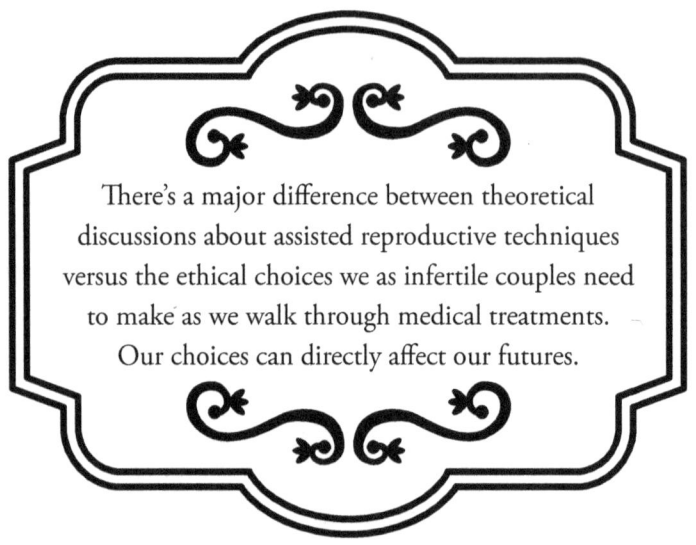

There's a major difference between theoretical discussions about assisted reproductive techniques versus the ethical choices we as infertile couples need to make as we walk through medical treatments. Our choices can directly affect our futures.

When I was right on the brink of another failed cycle or was feeling emotionally fragile from fertility drugs, I found that making a good moral choice was more difficult than I ever dreamed it would be. That was compounded by the knowledge that my time for having children was limited.

My purpose for including this chapter isn't to give final answers to all the theoretical ethical dilemmas, but to touch on some ethical issues you might encounter. Hopefully, this will allow you the chance to think through some biblical principles and determine your convictions before you need to make a quick decision during a time that may be highly emotional.

A doctor I visited once told me, "I think religion has no place in medicine. It should be kept totally separate." He didn't understand that for Christians, their awareness of God permeates their lives, and they can't separate or ignore the spiritual consequences of their actions.

On the other hand, the author of another Christian book I read stated that all Assisted Reproductive Technology (ART) was improper, implying that the less a couple did medically to have a child, the more spiritual they were. I don't find a biblical basis for this viewpoint either. I believe Christians can find help in making ethical decisions for using ART both by studying what God says in the Bible about creating life and by praying to ask God for his wisdom to align our hearts with his.

The Bible isn't definitive on some of the ethical issues of infertility testing and treatment, so there is room for disagreement about some choices. But the Bible can be used for guidance to explore several of the gray areas.

Biblical Principles and Guidelines

In looking for direct biblical instructions on infertility testing, treatment, and assisted reproduction, I did deep research. When I looked at several concordances under *Assisted Reproductive Technology*, I hoped to find the subject listed. I wanted to find a directive, such as "*Conceptions* 28:13, 'Do not participate in using in vitro fertilization to create life unless it is before sundown on the Sabbath. Fertilize no more than two eggs and replace them within seventy-two hours without tampering with them. If you do this, it shall be well with your household, and your quiver will be made full.'"

I didn't find that. But I did find some key biblical principles that apply to bringing life into the world, marriage, our intentions, and what to consider when our decisions affect others.

Human Life

God gives life and is ultimately in charge of creating life.
"The Lord God formed a man's body...and breathed into it the breath of life. And man became a living person" Genesis 2:7.

"He himself gives life and breath to everything" Acts 17:25.

Even before birth, God values each human life, knows it intimately, and has a purpose for it.
The verses below show God's connection with each soul and that his planned purpose for each person starts before birth or even conception.

God said to Jeremiah that he had planned his life and had a purpose for it before he was born. "Before I formed you in the womb I knew you, before you were born I set you apart" Jeremiah 1:5 NIV.

David said to God, "All the days ordained for me were written in Your book before one of them came to be" Psalm 139:16 NIV.

In Luke1:36, the angel told Mary that Elizabeth was in her sixth month of pregnancy. Mary left right after conceiving Jesus to visit Elizabeth. In verses 41-44, Elizabeth said to Mary, "As soon as the sound of your greeting reached my ears, the baby in my womb leaped for joy" NIV. So when Mary and Elizabeth saw each other, Elizabeth's baby (John the Baptist) was spiritually aware of Mary's baby (Jesus) who had just been conceived.

Each human being is created in God's image and so has incalculable value.
"Then God said, 'Let Us make man in Our image, according to Our likeness'" Genesis 1:26 NASB.

"Not one sparrow… can fall to the ground without your Father knowing it. And the very hairs of your head are all numbered. So, don't worry! You are more valuable to him than many sparrows" Matthew 10:29–31.

"God loved the world so much that he gave his only Son so that anyone who believes in him shall not perish but have eternal life" John 3:16.

God created people as eternal beings.
"Jesus told her, … 'He is given eternal life for believing in Me and shall never perish'" John 11:25–26.

"God has given us eternal life" 1 John 5:11.

Marriage

Marriage is given to us as a picture of God's love for us, so anything that would damage that image of God's faithful and pure love for us is warned against.
Emotional and physical fidelity is essential to a Christian marriage. God considers sexual relations outside of marriage to be damaging.

"God will rejoice over you as a bridegroom with his bride" Isaiah 62:5.

"Honor your marriage and its vows, and be pure; for God will surely punish all those who are immoral or commit adultery" Hebrews 13:4.

God originally linked the act of intimacy, of two becoming one, with procreation.
God created man and woman and instructed them to be fruitful. Sexual union is much more than a way to bring genetic material to life. Marriage includes the emotional, spiritual, and relational bond that God wants to grow into a beautiful picture of his love.

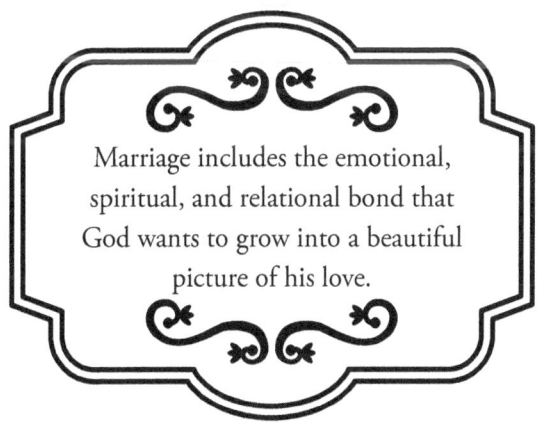

"This explains why a man leaves his father and mother and is joined to his wife in such a way that the two become one person" Genesis 2:24.

"God said to them, 'Be fruitful and multiply, and fill the earth'" Genesis 1:28 NASB.

Some people believe this is a corporate command for mankind that has been fulfilled since humans now *fill the earth* by living on every continent. Others believe it's an individual command to every married couple to have children or adopt them. Still others interpret this verse as a direction to multiply the talents and gifts that God has created within you.

Intentions

God cares about our motives.

Children are meant to be a natural outcome of marriage, but since children aren't coming to us *naturally*, we have the time to examine our motives for having them. Are we pursuing children because God is directing us to do so? Or are we pushing God out of the picture and turning to medicine as an alternative to trusting God? Are we transferring our trust in God to a doctor or a technique? We need to invite God, our Healer, into our medical quest for answers. How we walk this journey matters.

We need to invite God, our Healer, into our medical quest for answers. How we walk this journey matters.

"But the Lord said to Samuel, '... Men judge by outward appearance, but I look at a man's thoughts and intentions'" 1 Samuel 16:7.

Decisions That Involve Others

We aren't to hurt others, but to think of the other person also and let love always govern our actions.
We shouldn't use others to get what we want if it would cause them harm. This includes our spouse, anyone who would offer sperm or eggs to enable us to become pregnant, future children we might conceive, and society as a whole. We need to consider the impact of our choices on all those affected.

"Love your neighbor as you love yourself. Love does no wrong to anyone" Romans 13:9–10.

God demonstrated a certain flexibility in the Old Testament by not admonishing some alternative conception methods.
I found this third principle surprising and remarkable. In Deuteronomy 25:5–6, as part of the *Levirate Law*, God required a man to marry and take responsibility for his brother's childless widow specifically to give her a child. Some Christians believe that the modern practice of donor insemination allows a man with the characteristics of a brother to donate sperm to ease another's childless state. For further information on the Levirate Law, see Genesis 38:6–8; Ruth 4:1–10; and Matthew 22:23–30.

I was also amazed at the story in Genesis 30. Both Rachel and Leah used their maids Bilhah and Zilpah to produce children with Jacob. God didn't reprimand them for the practice of surrogacy. Instead, he honored the children born of those unions by making the sons—Dan, Naphtali, Gad, and Asher—part of the twelve tribes of Israel.

Of course, one of the major differences between modern surrogacy and Old Testament surrogacy is that the sexual act has been removed from the equation. Another difference is that in Old Testament times, the surrogate lived as part of the family.

The Old Testament has other examples of concubines becoming surrogates. In one of these accounts, Hagar specifically produced a child because Sarah, Abraham's wife, was infertile. But the account illustrates that surrogacy wasn't God's plan for Sarah and Abraham. Genesis also records the jealousy and discord this arrangement caused.

God wanted Abraham and Sarah to trust him for Sarah to become pregnant. Instead, they sought their own alternative because of impatience in Genesis 16:1–3. God eventually gave them the biological child they desired in Genesis 21:1–7.

Because these Old Testament situations don't directly relate to the situations and culture of today, they may lead to two differing viewpoints. The first view is that God demonstrated his flexibility in allowing alternate ways of conceiving children in these Old Testament situations, so the same flexibility applies to modern situations of childlessness. The other view is that God allowed deviation from the norm only to accomplish a specific purpose for those times. Since those specific cultural purposes no longer exist, we shouldn't assume God allows alternate methods of conception today to fulfill our desires.

Responding to Biblical Principles and Guidelines

God has given us biblical principles to guide us when he doesn't provide direct instruction. If we have a choice to make that's not spelled out in the Bible, we're given the freedom to choose—based on the principles God has given us. As Christians, we're in a relationship based on God's love, but the freedom this offers also includes a great responsibility to act in love toward him too. If we truly love God, then we won't want to do anything contrary to his desires or anything that would cause him sorrow. We can carefully search for the path God has for us by studying what God tells us in the Bible and seeking the leading of the Holy Spirit in prayer.

Praying for Wisdom and Direction

Prayer is such an important benefit in a Christian's decision-making process. Rich found that the decisions he and his wife needed to make during treatment were so important that prayer became second nature. He said:

> We were aggressive once we started medical tests and treatments, but every time there was a choice, we sat down and asked ourselves if this was a direction God might want us to go. Then we prayed and slept on it. A door either opened or closed in our minds.
>
> These are heavy decisions. What you may decide in a few seconds, you may need to live with for the rest of your lives.

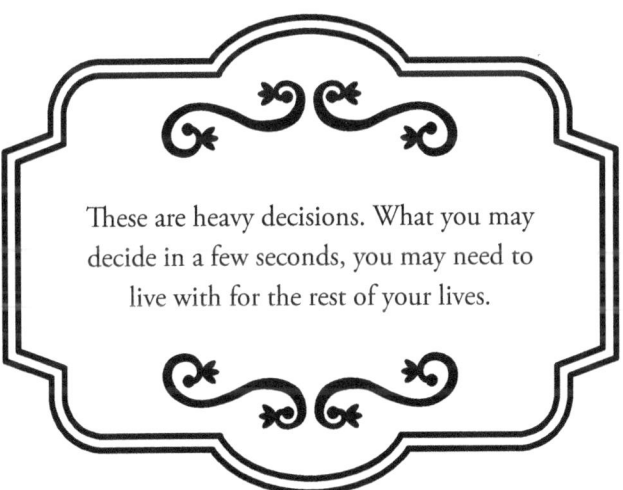

These are heavy decisions. What you may decide in a few seconds, you may need to live with for the rest of your lives.

Before making any major decision, we need to ask God to guide us and give us wisdom in our choices both individually and together as a couple (James 1:5). Ask the Holy Spirit to guide in unity so both have peace about the decisions.

Your Personal Journey

1. Have you and your spouse prayed for wisdom and direction both alone and together? If not, consider it now.
2. What additional Bible verses can you find that apply to the creation of life or principles that could guide your decisions? (Biblegateway.com is a wonderful site to use in searching for Bible words or phrases.)
3. If you still don't feel sure of which direction to take after biblical study and prayer, consider seeking some wise counsel to help you gain clarity. Can you think of someone wise you could talk to, someone who may have been down this path already? Perhaps a pastor or a counselor who would honor your values? Pray about talking to this person.

6
Encountering Ethical Issues within Assisted Reproductive Technology (ART)

Love does no wrong to anyone.
—Romans 13:10

The inability to tell good from evil is the greatest worry of man's life.
—Cicero[17]

I waited in the cold hallway of the university hospital early in the morning. Two other women had arrived before me. I looked at them curiously. Were they here for the same reason I was? Of course, I didn't ask. Soon a technician appeared and opened the lab door. The woman before me reached under her coat to bring out a little specimen cup. Ah, she was here to have her husband's sperm washed also. Then the technician called my name. I took out the little jar that I'd tried to keep warm while waiting. I watched as they wrote my husband's name on it.

I was keenly aware of the time constraints involved in today's procedure, so I wanted to stay close. I read in the hospital library as I waited the two hours for the wash to be done. At one hour and fifty-five minutes, I headed back to the lab to pick up my husband's newly washed sperm, smiling at a silly thought of the little guys singing in the shower as they all scrubbed up.

I tucked the vial of sperm back into my coat and headed out for the twenty-minute drive to my doctor's office. I missed a turn. As I rerouted, I realized I was clenching my jaw. What if I was late and the doctor didn't hold my appointment? I finally arrived at the office only a few minutes late. The supportive nurse performed the simple and painless insemination.

After twenty minutes I drove home. I kept feeling strange that Mike wasn't with me. I felt disconnected from him. I decided that if we did this again, I'd want him to come with me.

I was astonished when my period didn't come in two weeks. I started to feel pregnancy symptoms, but I'd been down that road so many times. I didn't want to run the risk of another negative pregnancy test. So, I waited... only a day or two.

I couldn't believe it when the nurse said the test was positive! I was thrilled!

A few hours later a thought suddenly popped into my mind. What if they mixed up the sperm samples at the lab? I hope the child I'm carrying is Mike's.

I'd never even considered the possibility of a mix-up before. I probably wouldn't have thought of it then, if there hadn't been two other women waiting with semen specimens at the lab. It was difficult to believe after so much struggle that a pregnancy had resulted.

I had tried to protect myself by not thinking of a possible positive outcome. Then, when the procedure worked, I realized I'd never thought through the possibility of a mix-up. Because the hospital had the reputation of being one of the top teaching hospitals in the country, I'd naively treated the procedure like a blood draw.

When against all odds, fertilization occurred, I suddenly felt a deep parental responsibility. The steps we'd taken had resulted in a new human forming. Why hadn't I asked more questions before the procedure? Why hadn't I asked to meet the lab personnel or asked what procedures they had in place to prevent a mix-up? Why hadn't I asked to watch to ensure I left with the same sperm I brought in?

A few months later I miscarried that baby.

Ethical Choices We May Encounter

Is it possible to use IVF while still respecting God as the Creator of human life?

Couples on the front lines of wanting to use reproductive technologies often face deep questions such as how to best respect God's role in creating a life. We may need to make decisions based on whether we believe that God breathes a soul into a human life at conception. It's important to think through these questions, such as when life begins, then make decisions that align with our values.

We can choose within IVF procedures to align our testing and treatments with our ethics. It helps to ask ourselves and our partners where our ethical boundaries lie before we get into the treatments.

Since creating and caring for embryos is more complex, ethical issues regarding embryos are discussed in chapter 7.

Masturbation

One of the first issues a couple may encounter in testing is the expectation of masturbation to obtain a semen sample. Masturbation for sexual gratification is considered immoral by some conservative Protestant churches, the Roman Catholic Church, and Orthodox Jews.

Masturbation to obtain a sperm sample, for other than the most conservative Christians, isn't viewed as an ethical problem.

"Masturbation in this situation is not being done for erotic pleasure," said Dr. Grounds, a former chancellor at Denver Seminary. "I see no problem with this even if someone felt masturbation for personal erotic pleasure was wrong."

The important thing is to also communicate honestly as a couple about any personal concerns with masturbation from both the husband's and wife's viewpoint. The couple may need to discuss the ethics of this choice in the context of their relationship, past addictions, or whether it may trigger other behaviors.

Special seminal collection condoms

If after discussing this issue with your spouse, either of you feels uncomfortable with masturbation to obtain a semen sample, using a special collection condom during intercourse to collect the sample is a medically approved option.

Special seminal collection condoms contain no spermicides and have a coating to let the sperm slide out easily. Research comparing the seminal characteristics of ejaculates collected during intercourse (collected in a sterile condom) versus masturbation has shown up to 39% better results.[18][19][20][21]

You will need to coordinate the timing with your doctor to deliver the sperm sample to the lab within a short time (1-2 hours) of obtaining it. Ask your fertility specialist for the brand they recommend.[22]

Pornography in Fertility Clinics

Clinics may offer pornographic videos or media to assist men in providing a semen sample. Mounting medical and social evidence of the dangers of pornography supports the biblical warnings to refrain from these materials.

If you or your doctors aren't aware of the issues involved with the use of pornography in fertility clinics, here are some brief discussions of the issues and three sites to find out more information.

Medical Evidence Against Using Pornography
Medical studies have begun to identify how highly addictive pornography can be to the human brain. Recent medical studies show that:

- Viewing pornography triggers brain activity that mirrors the brains of drug addicts as shown on fMRI scans. It causes the brain to pump out chemicals that lead to profound and lasting changes in the brain while reducing the area of the brain that enables us to function as humans.[23][24]
- Viewing pornography causes the brain to literally rewire itself, creating new neuropathways that are especially heightened and strong when accompanied by masturbation and climax.[25]
- Viewing pornography is causing sexual dysfunction in men, often leading to less sex, less satisfying sex, or no sex at all.[26]
- Viewing pornography just once can change brain chemistry.[27][28]

Social Evidence Against Using Pornography
Marriages already strained by infertility risk further damage when fertility clinics introduce pornography into their sexual relationship. Psychological and sociological studies on pornography have begun to show how devastating pornography is to intimate relationships (as well as our society). These studies show that:

- Pornography use affects marriages negatively. Three out of five divorces are now directly related to pornography use.[29]
- Pornography use causes less child-centeredness during marriage and a reduced desire for female children.[30]
- Pornography use increases the likelihood that the viewer will have an affair.[31]
- Pornography use creates acceptance of violence against women—the vast majority of porn portrays sexually debas-

ing, demeaning, aggressive, and misogynistic practices toward women.[32] [33]
- Pornography use lowers women's sense of their own sexual value as well as their perceived sexual value to men.[34]
- Pornography use participates in sex trafficking by driving and fueling the demand for sex-trafficked victims.[35]

Biblical Warnings Against Using Pornography

The Bible warns that pornography is destructive for Christians.

- Matthew 5:28 makes it clear that sexually fantasizing about anyone other than a spouse violates the marriage relationship.
- When the Bible talks about sexual immorality, it often uses the Greek word *porneia*, which is the root of the English word pornography. (Matthew 15:19, Mark 7:21, 2 Corinthians 12:21, Galatians 5:19, Colossians 3:5, Revelation 9:21)

With the easy access to internet pornography available, pornography addiction has become a crisis that currently threatens to overwhelm and has the power to bring down the Christian church.[36] For more information on the destructive effects of pornography, visit:

- https://pornharmsresearch.com/
- https://www.fightthenewdrug.org/
- https://www.yourbrainonporn.com/relevant-research-and-articles-about-the-studies/porn-use-sex-addiction-studies/cambridge-university-brain-scans-find-evidence-consistent-with-addiction/experiment-that-convinced-me-online-porn-is-the-most-pernicious-threat-facing-children-today-by-ex-lads-mag-editor-martin-daubney/

While it's a tremendous pressure for a man to need to deliver a sperm sample on a schedule, offering pornography as a stimulation isn't the simple solution it's claimed to be. Feel free to discuss other options with your doctor, such as collecting the sperm sample at your nearby home, having both husband and wife present in the *collection room* at the clinic, or using a collection condom at a nearby hotel. One IVF clinic provides an apartment above the clinic for out-of-town couples to stay in and also allows couples to use it at collection time.

Cheryl spoke of how the introduction of pornography affected her marriage years after she was finally able to give birth to a child. She said:

> I didn't understand the lure of pornography for my Christian husband, James. He'd said he believed that masturbating to porn was the same as having an affair, but he rationalized using porn offered in the doctor's office because of the time pressure.
> Later, he began to seek porn out on the internet. About a year later, I suspected this was happening, but James reassured me it wasn't a problem and refused to install safety software to block pornography on his laptop.
> But he was hooked. He tried to fight it for years and felt so ashamed. But pornography was such a powerful force, like a drug. I still don't know how pornography could become more real to him than me, but it did. He started to suggest we act out porn scenes he'd watched, and became enraged when I wouldn't. His drive to look at, then act out pornography became so great that after years of trying to fight it, he finally chose pornography over our marriage. He's living a defeated life, and our marriage is broken.

Our much-awaited young son now shares time between our separate homes.

Freezing Sperm or Eggs (Cryopreservation)

Another decision we may face is whether to freeze either sperm or eggs (separately). The Roman Catholic church and other conservative orthodox religions still see this choice as wrong because it removes the creation of life from the marriage act as a means of achieving pregnancy.

For others, because a human life hasn't yet been conceived, the ethics of the decision to freeze sperm or eggs revolves around assuring that the sample won't be used for any other purpose and ensuring that any storage failure concerns are minimized (lab safety).

Note: Although sperm have a better success rate at surviving the freezing process, survival rates for frozen eggs continue to improve.[37]

Donor Eggs or Sperm

Using Donated Sperm or Eggs

ART also opens the door to the option of using donor gametes or embryos because it allows the separation of intercourse from procreation. When a husband's sperm or wife's eggs are not healthy enough for conception, donor sperm or eggs can be introduced to obtain a pregnancy.

In a Donor Insemination (DI) procedure, the donor's sperm (usually from an anonymous donor) is washed, concentrated, and placed in the wife's vagina, cervix, or uterus using a sterile syringe. This procedure is relatively inexpensive.

In an IVF cycle using donor egg(s) (from either an anonymous or known donor), the donor egg(s) are fertilized with the husband's sperm using the same process as in a typical IVF cycle.

An IVF cycle using both donor egg(s) and donor sperm is most often done through the transfer of a donor embryo (also called embryo adoption). The procedure is the same as a typical IVF cycle except that the couple doesn't contribute genetically to the child.

The Infidelity Question of Using Donor Eggs or Sperm

While procedures that use donors within DI and IVF differ, the unique ethical issue they raise is the introduction of a third party within the marriage. Many Roman Catholics and conservative Protestants view DI as a violation of the *one flesh* that God originally intended for marriage and believe it's similar to infidelity. To many in the Christian faith though, there is no direct correlation between infidelity and using donor eggs or sperm because sex isn't involved.

Dr. Grounds talked about this distinction. He said:

> Some would say that if two are joined together, it is God's intention they produce children, that if they cannot produce children, then the use of donated sperm or eggs is, in effect, a violation of their relationship as a married couple. But I don't see how you could oppose it as in any way violating the nuptial bond, because there is no physical contact whatever—nothing of a sexual or amorous nature.

There are Christian couples who have thoughtfully investigated using donor eggs or sperm, earnestly prayed about it, sought guidance from pastors or those well-versed in Scripture, then decided to proceed. Donna and her husband, Joe, decided on donor insemination after discovering Joe's zero sperm count. They now have two boys conceived through donor insemination. She said:

> We went to a lawyer and started the adoption paperwork, but we didn't feel any peace about it. It was expen-

sive and uncertain. We prayed about donor insemination, talked to a pastor, and felt that God had put us in an age where it was one of our options.

We chose not to make it public, just to tell a couple of family members because we thought that would be better for our children's relationship with their father. The sperm bank sent us a list of donor characteristics. For both children, the process was similar. We chose as many of Joe's characteristics as possible, like hair color, height, and blood type (so if our children ever needed a transfusion, they wouldn't learn about their genetic paternity during a crisis). I had to sign forms saying that although the sperm bank screened for diseases, if I contracted any, they weren't responsible. Joe had to sign a form saying that he could never claim the child wasn't his.

We had the sperm delivered from the sperm bank to my gynecologist's office. Joe was present during the inseminations in the doctor's office. With our first baby, we didn't conceive until after the third set of inseminations. That night of the last insemination, we went out and had an incredibly romantic evening. The pregnancy may have come from the physical seed of someone else, but it was from our union.

I did have a few worries once I got pregnant that the bank might have mixed up the vials, and I would give birth to a baby of a different race. That would have been hard to explain.

When Jay was born, he looked so much like me I was worried, but he's such a Daddy's boy. Jeffrey, our second, looks more like my husband....

My husband's father was very prejudiced about everyone when he was alive, so telling him about using a donor would have been a problem. I know that if we had adopted, he would have had a hard time also, though. My mother felt it was private, but not wrong.

We worried that it would constantly be an issue, but Joe says he doesn't even remember unless it's specifically brought up.

Positive impacts of using a donor

Those open to donor insemination see it as a valid option for Christian infertile couples today. They see the main impact from the use of donor gametes (sperm or eggs) on marriage relationships to be positive. Some Christians also base their positive view of using donor gametes on the flexible view of conceiving children as seen in the Old Testament. (See chapter 5 for a further discussion on this.)

A child conceived by one spouse and an anonymous donor has an advantage over adoption in that the child legally belongs to the couple immediately. This can make conception with a donor more attractive than adoption in some ways.

Cautions with using a donor

DI isn't a simple solution for male factor infertility, just as receiving donated eggs isn't a quick fix for female infertility. Sharon said she didn't think about some of the complex issues of using donor sperm before she and her husband used this method to conceive. She shared:

> I guess I really didn't think through the ethics of our decision. I was a new Christian, and we weren't attending any church at the time. We just decided to do it. I felt adulterous about it to begin with. But my sister said at least it would be half ours.

The psychological difficulties when using donor sperm or eggs are complex, as John Jefferson Davis, a professor of Theology at Gordon-Conwell Theological Seminary in South Hamilton, Massachusetts, writes:

> AID [Artificial Insemination by Donor] introduces an imbalance in the relationship between the husband and the wife. Her maternal functions have been fulfilled, but his paternal function has not. The AID child remains as a constant reminder of his biological failure, and the shadow of an anonymous third party clouds the relationship.[38]

Annette Baran and Reuben Pannor wrote the book *Lethal Secrets* about some long-term consequences of DI. They talked with older children and adults who had been conceived by DI, sperm donors, and infertile couples who used DI procedures. They found remorse on the part of some of the men who donated sperm once they had grown older and had their own families. It was then the men realized the deeper implications of what they'd done. The authors also found donor offspring who felt cut off from their genetic father's roots, similar to the way some adopted children feel.

They also found infertile men who struggled years later with their decision to have their wives conceive through DI. The following summary of one couple's experience shows some of the psychological undercurrents:

> During the period when Zack's wife was undergoing monthly inseminations of donor sperm, Zack experienced myriad feelings, ranging from anger, despair, fear, and anxiety to withdrawal and depression. He had readily agreed to the insemination for his wife when it was offered by the doctor as the obvious solution.
>
> He wanted and needed a fast solution because of the depth of his pain but he needed to recognize the ramifications of his loss in terms of family name, bloodline, genetic continu-

ity, and sense of immortality. Not only did he need to live through that pain and loss, but he needed to recognize how important the shared experience of biological parenting with Carly had been to him. Now not only was he not siring a child, but he and Carly together were not producing the progeny that would have represented their coupling and loving.

In our interviews... we became increasingly aware of how tentative the sterile husband's feelings about the use of donor insemination really were... but to deny their wives the experience of pregnancy was unthinkable for most of them. If they could not provide sperm, they had to let someone else do it for them.

To most of these men, that sperm was emotionally equivalent to infidelity.... The couple's relationship underwent subtle changes, and the balance of power was shifted.[39]

Some infertile men (and women) have reservations about using donor sperm (or eggs) even after their child is conceived and born. The further choice of confidentiality or openness about the procedure adds another layer of complexity. The premise of *Lethal Secrets* is that it would be better for the children's sake to do away with the secrecy so they're allowed to know their genetic heritage. The problem with this openness though, is that it insinuates the third-party donor into an even more prominent place in the couple's marriage.

For those contemplating using donor sperm or eggs, it's extremely important to listen closely to your spouse, voice all hesitations about this procedure, and give extra weight to any concerns from the partner whose infertility will not be cured by this procedure.

Discernment in donor decisions
Because of these problems mentioned, some Christians, such as Steve Zeisler, a former pastor at Peninsula Bible Church, see the use of donor sperm or eggs as unwise. He said:

I think it is much wiser... that a couple would be better off adopting a child whose genes are one hundred percent unrelated to them rather than attempting to have a child with genes fifty percent related that would mean one of them—husband or wife—would be excluded from that relationship. I think the emotional tangle between Sarah and Abraham that resulted from the situation with Hagar suggests some of the difficulties a couple would probably have with donor eggs or sperm. Once it becomes clear that God won't allow a child to be born except with third-party help, I think the wiser course then is to ask him for a child to care for who is already born, as in adoption.

In the best scenario, using a donor to help you create a baby enables both you and your spouse to have the family you desire with minimal regrets for either of you. You draw closer as husband and wife because of the shared experience of parenting.

In the worst scenario, the child exacerbates an imbalance and tension already in your marriage. And one or both of you never recovers from the fact that your child isn't genetically the infertile spouse's.

Surrogacy

Surrogacy is when another woman agrees to carry a child for a couple. It can involve, 1) the husband's sperm and wife's eggs fertilized through IVF, 2) the husband's sperm and the surrogate's eggs fertilized either through IVF or DI, or 3) donor eggs and donor sperm fertilized through IVF.

The main concern with surrogacy is the involvement of a known third party introduced into the marriage and the resulting changes in the couple's relationship. It can also cause confusing and painful maternal feelings on the part of the surrogate. When the surrogate has no genetic tie to the child, as in the case of using the husband's sperm and wife's egg(s), it's hoped that she would not bond with the child as strongly as if it were genetically fifty percent her child, but no one knows how strongly a surrogate will feel toward a baby she is carrying until she's already carrying the child or even past delivery.

God allowed a form of surrogacy (with concubines) during a certain period of Israel's history, but it wasn't always beneficial. For instance, it caused pain and rivalry between Sarah and Hagar, depression for Sarah, disharmony within Sarah and Abraham's marriage, pain in Ishmael's life, and warring of subsequent generations and nations.

"You need to look at what is God's intention in marriage," said Dr. Vernon Grounds, a former chancellor at Denver Seminary. "If the woman is unable to carry the child, would it be better for her to accept that as a limitation rather than having a child produced by another woman who in fact is the mother?"

The type of surrogacy where the embryo is created through IVF, then carried by a surrogate who has a genetic tie, is sometimes done by a sister, another relative, or friend. This option still involves a known third party in the marriage/reproductive relationship.

The laws on the parentage of a baby born by surrogacy vary for each state. Even when the biological parent's sperm and eggs are used, they will often still need to legally adopt the baby after delivery.

Acting on Our Decisions

After we've developed convictions about which choices we feel would honor and respect God, we can talk to our doctor about them. Is the doctor willing to support our beliefs? Do we feel comfortable placing our convictions in the doctor's hands to be conscientiously followed? If we follow our deep moral values and uphold our respect for the miracle of life within fertility treatment, I believe we can honor God through our choices.

As we discuss these choices with our doctor, consider how the decisions we make might help another couple at the clinic making these same choices later. This is still a new field, so doctors are finding their way through the options as well. In educating our doctor, we may be paving the way for future patients to be offered better options for treatment.

In the end, the decision to use Assisted Reproductive Technology to try to become pregnant is an individual choice, but we're not deciding in an ethical vacuum. We remain responsible directly to God for our decisions. Our freedom of choice in the areas in which the Bible isn't specific gives us an even greater responsibility not to be ignorant of what God has told us in his Word, but to diligently seek to understand it.

If after searching Scripture and praying about it, we believe that a particular approach is wrong, then it's wrong for us, and we shouldn't do it. As Christians, our choices should be based on a right attitude of respect for God, studying what God says in the Bible to instruct us, and asking God to lead us to make the right choices as we partner with him in creating life.

Your Personal Journey

1. What statements or activities from a medical professional would you consider a red flag that would cause you to change specialists or labs for your ART treatment (ex., signs of disrespect or shoddy care)?
2. What ethical decisions have you needed to make or will you expect to make in dealing with your infertility treatments?
3. On what did you (or would you) base your decisions?
4. Consider answering the following additional questions to create a belief statement and assist you in communicating with your doctor.

Questions & Options about Assisted Reproductive Technology (ART) to Think Through and Discuss Together*

These questions are meant to help you consider some ethical issues you may encounter in ART testing and treatment. Check the questions you'd like to discuss or research further. Consider answering the questions alone and/or together that may apply to your situation and add any other questions you might have. Answering these questions can also help you write a personal belief statement and assist in communicating with your doctor.

General Assisted Reproductive Technology (ART)

☐ What decisions will we need to make during this test or treatment?

☐ Have we prayed about this test or treatment? What do we believe God is leading us to do next?

☐ What do we need to ask about before proceeding with this next test or treatment?

Masturbation

☐ Are we comfortable with this test or procedure if it requires the husband to produce a sperm sample by masturbation?

☐ What method of obtaining the sperm sample are we most comfortable with?

☐ What boundaries in this test or treatment do we not want to cross?

---

* Find this printable list of ethical questions at: AchingforaChild.com.

Pornography

- [ ] After looking at the three websites that discuss the issue of pornography in this chapter, what is our belief about the use of pornography?
- [ ] Where are our boundaries regarding the use of pornography in fertility clinics?
- [ ] What alternative(s) to using pornography are we most comfortable with?
- [ ] What steps will we take to ensure we protect our marriage and not degrade another person to create our child?

Eggs and Sperm

Freezing Eggs or Sperm

- [ ] Are we comfortable with the option to freeze our eggs or sperm (separately)? Why or why not?
- [ ] What is the plan for any eggs or sperm we have frozen that we're not able to use?

Donor Eggs and/or Sperm

Donating Eggs or Sperm (Gametes) to Others

- [ ] To what degree do we feel responsible for the eternal life of a child created by our eggs or sperm?
- [ ] How important to us is the ability to share our faith values with a child created from our eggs or sperm? Have we investigated options to donate our eggs or sperm to a couple who shares our faith?

Receiving Donated Eggs or Sperm

- [ ] Are we comfortable using the sperm or egg of a donor to conceive our child? How would introducing a known or unknown donor affect our marriage relationship?

- [ ] How would the spouse who won't have a genetic tie to our child plan to grieve their loss of a genetic connection to any child?
- [ ] What current testing and controls are in place to prevent a donor from passing communicable or hereditary diseases to us or our child?
- [ ] Would we choose to tell our child of their biological parentage or keep it confidential? At what age would we share this information?
- [ ] If we choose to tell our child, and the donor is anonymous, how might we deal with his/her feeling something's missing from their life because they don't know half of their genetic roots?
- [ ] If we choose to keep our child's genetic parentage confidential, how would we deal with the possibility of our child accidentally finding out their true genetic heritage (ex., by a medical emergency, the results of a DNA testing kit, or someone who knew of our infertile condition sharing information)?
- [ ] Have we considered the rare chance that our child born from donor gametes could grow up to marry a genetic half-sibling?
- [ ] What are the laws in our country/state regarding paying for donor sperm or eggs? Do we agree with them?

Surrogacy

- [ ] Are we comfortable using a surrogate to conceive or carry our child for us? Why or why not?
- [ ] What role would we envision the surrogate playing in our family's life before and after the birth of our baby?
- [ ] What effect would introducing a known and fertile surrogate have on our marriage relationship?
- [ ] How would we plan to handle any emotional issues of the surrogate's spouse and/or other children?
- [ ] Have we considered how using a surrogate might cause confusion in our child's life? How would we handle this?

- [ ] What plans would we make for our child if we were to die before the surrogate gives birth?
- [ ] What are the laws in our country/state regarding:
    - [ ] if our baby is born with a severe physical disability?
    - [ ] if a surrogate changes her mind and wants to keep our baby?
    - [ ] payments for surrogacy?
    - [ ] Do we agree with these laws?

Personal Belief Statement about ART (Assisted Reproductive Technology) Testing & Treatment*

Our personal beliefs regarding our testing and treatment:

_____
_____
_____
_____
_____
_____
_____

Guidelines we would want followed regarding our testing and treatment:

_____
_____
_____
_____
_____
_____
_____

What we don't want regarding our testing and treatment:

_____
_____
_____
_____
_____
_____
_____

---

* Find this printable list of ethical questions at: AchingforaChild.com.

Additional questions we want to ask our doctor:

_____
_____
_____
_____

Questions & Beliefs about Assisted Reproductive Technology (ART) to Print and Discuss with Our Doctor*

Write down your personal belief statement before you need to decide about ART testing or treatment. Check the questions you'd like to ask, then take this list with you when you go to your doctor visit to discuss your treatment plan. These questions are meant to help open a discussion with your medical professional about some ethical issues related to ART. Revisit your statement before deciding on treatment.

Masturbation

☐ Do you recommend sperm-collection condoms for obtaining sperm samples? Do you recommend a particular manufacturer?

☐ What other options besides masturbation for collecting a sperm sample are available (ex., collecting the sperm sample at our nearby home, having the wife present in the collection room at the clinic, using a collection condom at a nearby hotel)?

Pornography

☐ Do you offer alternatives to using pornography to assist in obtaining sperm samples (ex., a room where both husband and wife can obtain the sample together, the option to bring a sample from home, a pornography-free sperm sample collection room)?

☐ Pornography information sites to share with your medical professional:

---

* Find this printable list of ethical questions at: https://Achingfora Child.com.

- https://pornharmsresearch.com/
- https://www.fightthenewdrug.org/
- https://www.yourbrainonporn.com/relevant-research-and-articles-about-the-studies/porn-use-sex-addiction-studies/cambridge-university-brain-scans-find-evidence-consistent-with-addiction/experiment-that-convinced-me-online-porn-is-the-most-pernicious-threat-facing-children-today-by-ex-lads-mag-editor-martin-daubney/

Eggs and Sperm

Freezing Eggs or Sperm

☐ What are your lab's survival rates for frozen/thawed eggs or sperm? How do those rates compare to the national average?

☐ How does using frozen vs. fresh eggs or sperm affect your lab's live-birth success rates?

☐ What would be the typical plan for our frozen eggs or sperm if we died before we could use them? (Consider putting a clause in your will regarding your frozen eggs or sperm.)

☐ What lab standards or protocols do you have in place to avoid mix-ups and protect the chain of custody for frozen sperm and eggs? (Look for things such as a *double-witnessing* approach where two embryologists check that all materials match before moving samples or performing procedures to verify an unbroken chain of custody.)

☐ What protocols do you have in place to protect cryo-preserved eggs and sperm from equipment malfunctions?

☐ What is the storage security track record at your lab?

Donated Eggs or Sperm

Receiving Donated Eggs or Sperm
☐ What current testing and controls are in place at your lab to prevent donors from passing communicable or hereditary diseases on to us or our child?
☐ What protocols do you have in place to limit the number of children born from one donor?
☐ What are the laws in our country/state regarding the parentage of children born from donor eggs or sperm?
☐ What are the laws in our country/state regarding payment for donor eggs or sperm?

Donating Eggs or Sperm
☐ Does this clinic offer the choice to donate to a couple who shares the same faith?

Surrogacy

☐ What are our country's and state's laws regarding:
  ☐ the parentage of a child born through surrogacy?
  ☐ if the surrogate changed her mind and wanted to keep the baby?
  ☐ if the surrogate sustained an injury from carrying our child?
  ☐ if the baby was born with a disability?
  ☐ if we were to die after the surrogate was impregnated, but before she gave birth?
☐ Do you have a sample surrogacy contract we could take home and look over?

Medical Professional, Clinic, & Lab

- [ ] What decisions will we need to make during this test or treatment?
- [ ] How might the results of this test or treatment affect our future treatment?
- [ ] Would you be comfortable working with us and honoring our reproductive convictions?
- [ ] What procedures would be implemented to ensure that our convictions are honored?

Since there are currently no laws or enforced regulations regarding clinics or labs:
- [ ] Is this clinic a member of the Society of Assisted Reproductive Medicine (SART)? (Membership offers higher standards & accountability through verified success rates.)
- [ ] What lab standards or procedures do you have in place to ensure the chain of custody for sperm and eggs? (Listen for protocols such as a *double-witnessing* approach where two technicians check that all sperm or egg identifiers match before moving samples or performing procedures.)
- [ ] Will any services involving our sperm or eggs be outsourced?

Personal Beliefs We Want to Discuss with Our Doctor about Our ART Testing & Treatment[*]

Beliefs we want to discuss with our doctor:

_____
_____
_____
_____
_____
_____
_____
_____

Additional questions we want to ask our doctor:

_____
_____
_____
_____
_____
_____
_____
_____
_____

---

[*] Find this printable list of ethical questions at: AchingforaChild.com.

Requests we have for our doctor:

_____
_____
_____
_____
_____
_____
_____

7
Facing Ethical Issues about Embryos

If you want to know what God wants you to do,
Ask him, and he will gladly tell you,
For he is always ready to give a bountiful supply of wisdom
To all who ask him, and he will not resent it.
—James 1:5

The difficulty in life is the choice.
—George Moore[40]

I continued through the medical tests and treatments until the next option for me was to try the fertility drug Pergonal combined with an intrauterine transfer. If things went well, I could fit in two cycles of Pergonal treatment before our insurance changed. This was important because, without this insurance, we couldn't afford the thousands of dollars out-of-pocket that each Pergonal cycle would cost. Again, we held hope that this new treatment would fix our problem.

Everything looked great midway through the first cycle of Pergonal. The latest ultrasound showed that two eggs on the side with my good fallopian tube were maturing well. With each ultrasound, I became intimately aware of the earliest stages of my eggs' development. On the way home from one ultrasound appointment I found myself saying to God, "Lord, I pray that one of these two growing eggs will become our next child." Then I started laughing at myself. Now that I knew more information earlier in each cycle, I was already feeling maternal toward my eggs before they were even fertilized!

I went in the next day—the day the two eggs should have finally grown large enough to be released—excited to take the next step. The ultrasound showed that overnight though, several more eggs had grown large enough to now have a chance of also becoming fertilized and producing a baby.

I now had at least seven *potentially viable eggs this cycle*. If I chose to take the hCG shot to release the eggs and proceed with the insemination, the doctor explained that meant I could possibly become pregnant with seven *babies this cycle!*

I was stunned. I now faced a choice of no baby or possibly seven. And I'd gone through such effort and pain on this cycle! I told the doctor that pregnancy reduction wasn't an option for me.

My belief that life is given by God solidified during my years of infertility treatment. I was filled with wonder at the intricacies of the reproductive process up close, including all the marvelous changes and development that happen so quickly once an egg and sperm join. My awe at how early a fetus's brain waves and heartbeat start strengthened my convictions against abortion. And knowing that an embryo had all it needed genetically as a full human being, so all it needed was proper nurturing, sealed the deal for me. I didn't want to finally create, then be responsible for taking the life of my own child or children.

The doctor seemed surprised at my decision against pregnancy reduction. He told me I had about a 5 percent chance of a multiple pregnancy with triplets or more. It was so hard to come that far then *choose to stop. I agonized. Could I possibly play the odds, with the hopes that we'd only have one or two babies? But then I thought about how excruciating it would be to get pregnant and find out four or five babies were developing.*

I also had medical reasons to believe my body couldn't carry that many babies to term. So if I were to become pregnant with high-multiples, I would need to decide if I wanted to end the lives of some of my children with the hopes that I could carry a few of them to term.[41] I felt so strongly against abortion that I never dreamed I'd ever consider it as a possibility, much less a realistic option. It was incredible that wanting a baby so badly would make me now consider abortion.

I agonized, if we abstain from sex and don't let the sperm near the eggs (the ones I'd already bonded with), they would never produce life anyway....

But if I gave them a chance, I might have to take life from one or more of them....

But that would at least give the chance of life to two.

It was so difficult for me to deny the possibility of life to the eggs I'd already thought about as my future children.

I also wasn't in the best physical or emotional shape to think through this enormous decision. My abdomen ached, and I felt nauseous from the Pergonal. I had bruised arms from blood-draw needles, and my hips were sore from the medication injections. Unrelated to the infertility treatments, I'd also come down with laryngitis and a sore throat. On top of all that, I'd broken my right foot. So I was hobbling around on crutches with my foot in a cast.

Yet, I was only given the next five hours to make this choice—either take the hCG shot to release the eggs—to use these lovely eggs that were doing so well that we'd worked so hard to grow or miss the opportunity altogether.

I cried all the way home. I struggled to process it. Kneeling by my bed, I prayed. Next, I tried to call Mike at work, but he wasn't reachable. I didn't want to look at the long-term negative possibilities.

I wanted to think about the fact that I finally had a good chance to get pregnant that month. To help clarify my thinking, I began to write in my journal.

As I saw in black and white what I was thinking, I started to see what a major compromise in my beliefs I'd be making. If I chose to inseminate those eggs, I'd always know that I'd consciously chosen to open myself up to the possibility of a pregnancy reduction.

I knew that others had successfully delivered four, five, or more babies. But I also knew that as the number of babies being carried went up, the odds that they'd all survive went down. I'd been given information that I wasn't a good candidate for carrying a high-multiple pregnancy.

I also didn't want to place myself in a position where I'd need to stand up to a doctor who might encourage me to have a pregnancy reduction because without it I'd most likely lose all the babies I'd be carrying.

While this event happened within my body, it brings to light some of the questions about ethics and specifically about embryos that couples may face. We may need to make quick decisions when going through IVF and other treatments where the option of creating multiple embryos exists.

Infertile couples may have a hard time visualizing themselves with one baby, much less five, six, or seven. But many have been caught in this same situation. The over one million embryos in cryopreservation today are evidence of this dilemma. We need to pray and think about our decisions beforehand, so we can make proactive choices based on what we believe is true. Of course, there are times when we may end up with more babies than we'd planned, as can be true with typical pregnancies. That's where trust comes in. We do our best and trust God to take care of the rest.

As Socrates once said, "The unexamined life is not worth living." Congratulations. We'll never fall into the category of people with unexamined lives in this area again.

More Embryos vs. Fewer Babies Dilemma

With IVF, a woman is usually given fertility drugs, then the mature eggs are taken from her ovaries and placed with her husband's sperm in a sterile solution in a petri dish. After about forty-eight to seventy-two hours, the eggs are checked to see if they've fertilized and are dividing well. Then the fertilized eggs can be transferred into the wife's uterus. This procedure typically costs thousands of dollars.

The reason doctors attempt to stimulate a woman's ovaries to mature more eggs during each ART (Assisted Reproductive Technology) cycle is that 1) usually not all eggs will fertilize, 2) not all embryos will develop correctly, and 3) not all embryos that are transferred will implant in the uterus. So, a larger number of mature eggs during a cycle gives a better chance at overcoming these hurdles to result in a pregnancy.

Many factors, including age and egg quality, also affect success at each stage. For instance, the success of ART producing a live birth for women over the age of forty-two using their own eggs is currently only 1–3 percent.[42] But, as with all odds, there are times when nothing works and times when everything works too well.

There is still much that we can't control in this process, as Donna and Chuck found out. Donna said:

> Chuck and I were so careful throughout our treatments, trying to balance our best chances of getting pregnant without having a multiple birth. We were so happy when we first found out I was finally pregnant. We were so thrilled and willing to do everything possible to help make sure the baby could be born healthy.
>
> Then we found out we were having triplets, and we were scared. I needed a whole medical team to get me through the pregnancy and help care for all the babies once they were born. We often had close calls with their lives both be-

fore and after they were born. They had to spend months in the NICU, and everyone who cared for them had to learn how to care for their medical needs too. We're so thankful they survived, but it was a very scary journey.

Embryo Questions within Treatment

Some of the questions a couple may face within the IVF process or other fertility treatments include:

1. How many eggs do we want to attempt to fertilize this cycle?
2. How many embryos will we choose to have transferred into my uterus this cycle?
3. How will we choose to handle any remaining embryos (transfer, freeze, donate, or destroy)?
4. How would we deal with a large multiple pregnancy (quadruplets or larger) if we choose to transfer multiple embryos during one cycle (carry all to term or choose pregnancy reduction)?

One of the biggest concerns for couples using ART is the potential for a multiple pregnancy. For this reason, most reputable labs and specialists follow guidelines that limit the maximum number of developing embryos to transfer. These guidelines may differ between specialists and labs, and may also differ depending on the woman's age. Ultimately, we're the ones who will live with the results of our choices, so knowing our ethical boundaries is necessary to advocate for ourselves.

Respecting Human Life

How can anyone know more than we, the infertile couples who ache to have a child, how precious the miracle of life is? I can't think of anything more devastating for a couple who has struggled to become pregnant than to be told that all of our babies will probably die unless we choose to take the lives of some of them.

Because of this ethical dilemma, some have said that if we believe pregnancy reduction is wrong, then ART or using fertility drugs aren't ethical options for us. Rather than closing the door to these treatments altogether though, preventative measures can also be taken within the treatments to allow us to still follow our ethics.

Once an egg is fertilized, a human life has begun, so the ethical decisions become much more complex. Aligning our decisions with our ethics is the goal. The best time to make these decisions is before any of our embryos are created.

Ethical Creation of Embryos

The opinions about IVF within Christian communities vary. Echoing one common belief among Christians with a high regard for the Bible, Pastor Steve Zeisler said, "I don't think in vitro fertilization is wrong in and of itself.... That conception should take place in a dish and then the fertilized egg is placed back in the woman, does not seem to be beyond what is biblically proper."

Yet there are those, for instance in the Roman Catholic Church, who still consider this procedure wrong. Their belief that creating life only belongs within the sanctity of the marriage union doesn't allow for natural conception to take place outside of the wife's body.

Lori was shocked to find that the stigma against the procedure extended to her child. "When I went to have my baby baptized in the Roman Catholic Church," said Lori with her eyes wide, "I was told that she was less 'ensouled' than a natural-born child because she was conceived by IVF."

Choices We Can Make Within Treatment

Couples seek ART treatment because of their *lack* of children, so it's natural for them not to consider what might happen if they create or transfer *too many* embryos. It's important to think through this possibility though and some options to avoid it. You're the one who needs to live with the results of your choices and bear the responsibility for any embryos you create. So, knowing your ethical boundaries is necessary to advocate for yourself. Later in this chapter, possible consequences of these choices are discussed further.

Option 1: Creating Fewer Embryos

With careful ultrasound monitoring and some strategic choices, the risk of high multiples can be kept to a minimum without resorting to a pregnancy reduction. If our use of fertility drugs causes a large number of mature eggs one cycle, which means the number of potential embryos is high, we can choose to create fewer embryos by:

- Stopping treatment that cycle—Avoid intercourse or insemination to ensure no chance of pregnancy that cycle.
- Aspirating extra eggs—For cycles that will include either normal intercourse or insemination, extra mature eggs can be aspirated before fertilization. As with IVF, the aspiration procedure suctions out mature eggs with a needle. In this case, any extra eggs could either be discarded or frozen, leaving one or two mature eggs in the ovaries. This would allow the woman to proceed with an hCG shot and normal intercourse or insemination but lowers her concern of creating a high-multiple pregnancy. (This option wasn't yet available at the time of my decision at the beginning of this chapter.)

- Fertilizing only the number of eggs to transfer and carry to term if fertilization is successful—With IVF, the couple can choose to attempt fertilizing only the number of eggs that they'd transfer and carry to term if fertilization does take place. At this point, any extra eggs retrieved could also be frozen before fertilization occurs. (Sperm could also be frozen separately at this time if needed.)

It's important to notify your doctor if you plan to choose one of the options that limit the number of embryos created. Also, ask how this choice will affect the success rates you've been quoted for a particular procedure.

Option 2: Transferring Fewer Embryos

Most reputable labs and specialists will follow guidelines that limit the maximum number of developing embryos to transfer. These guidelines may differ between specialists and labs, and they can differ depending on the woman's age or the quality of her eggs.

While transferring fewer created embryos helps lower the potential for a multiple pregnancy, it can also create problems with *leftover* embryos if more embryos were created than transferred.

Option 3: Transferring all Embryos Created

If several embryos develop during a cycle, the specialist usually consults with the couple to decide how many embryos to transfer back to the woman's uterus with the hope that one will implant. The couple will also need to decide what to do with any created embryos that they choose not to have transferred.

This may include transferring embryos that have been graded as lower-quality than optimal, so be sure to discuss this with your doctor. Preparing to deal with the consequences of a multiple pregnancy needs to be considered with this option.

Making Decisions for *Extra* Embryos Created But Not Transferred During Treatment)

Option 1: Freezing Your Extra Embryos (cryopreservation) for a Later Transfer Cycle

You may be given the option to freeze any embryos created but not transferred to your uterus. If the current IVF round fails, you'd then be able to have these frozen embryos transferred during a future IVF procedure. If the current IVF round succeeds, you'd be able to have your frozen embryos transferred in a future IVF procedure when/if you later desire another child.

The drawback with this option is that couples need to decide what to do if this procedure works too well. They might be left with *extra* frozen embryos but feel their family is complete.[43]

Freezing and Thawing Safety Issues

Couples may be concerned with whether freezing embryos could harm them or the children later born from them. Not all embryos survive the freezing/thawing process, but with newer freezing techniques, the survival rate of frozen embryos has increased significantly.[44] And studies show the overall outcomes for babies born from fresh vs. frozen embryos are quite similar.[45]

Since the process of freezing will inevitably destroy some embryos, some believe freezing embryos is unethical. Dr. Vernon Grounds, a former chancellor at Denver Seminary, considers it immoral to participate in any process that allows human life to perish. He views freezing embryos as "initiating a process that is inevitably bound to kill some of them. Deliberately fertilizing some eggs, then deliberately allowing some of those eggs to die, isn't that killing off potential human life as in an abortion?"

Others, including many doctors, see embryos that don't survive the freezing/thawing process as embryos that probably wouldn't have developed further nor embedded in the uterus. Their views are strengthened by the fact that even though eggs often fertilize each month during a natural cycle, they don't all implant, so many leave the body during menstruation. These specialists feel that if more embryos are created than the couple wants to transfer, freezing the embryos follows the principle of giving them the best possible chance of survival.

Legal Issues and Changes in Circumstances
One unexpected result of the popularity of freezing embryos is that currently, there are over one million frozen embryos in storage. These embryos aren't simply tissue but are the earliest stages of a million unique people. They each contain their complete DNA and have everything they need to live if only they're nurtured. We need to protect them and consider their needs too.

Complex questions can arise when a couple's medical, financial, or practical circumstances change. These changes can affect a couple's choice or ability to keep their embryos frozen or pay for another IVF procedure. Couples with frozen embryos may divorce or one or both parties may die, which can leave their stored embryos in limbo. *Custody battles* and even the right to destroy frozen embryos are currently being fought in our courts. If you choose to freeze embryos, consider including directions for their future in your wills.

Ongoing Costs to Keep Embryos Frozen
There is currently no time limit for cryo-preserved embryo storage in the U.S.[46] A couple must pay several hundred to several thousand dollars each year to keep their embryos frozen. This is a significant cost for most. A couple with frozen embryos will need to make yearly decisions on how to proceed when the cryopreservation bill comes due.

Option 2: Donating Your Embryos to Another Infertile Couple for Adoption

Many embryo adoption agencies or clinics offer the opportunity to donate your extra embryos to other infertile couples. Snowflakes was the first adoption agency to include embryo adoptions.

Responsibly choosing a family for your child's physical and spiritual well-being

The issues involved in donating your extra embryos to another infertile couple to adopt are similar to that of a woman placing her baby for adoption. Usually, this decision is made after a couple has had one or more children through IVF and now feels unable to raise their remaining embryos.

In addition to wanting to ensure your children will be raised in a safe, nurturing, and godly home, you'll still need to mourn the loss of parenting those children yourselves. You may always wonder if those children are okay.

As Christians, we hold responsibility for the children who are created from our sperm or eggs. As with a Christian placing a child for adoption, it would be tragic to participate in the creation of a life, then not take steps to ensure the child will be introduced to a relationship with Jesus.

Many of these issues can be alleviated by choosing an embryo adoption agency or clinic that allows you to choose the future family for your embryos or at least designate a family of similar faith. You may also choose to meet a child born from your adopted embryo at age 21, choose an open adoption with ongoing communication with the future family, or choose a closed adoption. In this decision, also consider the child's perspective. He or she may feel drawn to know their genetic parents.

Option 3: Transferring All Created Embryos into the Wife's Uterus, No Matter How Many
The issues with this choice are discussed in the Pregnancy Reduction section later in this chapter.

Option 4: Discarding Extra Embryos, Destroying Them, Allowing Them to Die, Donating Them to Science, or Choosing a Compassionate Transfer
Although the Bible talks about God being involved with children while they're being formed in their mother's womb, the Bible doesn't pinpoint the exact moment of ensoulment. Does God breathe a soul or eternal life into a new human at the moment of conception? Does it happen when the fertilized egg touches and implants in the uterine wall? Is it later?

Since that moment is only something God knows, we need to weigh with great concern whether creating embryos, then letting them die could represent killing an eternal being with a soul. Does our choice respect the immense value of human life?

Rather than having problems with the idea of fertilizing a human egg in a dish, many Christians are more concerned with whether the resulting embryo is being treated with the respect a human life deserves. Are any embryos stopped from developing after fertilization occurs because they aren't identified as high-grade developers?

Dr. Alan McNickle, a former theology professor at Moody Bible Institute, voiced his concern this way, "In the matter of IVF, one problem is that the technology appears to be indiscriminate in what happens to the harvested eggs that are fertilized but then are essentially lost. This seemingly casual attitude toward the value of human life is disturbing."

It serves us well to look into how embryos are treated in the labs we choose. IVF may be an ethical choice for Christians depending on what choices they make within the procedure. For instance, Christians who strongly value the right to life may choose to ensure their core values are adhered to during an IVF procedure by asking their trusted doctor to agree that he or she will attempt to fertilize only the number of embryos they're willing to carry to term. Or the couple may feel comfortable choosing to freeze some embryos if they're assured the embryos will be given a chance to be nurtured to a full life.

Many Christians believe that destroying *extra* embryos, discarding them, allowing them to die, or donating them to science aren't options that honor the respect due to human life. The choice to discard embryos includes donating them to science because the embryos aren't meant to survive.

Some couples have chosen a procedure called a *compassionate transfer* when unforeseen issues have arisen for their remaining embryos. In this procedure, any remaining embryos are transferred to the wife's uterus during a time when pregnancy isn't possible.

Further Issues When Too Many Embryos Implant

Pregnancy Reduction (or Embryo Reduction)
A pregnancy reduction is when a doctor deliberately interferes with one or more of the fetuses, causing them to die. The reason that pregnancy reduction needs to be addressed is because fertility drugs can create more eggs during a woman's cycle. This increases the chance of a pregnancy but also increases the chance of a multiple pregnancy. The procedure is done because the chances of survival for each fetus go down in inverse proportion to the number of fetuses in the womb at one time.

Pregnancy reduction is usually done between ten and a half weeks and four months gestation by injecting a solution into the amniotic sac. Deciding which fetus to *reduce* might not be done according to which one is weaker, but by which fetus is easiest to reach with the needle. Then the fetus is either absorbed back into the uterus or is expelled through a partial miscarriage. This procedure can occasionally cause all of the fetuses to be miscarried.

Deanna had been pregnant three times, but she had lost all three babies at various stages of her pregnancies. She was apprehensive when she found out she was pregnant again, but this time with triplets!

As she and her husband Richard began to get used to the idea over the next couple of visits, the doctor told them of possible problems, particularly with two of the babies who shared the same gestational sac. Additionally, Deanna previously hadn't been able to carry one baby to term, much less three. The doctor gave her three choices, 1) keep all the babies and very probably have a difficult pregnancy or miscarry them all, 2) have a pregnancy reduction (abort one or more of the fetuses to give the others a better chance at survival, or 3) abort the whole pregnancy and start over again.

Richard and Deanna were frightened about what lay ahead, but they felt strongly that they didn't want any abortions. One of the doctors in the practice took them into his office and in Deanna's words "put extreme pressure on us to abort the two babies in the same amniotic sac." He told them the babies had less than a twenty percent chance to live and the only way to significantly raise the odds of survival was to *reduce* the pregnancy.

"But we've never seen an ultrasound that looked so good in any of Deanna's other pregnancies," Richard told him. "We can see all of their strong heartbeats and even their arms and legs."

The doctor spoke more insistently, saying yes, the ultrasound of the babies looked good, but Deanna and Richard should spend some time in a neonatal intensive-care nursery. He warned them that if the babies lived, they might be attached to tubes for the rest of their lives. He told them that since the pregnancy was now four months along, they only had two days to decide since after that the reduction process would be more difficult.

Richard and Deanna chose to keep all three babies despite the difficulties, but they were unnerved by the pressure that was put upon them to reduce their pregnancy.

Deanna eventually gave birth seven weeks early to two girls and a boy, who after much medical support, grew into healthy children.

Justified as saving the lives of the siblings

If you're reading this book, your heart cares about having and protecting children. I can't think of more difficult news than being told you need to sacrifice one of your children for the sake of another.

A doctor who suggests a pregnancy reduction because a woman is carrying too many babies to survive is sometimes compared to an abortion to save the life of the mother. This procedure is recommended to save the lives of the siblings.

The difference is our ability to make a protective choice before the babies are created. Steve Zeisler, a former pastor at Peninsula Bible Church, commented on the idea of a pregnancy reduction being compared to an abortion to save a life, "I think there is a significant difference, in that the group of siblings who will be sacrificed, were usually placed in danger by the choice of the doctor or the couple."

Justified as simply part of the mother's body

Though some may believe that a fetus is simply a part of a mother's body, John Stott says in his book *Involvement: Social and Sexual Relationships in the Modern World*, "An embryo, though carried within the mother's body, is nevertheless not a part of it. [This] is not only a theological but a physiological fact. This is partly because the child has a genotype distinct from the mother's."[47]

All an embryo or fetus needs for full human life is contained within it. All an embryo or fetus requires is the correct nourishment and nurturing to develop into a fully functioning and ensouled human.

Adopting Donated Embryos

Some couples may choose embryo adoption for the same reason that they'd choose to adopt a child. They value the lives of children who have already been created and need parents. This is true for embryos, as there are currently over one million frozen embryos. Embryo adoption can be either handled by an agency or sometimes by your fertility clinic.

Embryo adoption offers the adoptive parents several benefits, such as:

- It doesn't introduce an inequality to the marriage from the baby being connected biologically to only the husband or the wife. Both donor eggs and donor sperm are used to create the embryos.
- It offers the opportunity for the couple to experience a pregnancy and birth.
- It allows the adoptive mother to provide safety and nourishment for the baby during the pregnancy.
- It provides an opportunity to nurse the baby
- It carries a legal benefit because the baby belongs to the adoptive parents as soon as the donation has been completed.

Valerie and Jake decided to adopt an embryo because they wanted Valerie to have the opportunity to experience the closeness of pregnancy and ensure the child was cared for during the pregnancy. Valerie said:

We adopted Jeremy as an embryo from the Snowflakes program.[48] [49] We'd adopted our daughter, Natalie, when she was four years old. She had many difficulties due to her birth mom's drug addiction. We also have an open adoption with her birth mom, who still struggles with drug use. It's been quite a complex relationship.

With Jeremy, we wanted to give him the best start to life. We also chose an embryo adoption program that offered us the option of a closed adoption until he's twenty-one. When he's twenty-one, he'll be able to meet his birth parents, but we're hoping he won't feel as conflicted growing up as Natalie has felt in her relationship with her birth mother.

Also see chapter 15 for more adoption-related matters.

Further Embryo Awareness Issues Variations in Quality Testing Methods, Protocols, and Labs

Embryo Quality Testing

Reproductive specialists monitor the developing embryos and select the healthiest ones, based on a rating scale, to transfer back to the woman's uterus. However, the methods used to judge the viability of healthy embryos vary. Different countries and even different reproductive centers grade the health of embryos on several factors. These factors aren't consistent.

In most cases, embryos with irregularities are automatically discarded/destroyed. Often the specialists or labs see these irregularities as incompatible with life. Ask about how your lab grades embryos and voice your preferences.

Mix-ups at Labs

Horror stories of unrelated babies being born to couples caused by embryo mix-ups are in the news as well as stories of doctors using their own sperm to fertilize the eggs of patients. Though rare, these give reason to ask about the standards and procedures in place at the clinic and lab you're using. Ensure that the right protocols are in place to protect the chain of custody for your embryos. Look for things such as a *double-witnessing* approach where two embryologists check that all materials match before moving samples or performing procedures to verify an unbroken chain of custody.

Equipment or Protocol Failures at Labs

Rare stories of equipment failures at cryopreservation labs also give reason to ask about what protocols are in place in the clinic and lab you're using to ensure the safety of your frozen and stored embryos. For example, does your lab have backup generators installed in case of a power failure? You can choose to work with a lab that will treat your embryos with the same reverence as other human life or that will agree to honor your beliefs in this matter.

After the Decisions

When Mike came home the night I was told I had seven viable eggs, he affirmed the choice not to do the insemination that month. Even though we were able to try Pergonal again a year later, when we got new insurance, I never got pregnant in the six cycles I was able to take it.

I was still relieved about the hard decision I made that month. I thanked God that I was able to come to the decision I did because it matched my core values. I came to realize how easy it could be to make a wrong choice in the emotions of the moment. I'm grateful I don't live with that profound regret today.

Going through this situation made me more aware of my vulnerability though. I have much more compassion for those who do live with regret for choices they may have made in the crisis of the moment.

Your Personal Journey

1. What are your beliefs about when life begins? Related verses: Jeremiah 1:5, Genesis 2:7, Psalm 139:13-16, Exodus 21:22-25, Luke 1:44.
2. What statements or activities from a medical professional would you consider a red flag? What statements or actions might let you know that you need to find a different specialist or lab to create or store your embryos (ex., signs of disrespect or shoddy care)?
3. What ethical decisions have you needed to make (or would you expect to make) in dealing with your embryos?
4. What core values do you hold that helped you make those decisions? If you haven't yet needed to make those decisions, what values would help you make future decisions?
5. Consider answering the following questions to create a belief statement and assist you in communicating your beliefs and requests with your doctor.

Questions & Options about Embryos to Think Through and Discuss Together*

These questions are meant to help you discuss some ethical issues you may encounter in creating, caring for, and storing embryos. Check the questions you'd like to discuss or research further. Consider answering the questions alone and/or together that may apply to your situation and add any other questions you might have. Answering these questions can also help you write a personal belief statement and assist in communicating with your doctor.

Creating and Transferring Embryos

- ☐ What decisions will we need to make during this treatment?
- ☐ How many eggs will we ask the doctor to allow to be fertilized?
- ☐ Will we choose to transfer all embryos that are created?
- ☐ What will we do with any remaining embryos that we don't have transferred to my (or my wife's) uterus during treatment (freeze, donate, or discard)?
- ☐ Could we choose to freeze our eggs and sperm separately rather than freezing embryos?
- ☐ What will we choose to do with any *lower-quality* embryos?
- ☐ If we choose to transfer more than two embryos during a cycle, what would we choose to do about the issues surrounding Pregnancy Reduction?
- ☐ In what instances would we be comfortable discarding/destroying embryos? (Discarding includes donating embryos to science because they aren't meant to survive.)

---

* Find this printable list of ethical questions at: AchingforaChild.com.

- [ ] Have we prayed about this? What do we believe God is leading us to do?

Planning for Created Embryos

Freezing Embryos
- [ ] What do we understand about how the freezing/thawing process affects embryos?
- [ ] What is a typical freeze/thaw survival rate for embryos?
- [ ] What is our plan for our frozen embryos if we're able to successfully have children and feel our family is complete, but we still have additional frozen embryos?
- [ ] What is our plan for our frozen embryos if we were to die before we could have them all transferred? (Consider including directions for frozen embryos in your wills.)

Donating Our Embryos for Adoption
- [ ] What protections would be provided for our embryo/child?
- [ ] Would we prefer an open or closed embryo adoption?
- [ ] To what degree do we feel responsible for the eternal life of a child created by our eggs or sperm?
- [ ] How important is it that a child born from our embryo(s) is introduced to our faith? What options do we have for our embryo(s) to be donated to a family of similar faith?
- [ ] What steps do we want to take to protect our child's physical and spiritual future?

Discarding/Destroying Our Embryos
(Discarding includes donating to science because the embryos aren't meant to survive.)
- [ ] What procedures to protect their lives and dignity would be provided for our embryo(s)?

Compassionate transfer
- [ ] Would we choose to transfer any remaining embryos that we didn't use to my (or my wife's) uterus during a time when pregnancy isn't possible?

Adopting or Receiving Donated Embryos

- [ ] Are we comfortable with receiving or adopting a donated embryo? How would introducing a donated embryo affect our marriage relationship?
- [ ] What would we want to know about the embryo donors?
- [ ] Have the embryo donors been screened for illnesses?
- [ ] What level of contact, if any, would we want with the biological parent(s) of our adopted embryo before and after the birth of our baby?
- [ ] Would we choose to tell our child about their biological parents or keep it confidential? At what age would we share this information?
- [ ] If we choose to tell our child about adopting them as an embryo, but the donors are anonymous, how might we deal with our child feeling something's missing in their life because they don't know their genetic roots?
- [ ] If we choose to keep our child's genetic parentage confidential, how would we deal with the possibility of our child accidentally finding out their true genetic origin (ex., by a medical emergency, the results of a DNA testing kit, or someone who knew of our infertile condition sharing information)?
- [ ] Have we considered the rare chance that our child born from a donated embryo could grow up to marry a genetic half-sibling? What are some precautions to take to avoid this?
- [ ] What are the laws in our country/state regarding:
- [ ] the legal parentage of donated/adopted embryos?
- [ ] payments for donated embryos?
- [ ] Do we agree with these laws?

Personal Belief Statement About Our Embryos*

Our personal beliefs about our embryos:

_____
_____
_____
_____
_____
_____
_____

Guidelines we would want followed regarding our embryos:

_____
_____
_____
_____
_____
_____
_____

What we don't want regarding our embryos:

_____
_____
_____
_____
_____
_____
_____

---

* Find this printable list of ethical questions at: AchingforaChild.com.

Additional questions we want to ask our doctor:

_____
_____
_____
_____
_____
_____

Questions & Beliefs about Our Embryos to Print and Discuss with Our Doctor*

Write down your personal belief statement before visiting your doctor for treatment that would involve creating embryos. Check the questions you'd like to ask, then take this list to your doctor's appointment to discuss your treatment plan. These questions are meant to open a discussion with your doctor about ethical issues related to ART. Revisit your statement before deciding on a treatment.

Creating and Transferring Embryos

- ☐ How many eggs do you typically attempt to fertilize per cycle?
- ☐ How many embryos do you recommend transferring? Do you recommend transferring all embryos that are created?
- ☐ Would knowing that we wouldn't want a pregnancy reduction affect the number of embryos you would transfer?
- ☐ How often do you recommend pregnancy (or embryo) reduction?
- ☐ What do you typically suggest couples do with any *extra* embryos (freeze, donate, or discard)?
- ☐ What would be the plan for *lower-quality* embryos?
- ☐ Could we choose to freeze our eggs and sperm separately rather than creating/freezing embryos?
- ☐ What other decisions will we need to make during our treatments?

---

* Find this printable list of ethical questions at: AchingforaChild.com.

Planning for Created Embryos

Freezing Embryos
☐ Discuss with us how the freezing process might affect our embryos.
☐ What is your lab's survival rate for frozen/thawed embryos? How does this compare to the national average?
☐ What would be the plan for our frozen embryos if we're able to successfully have children and feel our family is complete, but we still have additional frozen embryos?
☐ What would be the plan for our frozen embryos if we died before we could have them all transferred?

Donating/Placing Our Embryos for Adoption
☐ What is the screening process for potential embryo adopters?
☐ What role would we as the biological parents play in the adoptive family's life before and after the birth of a baby born from our embryo?
☐ Does this clinic offer the chance to donate our embryo(s) to a family who shares our faith?

Receiving/Adopting Donated Embryos

☐ What information would we receive about the embryo donors?
☐ Have the embryo donors been screened for hereditary diseases?
☐ What level of contact, if any, would be typical between the biological parent(s) of our adopted embryo and us before birth? After birth?
☐ What are the laws in our country/state regarding:
  ☐ the legal parentage of children born from embryos we adopted?
  ☐ payments for donated embryos?

Medical Professional, Clinic & Lab

☐ Would you be comfortable working with us and honoring our reproductive convictions?

☐ What procedures would be implemented to ensure that our convictions are honored?

☐ What procedures will be provided for our embryo(s) to protect their lives and dignity?

Since there are currently no laws or enforced regulations regarding fertility clinics or labs:

☐ Is this clinic a member of the Society of Assisted Reproductive Medicine (SART)? (Membership offers higher standards & accountability through verified success rates.)

☐ What lab standards or procedures do you have in place to ensure an unbroken chain of custody for sperm, eggs, or embryos? (Listen for procedures such as a *double-witnessing* approach where two embryologists verify that all identifiers for embryos match before moving samples or performing procedures. Some labs offer photos and/or lists of embryo characteristics to parents before freezing and again after thawing to ensure they match.)

☐ What reassurances do you offer that our embryos will be well-cared for? (Some labs offer an app for parents to watch the cryopreservation tanks where their embryos are stored. All cryopreservation facilities should be equipped with backup generators.)

☐ Will any services involving our sperm, eggs, or embryos be outsourced?

☐ What are the costs, both short-term and long-term (including embryo cryopreservation storage costs)?

Personal Beliefs We Want to Discuss with Our Doctor about Creating, Caring For, and Storing Our Embryos[*]

Beliefs we want to discuss with our doctor:

_____
_____
_____
_____
_____
_____
_____
_____
_____
_____

Additional questions we want to ask our doctor:

_____
_____
_____
_____
_____
_____
_____
_____
_____
_____
_____
_____

---

[*] Find this printable list of ethical questions at: AchingforaChild.com.

Requests we have for our doctor:
_____
_____
_____
_____
_____
_____
_____
_____
_____
_____
_____

Part III

Why Do We Ache This Deeply?

8
Feeling Broken

Save me, O my God. The floods have risen.
Deeper and deeper I sink in the mire; the waters rise around me.
I have wept until I am exhausted; my throat is dry and hoarse;
my eyes are swollen with weeping, waiting for my God to act.
—Psalm 69:1–3

When my spirit was overwhelmed within me,
You knew my path.
—Psalm 142:3 NASB

I didn't know how long I'd been lying across the bed. The sun was going down, and I knew I should get up and do something. But I felt like someone had pulled a plug and drained all the life out of my body. I had no control over the tears that continued to run down my cheeks. My body had betrayed me once again. I had vowed not to get my hopes up anymore, but this month the twinges of nausea and my period being a few days late had worn away my resolve. I couldn't deny the hope that had once again exploded in my heart.

But my period had come again that afternoon.

It was my fifth month on Clomid—the wonder drug that I had been sure would fix whatever hormones were off-balance. Even though my cycles had become more regular with taking Clomid, I still wasn't getting pregnant. Though I'd become more adept at tamping down my hopes each month to a more realistic level by now, it seemed with each new treatment they would skyrocket again.

A bothersome thought pushed its way into my brain again, then struck my heart with horror—what if I can never have a baby? Of course, it had been a hypothetical possibility before, but I had never seriously considered it. I'd wanted kids and loved babies my whole life. I couldn't even imagine not having children.

I tried to picture what my life would be like without children. My husband was so focused on his career, I knew children were secondary to his life purpose. The job I was currently doing seemed a sterile existence compared to creating new life and raising little people with eternal souls to become caring adults. I'd always been taught that as a woman, a major part of my life's ministry would be toward my children. I pictured our future home—cozy, but missing children's giggles, building blocks, and dolls. I thought of never being able to share the joy of discovery with my children, their first steps, their first taste of ice cream, their funny words, their fresh insights about the world, or their first kiss.

I pictured my place in our community, how people might view me for the rest of my life. Some would feel sorry for me thinking, *it's a pity, when she was younger, she desperately wanted children but was never able to have them. I wonder what's wrong with her?*

Or maybe they'd never understand the loss, instead thinking, *can you believe she made such a big deal about not being able to have a baby?*

They might even start to avoid me as if I had some sort of spiritual plague, thinking, *I hope she wises up and repents of whatever she's doing wrong so God can bless her with a baby. I won't get too close because I don't want it to rub off on me.*

Our joyous secret of trying to conceive had become a shameful secret. I felt embarrassed, like a child who doesn't want other kids to see her be disciplined by her parents.

The grief became unbearable. I felt I could no longer go on feeling this deep agony and sense of isolation. The only One who could have helped me through seemed to have turned his back on me. It was excruciating. My anguish-induced tunnel vision made nothing else seem to matter. I couldn't see myself ever finding anything else as worthwhile or even enjoyable in life besides mothering. I thought of ending my life to end the pain.

The sun set as I wrestled with this thought. Drained inside except for the ache at the picture of life without my own child, my arms yearned to hold him or her. I began to writhe from the internal pain and thrashed from side to side to try to escape it. I felt I was being torn apart.

"God!" I yelled out. "You promised not to test me beyond my endurance! But I'm the one living in this body, and I'm letting you know that this has gone beyond what I can bear! Have you forgotten me? Tell me, what have I done? Have I offended you so much that you would keep the common blessing of a child from me? I know you can do miracles, but you're choosing not to do one for me. Why? Aren't I loving you and obeying you to the best of my ability?

"I'll do anything, God, just tell me what it is! If you want one of my limbs, take it. I'll gladly pay the loss of a limb for a child. I'm so broken and despairing, but you still won't answer me. You've refused to gift me with my most precious dream. I can't go on like this. I need you to give me a child or take away this crushing ache."

No earth-shattering answer came as I lay empty before God. It wasn't until hours later that I finally felt drawn to call Mike. I was too scared to tell him the depth of my agony, but I cried as I told him my period had come again. He offered to come home, but I told him I would make it through the night, and I realized then that I would.

The Paralyzed Limb

Finding out we're infertile can feel like suddenly discovering one of our limbs is paralyzed. Everything may seem normal until we need to use the reproductive parts of our bodies.

ACHING FOR A CHILD

What if for instance, a woman on her way out the door in the morning reaches out to pick up her keys and finds her right arm won't move. Imagine her shock. She thinks, *that's strange, maybe I need to focus more on what I'm doing*. She concentrates and tries again. Her arm doesn't move. She's confused. She's never entertained the thought that her arm might not work.

The cold fear that something's dreadfully wrong begins to settle on her. She changes her plans for the day. She sees a doctor. She endures months of tests and treatments, searching for an answer. All the doctor can tell her is that there's always a chance her arm will spontaneously heal in the future, so keep trying to use it, but also keep in mind that it might never work right again.

So, she keeps trying. Each time she thinks of using her arm, a small, persistent hope rises in her—maybe this time it will work. But over and over, she's disappointed. Her hopes are crushed again. Meanwhile, she looks no different to the outside world. People are confused when she stops coming to volleyball games or won't shake hands.

When she finally ventures to tell some friends about her sadness, she hears a lack of understanding. *Well, at least you have your other arm*, friends say. Others offer, *at least it's not life-threatening*. A few times she hears cutting responses that make her feel shame, like it's her fault.

Then one day she finds some friends who seem to understand her hurt, who empathize without pitying her. She feels profound relief at their support. She holds on to these friends like a lifeline as she continues to work on fixing her body that still won't work like it's supposed to.

She'll experience a multitude of feelings on her own as she sorts through and realigns herself to her new reality without the use of her arm. Before she adjusts, her shock and fear will probably turn into questioning, anger, feelings of vulnerability, and deep sadness before she'll be able to reassess and see herself as whole again without the use of her arm.

And she continues to live with the hope that she'll wake up one morning to the miracle that her paralyzed arm has begun to function again as it was created to work.

With those of us facing infertility, we discover that a part of our body we had always counted on to work in creating and nurturing a baby until birth is disabled. To varying degrees, we go through a similar grief and reassessment process as we adjust to our new reality. We grapple with what this means to our self-image and life plans.

Grieving

Those of us unable to conceive a child may not experience a clean grief because our loss happens over an extended period of time—as a monthly cycle of hope and grief. This may also be the first disability we've encountered as women since it happens in our younger child-bearing years. We may not have developed good coping tools to deal with loss. For others, this new loss may be yet another grief piled on top of losses we've already experienced.

During this cycle of grieving our inability to have a baby, we also face related losses such as privacy, sense of control, time, money, career progress, and innocence. We may lose the ability to make plans, to move toward our perceived life purpose, to attain social credibility by having and raising children and grandchildren, to progress to the next life stage in adulthood, and to feel camaraderie with friends who are having children.

This is why many women view infertility as such a devastating experience in their lives. It affects so many areas.

What surprised me about grief was the way it kept blindsiding me when I least expected it. A day at church would start with no great emotional load, but a word or a song would set me off. I would have to leave church because I couldn't control my sobbing—not crying—uncontrollable sobbing. It took a while to regain my equilibrium.

I wanted to respond *well* to infertility. I wanted to breeze through it. I didn't want children to matter so much to me that I couldn't function in other areas of life. I not only felt shame because I'd failed in having a baby, I felt shame that I got depressed about my failure.

I finally realized that feeling this pain so deeply didn't mean I was less spiritual, only that my desire to have a baby was deeply ingrained in the core of my being. When I realized this, I could go to God for comfort and also open up more easily to others. Opening up myself to safe people eventually helped me to face my grief and come out on the other side of it. I learned there was nothing wrong with the intensity of my feelings. I simply needed to choose to honestly work through the grief process and learn to express my feelings in a healthy way.

As a note of encouragement to those who might be in the pit of grief right now, I've been amazed at the compassion and depth of character I see in people who have been willing to go through grief and lean into it. The ones who ignore the process often seem to build up walls and become unreachable or bitter. Those who allow themselves to feel their honest feelings, and make themselves vulnerable to God in the process, can end up as people of deep character. I admire and love being with people who have walked through and processed grief. I trust their wisdom because it's been tested through their journey of pain.

Reeling from Shock and Denial

Some individuals ease themselves gently into facing their infertility. Vicky and her husband, Steve, did this. Vicky said:

> Realizing that we were infertile dawned on me slowly. It started as a nagging doubt and grew into an awful reality. I was afraid to say the word *infertile* aloud for fear that speaking the word might make it so.

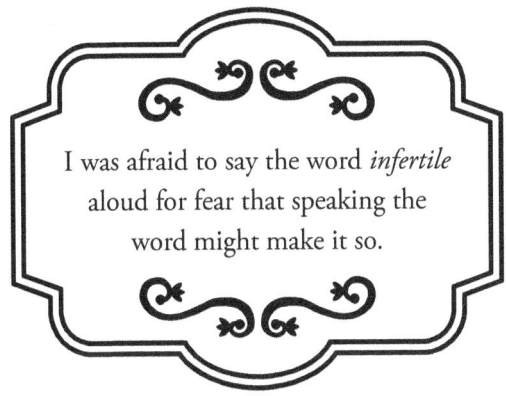

I was afraid to say the word *infertile* aloud for fear that speaking the word might make it so.

When I finally admitted to myself that something might be wrong, I then had to convince my husband. Here I was, trying to convince him of something I didn't want to be true! He's an optimist, and I was easily talked out of my doubts. Looking back, I think we were both in a state of denial.

My situation was somewhat different because my history of irregular periods offered some physical proof of a possible problem. I didn't deny we had an infertility problem for long, but infertility still shocked me. After all, my mom had no problem having four kids. She even got pregnant while using birth control! How could I be having problems when I came from those genes?

It was so hard to adjust our thinking. Since Mike and I had gotten married we'd been focused on not having a baby too soon. We thought once we stopped using birth control, we'd immediately get pregnant. We were stunned to find out it doesn't always happen that way.

For a time, shock and denial are valid responses to our infertility. It gives us a breather before we go into battle. I've had women call me for information about support groups although they didn't yet define themselves as infertile, even though they'd been trying to get pregnant for a couple of years. They'd want to ask a question about a doctor or find out what support was available if they should need it, but they didn't quite believe they fell into the infertile category yet. I've learned not to try to intrude on anyone in this stage, but to support and give any information requested, respecting each person's need to go through this phase of the grieving process in their own time.

Searching for a Cause or Reason

I don't know any infertile person (past the denial stage) who hasn't asked the question, *why?* We ask, *why is this happening?* Within this question we may also ask a deeper question, *why is God allowing this to happen to me?*

Part of the first question is our natural curiosity, *why isn't my body working right?* During the process of searching for causes and reasons, we might find ourselves wondering if something we did or didn't do caused our infertility. We may question nebulous things like the water we drank or medicine we took. Or we may question things with more direct consequences, like a known pelvic infection, rape, or abortion.

During this phase of questioning, a doctor can be a great support in helping us each search for specific causes of infertility in our unique body.

Another way to take care of ourselves during this phase is by becoming aware of other questions our infertility brings up. We can then investigate those questions too.

We can also build emotional support. Forming a network with other infertile couples, sharing with a caring friend, or seeing a counselor can help us name our questions and gain insights from others' struggles.

I address the deeper question about God in the next chapter, but I want to say here that we can hold fast to the truth that Jesus loves us and will be close by our side to help us deal with any scars from our past. Also, remember that God wants us to come to him with our questions. He welcomes our honest questioning because he loves us and wants to connect with us. We're told to pray and ask for answers. We don't have to stop asking questions until God gives us an answer. He's faithful and promises that if we seek him with all our whole heart, we'll find him.

We don't have to stop asking questions until God gives us an answer.

During this *why* phase we may need to keep checking the direction of our thinking against the facts. Pam explained how she needed to redirect her thoughts some days. She said:

> It's amazing how I can go off pursuing wrong directions in my thoughts about whether I might be responsible for some of this, trying to figure out an answer. Sometimes I can drive myself crazy with *what-if* questions. I have to remind myself to reel my thoughts back in and start again from what I know is true.

Frustration and Anger

I was confused and angry that every woman around me seemed to get pregnant and have babies so easily. Everywhere I looked, it seemed my friends, family members, and even women in the grocery store had swelling baby bumps. I was certain that all these pregnant women bombarding my vision had never needed to think about taking their temperature. What seemed natural for everyone else wasn't for me.

I found that needing to consider whether I'd possibly become pregnant next month or year frustrating too. The possibility seemed to affect every decision we made. Should we buy a two-door or four-door car? Should I take the promotion offered at work or prepare to be a stay-at-home mom? Should we move into a larger place? Should I buy this new pair of pants? Should I take this headache medicine?

At first, it was fun to wonder, but as the complexity grew over several years, prioritizing and juggling decisions while staying aware of potential future consequences wore us out. It was like constantly needing to make plans to live in two different countries at the same time. Because we frequently had to process these complex decisions, we both had a lower tolerance for everyday problems that cropped up. Anger or tears were often close to the surface because our emotional buffers were depleted, and we hadn't yet developed better coping skills.

Throughout this long season of infertility, I directed much of my frustration and anger at God for what I perceived as his rejection of me and my dreams. I discuss more about this in the next chapter.

Anger at Injustice

I also found myself infuriated at women who abandoned their babies to die after giving birth, women who abused their children, or women who gave birth to drug-addicted babies. I would rant and cry over the news reports. The injustice of it all!

Julie, a high school counselor, felt this too. She said:

> One thing that frustrates me in my job is that I work with a lot of pregnant teenage girls. I see this as a test of my spirituality right now, but I don't understand why I'm go-

ing through this! I'm newer to this infertility stuff, but I'm having to leave my job because it is just too difficult. Why are those girls getting pregnant and I'm not? I can't tell you how many I've dealt with this year.

Theresa focused a large part of her anger on doctors who hadn't listened to her. She said:

> For years, I've been trying to find the answer to my extremely painful periods. I'm so angry at the doctors for missing the obvious diagnosis of endometriosis ten years ago when they might have been able to do something to control it. Now it's throughout my abdomen.

Anger at injustice is valid. I've found the important thing about anger is to honestly admit it, then express it appropriately. Pretending we're not angry or stuffing our feelings causes other problems, but so does flying off the handle and hurting people with our anger. If we choose to be curious about our anger, it can help us understand ourselves and what we value. Anger can energize us to look for medical answers. It can also motivate us to search out more about God's character.

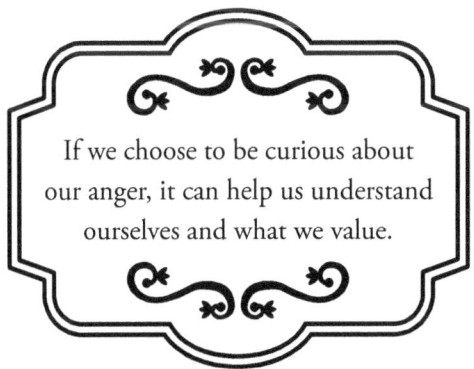

If we choose to be curious about our anger, it can help us understand ourselves and what we value.

Once we admit to feeling angry and identify the source, we can choose how to respond to it. Are we going to make different choices armed with our new knowledge? Are we going to forgive? Are we going to trust God to care for us when we're in this vulnerable position?

Destructive Anger

Sometimes we may find we're focusing our anger about our infertility on the ones closest to us—our spouse for not agreeing to a test or procedure, doctors for insensitivity, friends for not understanding, or even on ourselves for any number of reasons. We can try to determine if we're just frustrated and lashing out or if there's a specific problem we can address.

If we can identify a specific problem, we can address it without attacking the person involved. If we're angry at someone, we can speak the truth in love about their insensitivity or write them a letter. Talking, texting, or emailing when we're angry is rarely a good choice because it's too easy to say things we'll regret later, but the words will last forever. Writing a letter that we never send or writing in a journal can be a good way to process immediate anger before speaking to someone. God will help guide us too. Sometimes our first prayer can be, *God, help us want to forgive that person.*

If we find we're constantly dwelling on our own past mistakes and how they may have contributed to our infertility, this can inhibit us from moving through the grief process. God wants us to live in freedom. We can confess to God that we made wrong choices, accept his grace, and then move on. Guilt or sorrow from God will always motivate us to change for the better. Shame, on the other hand, destroys our soul, immobilizes us, and doesn't come from God.

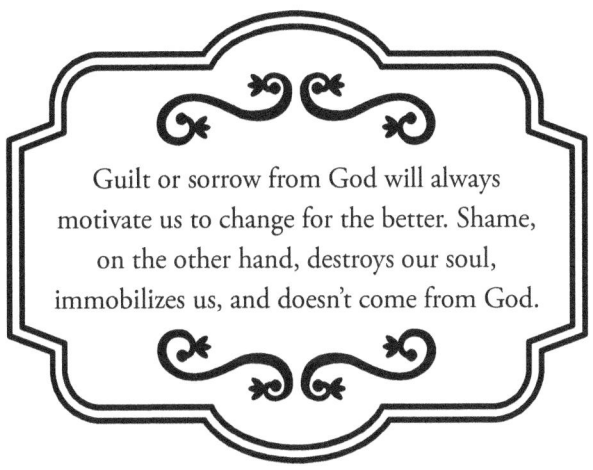

Guilt or sorrow from God will always motivate us to change for the better. Shame, on the other hand, destroys our soul, immobilizes us, and doesn't come from God.

Loss of Self-Esteem—Feeling Defective

I remember a storyline in an old TV show where a female character needed a hysterectomy because of medical issues. She was unable to hold her friend's baby because the child reminded her that she couldn't have children now. She told her husband she felt empty and worthless. She described that time seemed to be passing differently for her now, as if she were wearing a broken watch. Then she said, "I feel as if I'm broken." She felt she'd lost her wholeness as a woman, let her husband down, and now expected him to look at other women because she no longer had a uterus. Her feelings after a hysterectomy match those of some infertile women.

Infertility can feel like an emotional hysterectomy. Just as virility may be linked in men's minds with masculinity, being able to become pregnant and bear a child can be strongly linked in women's minds with their sense of femininity. When a woman realizes her hormone levels are so off that she can't become pregnant or her body betrays her and won't carry a child to term, she may begin to see herself as less feminine.

This is certainly not true in God's eyes. So, it's a good thing to think about how our identity has been affected by the core issue of the loss of our fertility. Satan can twist this and many other lies we may start to believe during infertility. He may use these lies to get a foothold in our hearts, making us vulnerable to temptation.

Whether it's a temptation to believe we're not loved by God or that we're worth less than women who have children, our temptations can often be related to our distorted view of ourselves.

Beth found that her infertility opened her up to temptations in a new way. She said:

> I found myself daydreaming about being attractive to other men. I had never been tempted to have an affair before, but suddenly I started thinking about a male friend at work putting his arm around me. I wanted to escape both what I felt was lacking in myself and the sadness in our marriage. I longed to feel feminine and desirable again. I had to watch myself.

Infertility can erode our sense of worth. We can lose our healthy or proper perspective, which is seeing ourselves as God sees us. But how do we get what we know in our heads into our hearts? It can take a lot of work, tears, and sweat. It may take going back again and again to what we know is true: God loves each of us, and we've been made in his image. We're valuable just as we are.

Feeling Vulnerable and Fragile

As the pain of infertility grows, we can find ourselves trying to avoid pregnant friends, baby showers, or Mother's Day gatherings. We each need to find our balance between participating in life and withdrawing a bit to pursue healing. This balance may be different within each phase of our grief. We can ask ourselves, *is this choice helping or hurting my healing?*

I felt so vulnerable and exposed when I was grieving intensely. As hard as I tried, I couldn't seem to function normally. I was confused and forgetful. At baby showers, I wondered if my destructive longings were similar to what a recovering alcoholic feels like at a cocktail party. Attending a baby shower would break through my fragile resolve to trust God. My focus would turn again to all I was denied.

When I felt my anger flare at an intrusive question during a baby shower one day, I knew I needed to back off from showers until my emotions weren't so raw. Even though I had worked through some of my grief, I still didn't have enough strength to keep from falling back into my negative ways of thinking. So, I stopped going to showers for a while. At the time, I thought it might be forever, but gradually I grew strong enough to attend and celebrate again while avoiding stepping into a downward spiral.

I began healing faster once I stopped isolating myself and found understanding people to share with. I felt freer to talk openly once I shed the stigma I felt from infertility. But I couldn't do that until I realized that it wasn't my fault. I chose to share our condition with a few close friends and family members I thought might be safe people. When they supported me, I began to tell others. When I encountered a hurtful reaction, I drew back and waited a while until I felt secure enough to share with someone else.

Find safe people to share with, then honestly share with them. For me, the most healing came from being able to talk with others in my wonderfully supportive infertility and pregnancy loss group. A safe community will speed our healing, so it's better not to isolate ourselves. Talking to another infertile person, a counselor, or joining an infertility support group are probably the safest ways to start. (You can find information about starting or joining a care group at: AchingforaChild.com.)

Find safe people to share with, then honestly share with them.

Sadness and Depression

Grief can be scary. We may fear that if we allow ourselves to feel all the sadness of our loss, we may never make it back out of the depths again. The strange thing about grief is that when we allow ourselves to face it, we're beginning the process of healing. When we acknowledge our need to grieve and choose to focus on it for a time, we begin building tools to deal with it. We need to lean into grief to deal with this enormous upheaval in our world. We may need to spend much of our time and energy for a while working through our sadness to incorporate the tragedy into our view of life.

Virginia first tried to ignore her grief. She said:

> I didn't know how to grieve. I kept trying to rationalize the situation—to put it in a box so I could put it on a shelf and forget about it. I learned though that grieving is a process. It's not logical, necessarily quick, or even finished at a specific time. I also learned it's okay to grieve, that you need to ask God's help and make choices to help yourself according to your need.

Your loss is real and valid. Many women feel an acute emptiness or hollowness when they're unable to conceive or when they lose a child during pregnancy.

Deanna described her feeling of extreme sadness this way:

> I felt like I was failing in the most important job that I could ever do. I completely withdrew from the whole world for a while. Right or wrong, that's the way I handled it. I had a hard time being around anybody. I would pretty much stay at home. I had a hard time going back to work after my miscarriage. I was scared to face everybody there.
>
> Each day was a challenge. Many days I left work crying. My arms literally ached, and I felt so empty. I didn't want to cook or clean. I left the house dark. I wasn't sleeping, so the doctor prescribed sleeping pills. I would take a sleeping pill and end up crying myself to sleep every night. It was a long process to recover.

When I finally realized I was infertile, I felt the most intense negative emotions that I'd ever experience in my life. I was despairing and disoriented. I was helpless to lessen a pain that was too great to bear. I felt I'd lost my confidence, purpose, strength, and self-worth. I remember reading a book about a woman who had been infertile for ten years. I couldn't *conceive* of living with my deep pain for that long.

What I didn't know then was that my infertility pain was the most intense in the first couple of years. After that, it gradually settled to a dull ache. After a few years, I'd worked through many of my misunderstandings with God, developed some coping tools, and connected with a support network of infertile friends. This made life so much better.

Christian music also soothed my heart and soul during this time in a profound way. I made a list of some of the songs I've found helpful. This is available at: AchingforaChild.com.

A song by Leslie Phillips hit the mark with me about how intense grief can feel and how we need to depend on God for each day's strength. Here are the words:

Strength of My Life

> I open my eyes to the sound of morning news.
> I wish for ten more minutes left to sleep.
> And as I get into the shower,
> The thoughts of facing one more day
> Overwhelm me and I begin to weep.
> And I've never felt
> Like I've needed your help so bad.
> Well, my tears are pushed away now
> For the sake of morning rush
> Till the Bible on the table catches my eye.

And I read that you are near to
The hearts that break with grief
And I realize that I don't have to try
To live life myself
Because you're ready to help me live.
And every day I look to you to be the strength of my life.
You're the hope I hold on to
Be the strength of my life today....

If you're despairing, pray that God will show you someone safe to share your heart with. Many people need help in walking through their grief. Ask others to pray for you. Join a Bible study group to focus on what is true about God. Remember Deuteronomy 30:20, "That you may love the Lord your God, listen to his voice, and hold fast to him" (NIV). I urge you to keep struggling with God to answer your hard questions. While it's normal to feel depressed, don't neglect to ask for help if you need it. God would want you to take care of yourself.

The Bible doesn't list an appropriate length of time to mourn, just that to stay open and soft to God while going through it. If severe depression lasts longer than about two weeks though, or you find yourself entertaining recurring thoughts about suicide, it's time to find a good counselor. You can ask your pastor, doctor, or friends for a referral to a good Christian counselor, psychologist, or psychiatrist.

And if you aren't overwhelmed by grief, that's also an appropriate reaction. People have a wide variety of responses to infertility, so no level of grief is better or worse than another.

I found that a major portion of my grief was because my image of a caring God was damaged. If he allowed me to go through this grief without answering me, was he trustworthy? If I couldn't depend on God, and I couldn't even have children, what reason did I have to continue? Infertility had such an impact on my view of God that I explore that in the next chapter.

Regaining a Sense of Balance

I had no dramatic miracle happen to me after the dark night of my soul, my low point of crying out to God that I described at the beginning of this chapter. I still had many nights of crying and frustration, but after that night I began developing a foundation that kept me from reaching that rock-bottom point of despair again. In hindsight, that time of laying myself bare to God was a turning point in my life. In opening myself up to him, I also opened myself to feel his comfort. In this process, my tunnel vision began to open too. I started to see God working in other areas of my life and began to feel hope that I would experience joy again. Discovering that God was holding and comforting me in my grief didn't erase my pain, but it opened the door to an intimate healing journey with him.

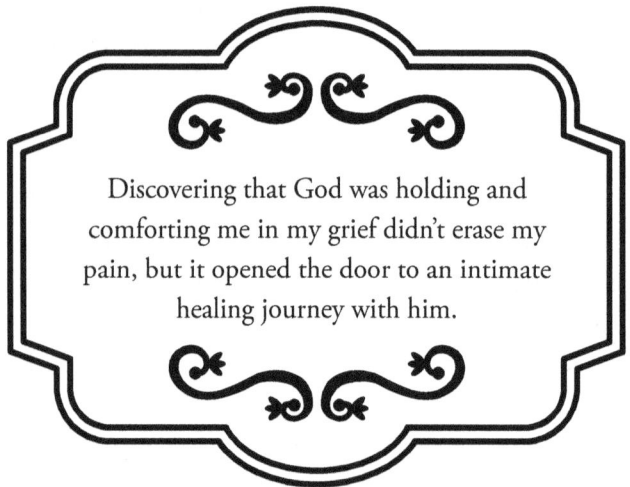

> Discovering that God was holding and comforting me in my grief didn't erase my pain, but it opened the door to an intimate healing journey with him.

While I was in the depths of my grief, I feared I would never recover. I realize now that my grieving was a normal, common process and although I couldn't imagine it at the time, hope and joy did come again.

My healing began after I was honest with God. I still found myself responding to my infertility with frustration or deep sadness sometimes, but these intense emotions usually lasted for days rather than for months. I began to feel hope for my future, that I could live even if I never had children. I could imagine that much of my life would still be enjoyable and that I could still become the unique woman God had created me to be. I learned I had the agency to make choices to move toward what I valued in other areas of my life.

Your Personal Journey

1. Were you shocked when you found out you were infertile? Do you or did you struggle to find a reason for your infertility? Have you found any answers yet?
2. Do you or did you feel angry and frustrated? Why? How have you expressed these emotions?
3. Have your feelings of self-worth or self-esteem been damaged by infertility? Do you feel vulnerable? How?
4. What makes you the most sad about your infertility?
5. Have you felt any times of healing from your grief over infertility? Describe them.
6. Which feeling related to your infertility is the strongest for you right now?

9

Desperately Questioning God

"O God my rock," I cry, "Why have you forgotten me?
Why must I wander around in grief…?"
For the eyes of the Lord move to and fro
throughout the earth that He may strongly
support those whose heart is completely His.
—2 Chronicles 16:9, NASB

> *Lord, I ask more questions*
> *Than you ask.*
> *The ratio, I would suppose*
> *Is ten to one.*
> *I ask:*
> *Why do you permit this anguish?*
> *How long can I endure it?…*
> *Do you see my utter despair?*
> *You ask:*
> *Are you trusting Me?*
> *—Ruth Harmes Calkin[50]*

I've trusted God to care for me for my whole life. But when infertility dragged on and on, I began to question my relationship with God and whether he cared about me.

David, who was called a man after God's own heart, was refreshingly honest and intimate when he talked with God in the Book of Psalms. When I discovered this, it gave me a new freedom to be honest with God too. I decided to follow David's pattern and write my own psalm to express some of my feelings to God.

A Psalm of the Childless

How long, Lord?
How long will my tears drench my pillow?
How long will you keep silent when I pray to you?
I cry out to you day and night from the very depths of my soul,
but you don't answer.
Don't you care about this anguish that touches every aspect of my life?
With one word, you could breathe life into me.
Why do you hold back?
Where is your compassion?
I search the Scriptures for answers, but there are no promises of a child for me.
Have I committed a great sin against you that made you turn your back on me?
Just show me what it is.
I'm willing to change anything.
I've confessed each sin you've brought to my mind.
I still struggle to do right, but it's because I love you, not because I'm afraid of you.
I've searched my heart and stand open to you.
Yet I watch people who don't even want children reproduce with ease,

some even abuse the children you've given them.
Why?
Is it because I'm not sincere enough in my asking?
Am I not praying hard enough, or long enough, or fasting?
Father, I know you hear when I pray.
Why won't you answer?
(10/5 Journal Entry, based on Psalms 69:3, 77:1–4, 88:1–3, 93:7.)

Spiritual Questioning

Christians who experience difficulty having children often go through not only a physical and emotional struggle but also a deep spiritual questioning. Sometimes they may wonder if a loving God exists at all.

Does Being Angry at God Mean I Don't Believe in Him?

I wanted to soar through my trials knowing my relationship with God was so strong that nothing would affect me. I expected that if I were strong spiritually and trusted God, I wouldn't experience deep pain or anger. When that didn't happen, I let myself be honest. I realized I felt confused, frustrated, and angry at God. Then I felt guilty.

Philip Yancey's book, *Disappointment with God*, helped me deal with this guilt I experienced at being angry at God. I thought that if I was angry at God, it meant I didn't believe in him, love him, or trust him. I found myself relating to the man Richard, whom Yancey wrote about. He said:

> Richard was feeling a pain as great as any that a human being experiences: the pain of betrayal. The pain of a lover who wakes up and realizes it's all over. He had staked his life on God, and God had let him down.... True atheists

do not, I presume, feel disappointed in God. They expect nothing and receive nothing. But those who commit their lives to God, no matter what, instinctively expect something in return.[51]

I realized that it was because I choose to follow Christ, and so presumed an intimate relationship with God, that I felt betrayed when I was hurt, but he did nothing to fix it. When I understood this, it freed me from constantly questioning if my relationship with God was close enough.

Maybe you can relate to the Bible's book of Job like I did because it deals with his questions about God that came from his deep pain and loss, both physical and emotional. It also shows Job's *helpful* friends (not helpful!) and how they made his pain worse.

Dr. James Dobson once said this about Job:

> What impressed me most about Job was that the most severe suffering he experienced was not from the loss of possessions or even the loss of his family, it was from the fact that he couldn't find God. He said, "I looked for him in the north country, the south. If I could just go find his throne and plead my case to him, I could make him understand." For a period of time God sealed the heavens and cut him off. He couldn't communicate with God for a time. Not only did Job go through that, but sometimes we pray to brass heavens too, yet God is there, just as he was with Job.[52]

Why, God?

My first reaction toward God was confusion. This didn't make sense! I'd always believed that if I committed myself to God, sincerely desiring to obey him, and following him as best I could, then he would bless me. It wasn't as if I were asking for something outlandish like never again experiencing pain, becoming rich beyond measure, or suddenly qualifying as the world's prima ballerina. I was simply asking for my body to work as God had originally planned. Was that too much to ask?

I was overwhelmed with longing for a child, my body broken, and God seemed detached and motionless.

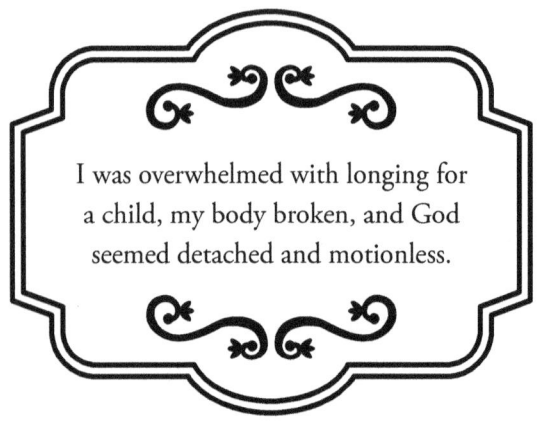

Yet I realized that, like Job, I didn't fully understand God's ways. I was the one in this relationship who wasn't all-knowing. So, I started to look at my faith to see if my beliefs could be based on any misconceptions.

Don't You Understand the Depth of My Pain?

I knew that if I ever was blessed with a child, and I saw her hurting as much as I was now, I would be moved to do something to help. Why then wasn't God moved by my pain? I wondered if God thought I was making a big deal out of nothing as some of my acquaintances implied.

Then I came across a telling verse in Isaiah 54:1 that says:

"Shout for joy, O barren one, you who have borne no child;
Break forth into joyful shouting and cry aloud, you who have not travailed;

For the sons of the desolate one will be more numerous
Than the sons of the married woman," says the Lord.
(NASB)

Isaiah uses the picture of a barren woman here to show how Israel will eventually be spiritually fertile through Christ. Brian Morgan, a pastor at Peninsula Bible Church in Cupertino, California, once taught about the three different terms in this passage that describe barrenness and how they indicate an intensification of pain. He said the last term *desolate one* is *a desolation so appalling it leaves the onlooker speechless.* That brought me to tears. It sounded like God really understood the depth of pain that barrenness can carry.

Other passages also show God's understanding of the distress that accompanies our inability to bear a child. In Proverbs 30:15–16 (NIV), the longing and desolation that barrenness brings are clearly understood:

There are three things that are never satisfied,
four that never say, "Enough!":
the grave,
the barren womb,
land, which is never satisfied with water,
and fire, which never says, "Enough!"

Through these verses, I learned that God did understand my pain. That helped, though I still didn't understand why he wasn't doing anything to fix it.

Am I Being Punished?

The next possibility I looked into was whether God was punishing me. I grappled with this question constantly during the first few years of our infertility. I thought our difficulties must be the result of personal sin. I confessed everything I could think of, but it never seemed enough.

After much prayer and study, I grasped the concept of corporate sin. Even if I confessed my sins and was right with God, I still needed to live in this corrupt and fallen world with the residual effects of Adam and Eve's sin. It's this continuing effect of corporate sin in our world that has resulted in bodies not working correctly, as with infertility, or even death, as with miscarried or stillborn babies.

Sandra Glahn explained she had a similar spiritual crisis that shook her when she was faced with infertility. In her book, *The Infertility Companion,* Sandra says:

> I had to face the fact that I had a mistaken perception of God. My life had gone fairly well up to that point, and I thought it might have something to do with my obedience. I secretly believed that if I continued feeding my *quarters* of obedience into God's cosmic vending machine, I'd get what I wanted. When that didn't happen, I realized that either something was wrong with my behavior or, the more helpless option, that God doesn't necessarily stick to such clear cause-and-effect arrangements. If the latter was the case, as I began to suspect it was, no amount of obedience would solve my fertility problem.[53]

The Bible also clarified for me that *many* problems have nothing to do with a person's sin. Job's friends kept telling him he must have done something bad to have caused his suffering, but they were wrong. We get a glimpse into what's happening in heaven and find that God isn't punishing Job at all. God allowed Satan the freedom to exercise limited power for a specific time to confirm that Job loved God for more than his blessings.

Elizabeth and Zacharias were also blameless but remained childless until late in life. God simply timed the birth of their child (John the Baptist) to accomplish something great (Luke 1:6).

In the Old Testament, there were times when God withheld children from people to draw their attention to his displeasure. In Genesis 20:17–18 (NASB) it says, "And Abraham prayed to God; and God healed Abimelech and his wife and his maids, so that they bore children. For the Lord had closed fast all the wombs of the household of Abimelech, because of Sarah, Abraham's wife." (Abraham was afraid of Abimelech, so he told Abimelech that Sarah was his sister when she was really his wife. Abimelech had unwittingly become involved in sin by taking Sarah as his wife.) So God has control over all his creation—including wombs—and may open and close them to accomplish his purposes.

God's specific plan for Israel was different though in many ways than his plan for Christians today. There are theological differences between a couple's infertility today as a medical issue and the Old Testament's barrenness as a punishment from God.

Ray S. Anderson, a professor of theology and ministry at Fuller Theological Seminary, once explained it this way:

> In the Old Testament, childbearing was considered crucial to the development of Israel as the people of God. The messianic hope of Israel is grounded in the birth of a child, the Messiah.... So, conception was interpreted as a mark of divine favor, and infertility as a sign of divine displeasure or indifference....
>
> With the birth of Jesus, however, we see a radical transformation of this emphasis on childbearing.... The primary metaphor is no longer conception, but adoption. The value of each person is centered on being a child of God, not in having children.

All this does not, of course, remove the frustrations and grief of the infertile couple. But it does remove the stigma and the feeling that infertility is a failure of prayer or a form of divine displeasure.[54]

At times we might even see a direct relationship between our past choices and our infertility. One woman in our group contracted a pelvic inflammatory disease (PID) during her wild youth that her doctor told her caused scarring that now blocked her fallopian tubes.

We encouraged her that God always forgives if we ask him. Once we've confessed, there's no question, we're forgiven (Psalm 103:11–13). God doesn't always choose to change the circumstances that result from our previous choices, but we can trust that he's lovingly working to change those circumstances into a good plan as we believe in his forgiveness (1 John 1:9) and forgive ourselves also.

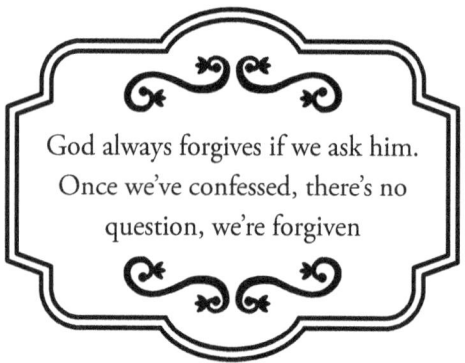

God always forgives if we ask him. Once we've confessed, there's no question, we're forgiven

I still don't fully understand why God left the effects of sin in the world, but I do understand that for some ultimately good reason he did, and we're affected by it. When I understood these biblical stories better, I was relieved to drop the added weight of struggling to find hidden sin that might be causing God to withhold a child from me.

Do I Lack Faith?

I slowly recognized that childlessness wasn't a punishment, but I still couldn't understand why God wouldn't fix me. If God wasn't punishing me, maybe he was playing a cruel game with me that went like this: I was doing something dreadfully wrong but didn't know what it was. God knew what I was doing wrong but wasn't going to tell me. I needed to figure it out on my own, then God would again love me and shower me with blessings. So, my job became finding out what would earn God's love again.

The part of faith I struggled so deeply to understand was God's promise for a good plan for my life (Jeremiah 29:11). I *knew* that God could heal me in a second and make me pregnant. That was what was so frustrating! I wanted to know *why* he wasn't doing it.

Since I was a young child, I believed in God because I saw him in our world. Each seashell, the heavens, our human bodies, they were all so intricately made. I felt it would have taken much more faith for me *not* to believe in a God who created and orchestrated life.

One person suggested that God might not be giving me a child because I lacked faith. I wondered, *am I in this dilemma because I have less faith than others around me? Could a lack of faith on my part be powerful enough to defeat God's good plan for me?* (Guilt seems to be one of my superpowers.)

I didn't attend a *health and wealth gospel* church, but a bit of that teaching can filter into any church. Health and wealth teachings say that if you follow Christ, you'll become healthy and wealthy. Since sickness and disability weren't part of God's original plan, followers of this teaching believe that people only become sick when they don't have enough faith. When someone gets sick, is born with a disability, or even has less money, they're taught that the difference is because they lack faith.

God wants us to hope in him, trust him, and have faith in him. But this belief can be twisted to heap an additional burden of guilt on the sick or disabled person when they're made to feel responsible. Now, not only are they hurting, but the guilt isolates them because they're made to feel spiritually inferior to others around them.

I felt such relief when I read the story about Jesus healing the paralytic man who was lowered through the roof of a home. In this story, Jesus healed this man because of his *friends'* faith. When Jesus saw *their* faith, he healed the man (Mark 2:2–5). If a lack of faith was truly an issue, the faith of those around the person needing healing seems to matter just as much.

Jesus taught us to pray about everything, so we do. We can study God's promises and hold on to them. God's promises are true, so we can trust them.

But the gospel truth that Jesus taught opposes the health and wealth gospel (Hebrews 11:36-40). We don't control God or his healing by our actions. When God chooses to heal someone, it's a wonderful gift. And God doesn't think less of us or play games with those who are disadvantaged by sickness, disability, or the multitudes born poor and living their whole lives in third world countries.

So, we can know we didn't cause our infertility by our faith deficit in comparison to the people around us. But with all Christians, we can ask God to help our trust in him continually grow. "I *do* have faith; oh, help me to have *more!*" Mark 9:24.

Do I Have a Major Character Flaw?

I also wondered if God knew something about me that would make me a terrible mother. Would I raise a child who would become an ax murderer? I knew I wouldn't be a perfect parent, but I'd had a loving Christian upbringing and thought I'd developed the capacity for love and many skills needed to parent a child.

In answer to this question, I found I simply had to look at examples of parents who abuse or even kill their children. I knew I could do a much better job than that.

Dana also understood the answer to this question when she got to know other infertile couples who would make wonderful parents. She said:

> I couldn't understand why God was doing this to me. I fluctuated between feeling unloved and guilty of some unknown sin. Why was God causing me so much sorrow? It wasn't until I joined an infertility care group that I turned around in my thinking. I realized that some women, even some beautiful, godly women, can't have children. It doesn't mean God doesn't love them or that they've done something to cause it. They just can't have children.

Just as no one is entitled to God's grace, no one lives a life that's *good enough* to earn the gift of children either. Children are gifts given to the undeserving. Of course, we still may wonder why we didn't receive the gift of children when others did, but it helps to know it isn't because we would be bad parents.

Children are gifts given to the undeserving.

Does God Really Love Me?

I probably memorized John 3:16, the classic verse about God's love, when I was five or six years old. I grew up in churches that emphasized the need to base our relationship with God on truth alone, not feelings. I still believe this, since our daily feelings can fluctuate, but somewhere the idea got twisted in my mind to mean I didn't need to feel anything for God. I simply needed to obey him. Likewise, since emotions weren't to be trusted, I couldn't trust the love that God said he felt for me was real. I figured God acted on my behalf more out of a sense of duty, like a contract. If I obeyed, he was then obligated to hold up his end of the bargain.

Thankfully, God used my infertility to break through my twisted thinking to reach my heart and emotions. I finally grasped that God doesn't only want obedience, he wants a relationship with me. A truly intimate relationship with God includes emotions, including the delighting in each other that comes from love. The light dawned on me that the Bible would have used the words *duty* or *obligation* if that's what God meant. Instead, the Bible uses the word *love*, a pure emotion of affection so strong he sent his Son to die for me.

Sometimes God goes out of his way to show us some of the many ways he's loving us. We can ask God to open our eyes to see other ways he's caring for us and blessing us while we're waiting for a child.

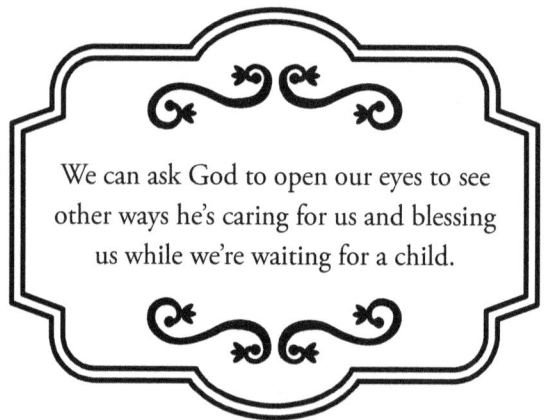

We can ask God to open our eyes to see other ways he's caring for us and blessing us while we're waiting for a child.

At one care group meeting, Sara shared this story of how God chose to help her see how he was caring for her.

I saw an ad for a new shade of nail polish. It wasn't pink and wasn't peach, but in-between so it went with anything. The color was called *shrimp*. I was so excited about this silly color. It was exactly what I had been looking for. I went everywhere trying to find it, but no one had it in stock. The makeup specialist at one store said it had been a special promotional item and wasn't available anymore. I kept looking but could never find it.

One day my husband and I were disagreeing about a job opportunity he had lost in Colorado. When he didn't get the job, he simply said, "I guess God guided us like we had asked for on that one."

But I was angry. I felt God had let us down again.

I was in this frame of mind when we went to the drugstore to pick up a prescription. While I was waiting, I muttered some of my anger to God. I mumbled, "Why couldn't you have given us that job in Colorado? Don't you know how much we wanted it? And don't you know how much we want a baby too? You just don't care. I couldn't even get that stupid *shrimp* nail polish!"

Well, I looked up then, and right in front of me was the makeup aisle. I thought, should I go look? No, I'll be struck by lightning if I walk down that aisle after grumbling to God. Should I, or shouldn't I?

Finally, I got up and walked over... and right there in front of me were three bottles of *shrimp* nail polish. This was the same store where I'd been told, "No, we don't have anymore, and we won't be getting it in." I laughed out loud and picked up the nail polish. I realized God was letting me know in no uncertain terms that he's in control of our lives and cares about everything connected to me, even down to *shrimp* nail polish.

Later, while in prayer, I felt him say, "Sara, I would never use you. I love you. I suffered and died for you. I care for your anguish. If you never did anything but know how much I love you, it would be enough."

God loves us. This isn't just an intellectual idea. He loves us deeply, tenderly, and passionately. And God likes us too. He longs for a relationship with us as much as we long for a relationship with a baby. Learning the depth of God's love will continue to be an ongoing process throughout our lives because it's part of our growing relationship with him.

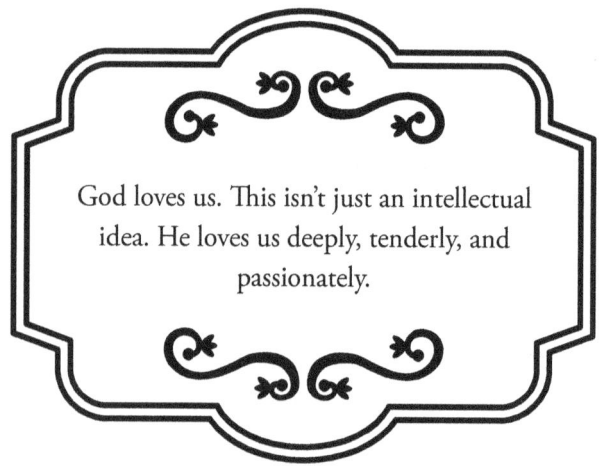

God loves us. This isn't just an intellectual idea. He loves us deeply, tenderly, and passionately.

A good request to ask of God is, *show me how you're loving me today*. This helps us anticipate, watch for, and notice ways God is loving us that we might otherwise miss during this huge trial.

Why Is God Making Me Wait?

Can I just say that waiting stinks? Even knowing God loved me didn't take away the pain of needing to continue to wait for my dream to be fulfilled. Was God making me wait because I wanted something wrong? Was God telling me to forget children altogether? I used to think if God told me I had to wait say, four more years before he would give me children, that would make my life so much easier. Knowing when children would be added to the picture certainly would've helped in making many decisions on medical treatment, jobs, cars, and housing. The real kicker in all this waiting was that I didn't even know if any children would ever come from it.

I had to investigate what waiting on God meant. Part of me thought waiting meant inertia. But I found learning to wait on the Lord didn't mean giving up. After praying for direction, I could lean on God for courage and guidance and anticipate him helping me while I took the next right step.

Many people can remain spiritually strong during a short crisis, but a long time of waiting in sorrow requires us to grow deep spiritual roots. Waiting reveals what we're made of as the false supports we've learned to lean on give way. The core of our soul becomes exposed as we wait. Focusing on God's love for us, remembering to thank God for what he has already given us, and watching for how he continues to bless us has the power to keep us persevering during long-term trials and waiting.

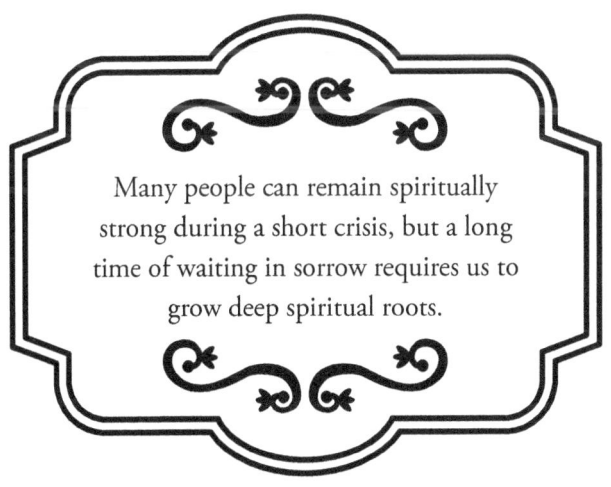

Many people can remain spiritually strong during a short crisis, but a long time of waiting in sorrow requires us to grow deep spiritual roots.

I remember when the revelation came to me that God was answering my prayers and blessing me in other areas of my life. Mike and I had just completed his first year at Denver Seminary and our first eighteen months of infertility. Due to unexpected circumstances, we didn't have enough money for the next two years of seminary. While God still wasn't answering our prayer for a baby, he provided a way for Mike to be accepted into a less expensive seminary, a scholarship that would pay all the tuition at this new school until graduation, and money for moving expenses that arrived from out of the blue. When I realized this series of miracles were happening to move us to another school, I was finally able to comprehend that God was still actively caring for us.

God wasn't withholding all blessings, including a baby, from us because he didn't like us. He continued to show his love for us in other ways while saying *no* right now to a baby.

If I hadn't needed to wait, I wouldn't have gone through the effort to press God for meaning in my situation. My relationship with him would have been weaker because I would have based it on false assumptions. I would have missed out on a clearer perspective on God and his relationship with me. Romans 5:3–5 states:

> We can rejoice too when we run into problems and trials for we know that they are good for us—they help us learn to be patient. And patience develops strength of character in us and helps us trust God more each time we use it until finally our hope and faith are strong and steady. Then, when that happens, we're able to hold our heads high no matter what happens and know that all is well, for we know how dearly God loves us, and we feel this warm love everywhere within us because God has given us the Holy Spirit to fill our hearts with his love.

Working Through Our Questions

When we encounter infertility, if our first reaction to God is fear, resentment, or anger, he longs for us to wrestle and cling to him as Jacob wrestled with the Angel. God intended that event in Jacob's life to teach him something important. Jacob was blessed because he didn't let go of God (Genesis 32:24-30). When our hearts break, we can choose to turn away from God and become bitter, or we can cling to him until we get the answers we need.

Don't give up the struggle until you've experienced God in a new way. In a sermon on 1 Corinthians 10:13, Gary Vanderet, a former pastor at Willow Glen Bible Church in San Jose, once explained what to look for when the pressure feels too great and we want to give up. He said:

> Paul doesn't say God won't allow us to be tempted beyond what we think we're able. God often takes us beyond that point. In fact, he must if growth is to be accomplished.... God must push us beyond what we think we can withstand by confronting us with more pressure than we think we can handle. But it's a controlled pressure, it will not be more than we can handle.
>
> "But with the temptation [God] will provide the way of escape also, that you may be able to endure it" (NASB). When pressure is active in the Christian's life, there's a counteractive power available from God.
>
> It's interesting that the word for *escape* is almost exactly the same word as *exodus*, a way out of the wilderness. When we're in the midst of the wilderness and we think we can't take any more pressure, we must remember God is right there with us. David wasn't resting in a green pasture when he wrote Psalm 23. He was in a wilderness—a desert.[55]

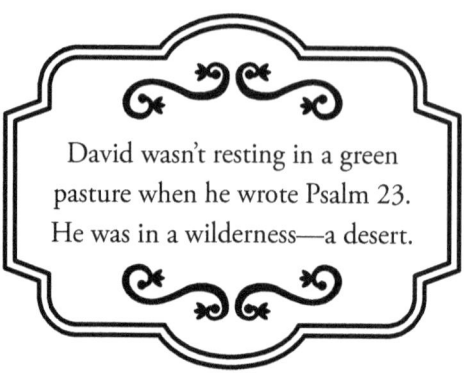

David wasn't resting in a green pasture when he wrote Psalm 23. He was in a wilderness—a desert.

If you feel there's no way out of your wilderness or barrenness and are tempted to become bitter, keep looking for the escape. God promises it will be there.

Choosing to be Honest and Trust

When I went through each struggle that came with infertility, I questioned why God allowed these agonies in my life. I still don't understand all the reasons why God chooses to do things the way he does. I recognize more though that my perception of something being unjust might be because of my ignorance, not because God is acting maliciously.

Sometimes we experience direct positive results when we follow God and choose his values as many verses in Proverbs state. But at other times, there's no direct correlation of blessing when we choose to follow God, except nearness to him.

When Christ asked to be excused from the suffering of the cross, God allowed his suffering to remain and suffered with him. He knew the enormity of the world was hanging in the balance, and the cross was the only way our relationship with God would be restored. Romans 8:32 says, "He who did not hesitate to spare his own Son, but gave him up for us all—can we not trust such a God to give us ... everything else that we can need?" PH.

Job, like Jesus, also continued to trust beyond what he could see, "Job is an example of a man who continued to trust the Lord in sorrow; from his experiences, we can see how the Lord's plan finally ended in good, for he is full of tenderness and mercy" James 5:11.

God's Response to Our Questioning

Comfort

The turning point in my grief came when I discovered God wasn't against me. Instead of my previous guess that God was sitting in heaven glaring at me for a poor choice I'd made, I now understood he was crying with me over the hurt caused by the global effects of sin. One night while I was praying, I felt God's presence and almost tangibly felt his hand reaching out to hold mine. I knew he was grieving with me. For the first time since the beginning of my infertility, I felt a sense of peace. I remembered this poem:

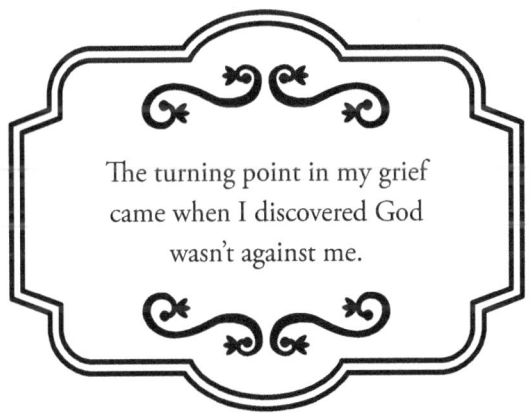

The turning point in my grief came when I discovered God wasn't against me.

Sometimes the Lord calms the storm,
Sometimes he lets the storm rage...
and calms the child.[56]

Going through infertility has caused me to change my whole concept of God. I know my understanding is still extremely limited, but I feel I've been reintroduced to the God of love and comfort. His comfort didn't feel like happiness at remaining infertile, but I began to feel more contentment. My confusion and turmoil dissipated. A quiet trusting took its place as I realized God's love toward me.

Ruth also found she was seeing God from a new perspective. She's facing infertility as a single woman because she's had both of her ovaries removed due to ovarian cancer. I thought her insight about Helen Keller's learning was profound. Because Hellen Keller was both blind and deaf, she spent years of her life unable to understand others or communicate well. Once she learned to communicate, she went on to Harvard and became a prolific author. Ruth explained how Hellen Keller's *aha* moment helped her relax and lean into God when she couldn't understand what he was doing. Ruth said:

> When Helen Keller kept being awakened by hands *spelling* into hers persistently, at first the movement felt like a game, just another stimulus. It was no more significant than the rest of the darkness around her. Then one day the movement against her palm burst with meaning. She learned.
>
> I feel like that with God. Maybe he's *finger-spelling* into my hands, and for long periods of time, it feels like just another stimulus, no more significant than the chair that's under me. I'm still in the dark, but maybe this movement under my fingers has meaning.
>
> I'm listening differently because I'm watching for God trying to communicate with me.

God anticipated there would be times we felt abandoned by him *as orphans in the storm* (John 14:16–18), so he gave us the Holy Spirit. Learning to connect with the Holy Spirit and asking to experience his presence and comfort is a prayer that pleases God. He promises to be near to the brokenhearted. "The Lord is close to the brokenhearted; he rescues those whose spirits are crushed" Psalm 34:18 NLT.

If I Know God Loves Me, Why Do I Still Hurt?

Does knowing God's comfort remove the pain? Virginia, who had gone through two miscarriages, said, "I've gained insights about struggling in my life because of this experience, but it still hurts too much to say I'm more grateful for those blessings than the babies I could have had."

God doesn't promise to take away all pain. Sorrow is a natural part of this life. We all want to be done with the grieving process. Those around us probably want us to be done with it too. While we're in the process of grieving though, we aren't failing or bad Christians.

When Christ died on the cross, he didn't have a beatific smile on his face. And he wasn't singing his way through the crucifixion. He cried out to God in agony and anguish. Yet who knew God more intimately than Christ? When we look at his suffering though, we're able to see the amazing, joyous result that came later and couldn't have come any other way. We see why he had to go through it because we're allowed to see more of the story.

Right now, we're just walking through each day of our story, this one page, unable to see the ending. But we can gather hope from knowing that the same loving God, who planned the story of Christ, also planned each of our stories. In time, something amazing will come from our pain too if we trust God to give us strength and heal our broken hearts (Psalm 147:3).

As we study God's Word, we can practice listening for him to speak to our hearts. Attending a Bible study group can also help us find answers. Joining Bible study groups has helped me so much. Even though I wanted to withdraw from everyone, so many issues became clear during discussions of the Word.

God promises to be with us through our pain. Comfort and courage come from knowing God waits with open arms. He holds us close and grieves with us whenever we're ready to take our pain to him.

Comfort and courage come from knowing God waits with open arms. He holds us close and grieves with us whenever we're ready to take our pain to him.

If we hang onto God, whether we're crawling up into his lap for comfort or wrestling with him for answers, he promises to bless us with a deeper relationship with him. Though we pray to God to fill our needs, he often answers by giving us himself. Our ultimate reward is intimacy with God.

Here's the end of the psalm I wrote to God.

A Psalm of the Childless (continued)

Help me to remember your compassion for me
and that you cry along with me
when I mourn the loss of my baby who will never live,

just like you cried at the death of Lazarus.
Restore my heart to you.
Let us be intimate once more.
Replace my anger with knowledge of your love and an unshakable trust in you.
Father, help me to walk so close to you
I won't fear my monthly failure to conceive.
Help my mind and emotions know you're taking care of me.
Turn me away from wanting any other plan but yours.
I'll recall the many gifts you've given to me
and miracles you've done for me in other areas of my life.
Bring them to mind when I forget and feel once again that you've forgotten me.
I believe your Word when you say, "Delight yourself in the Lord and
he will give you the desires of your heart."
If a child's not in your plan for my life,
then take away the intense desire that breaks my heart.
Replace it with a desire for whatever is in your unique purpose for my life.

In the midst of this turmoil I wrestle with in my heart and mind,
while I'm still waiting for answers to my questions,
while I still don't understand why,
while I continue to quake under this refining process,
help me not to cause another to stumble.
Help me to reach out through my pain
to comfort someone else going through a painful experience.
And the hardest of all, Father,
because it reminds me you haven't chosen this miracle for me yet,
help me to rejoice with someone who has just been given the miracle of a baby.

*Help me to react with love when others say hurtful things
about this, my softest spot.
You've promised to hear and listen to my prayers.
I'm choosing to trust you with my life and dreams.
You are trustworthy!
I know I'll again have reason to praise you
when I've traveled far enough to look back on this sorrow
through your eyes instead of mine.*
(Based on Psalms 37:4, 40:1–3, 56:8, 77:11, 112:7, 119:37.)

Your Personal Journey

1. Write your own psalm to God telling him your honest feelings about your infertility and your relationship with him.
2. Ask others to pray for you. Write down the names of two safe people who might uphold you in prayer and ask them to do that. If you can't think of two available people, ask God to provide them and to connect you with these future prayer partners.
3. Think of ways God has been faithful to you in the past. Write down ten times when God has helped you. Look at this list when you're having a tough day and don't feel loved by him.
4. Look for ways God is actively participating in your life now. What gifts is he currently giving you? Supportive relationships? A caring doctor? Look up some of the following verses and write down what they mean to you: Psalm 84:11, Psalm 103:5, Psalm 139, Psalm 142:3, Psalm 145:14, Isaiah 43:1–4, Jeremiah 29:11, Matthew 10:30, and James 5:11.

Part IV

Does Anyone Understand?

10
Learning to Cope—Self

He gives power to the tired and worn out,
and strength to the weak.
—Isaiah 40:29

For Jehovah God is our light and our protector.
He gives us grace and glory.
No good thing will he withhold
from those who walk along his paths.
—Psalm 84:11

I tried to keep up a brave front as I ate the latest piece of pink-and-blue-frosted cake. This was the third baby shower I'd attended that summer. I tentatively chose to go, steeling myself for the battle of emotions, because I wanted to celebrate my friend's happiness in becoming a new mom. I wanted her to see the tangible support of my presence. And I'd been doing better, learning to trust God more. So, I went but still tried to blend in with the furniture as much as possible, hoping no one would touch the still-raw wound of my infertility.

As insider pregnancy and birth stories flowed freely, I found myself slipping back into confusion and started praying again. Why, God? Why have you singled me out for this pain of infertility? Will I always be an outsider to motherhood? You know how important children are to us. Couldn't you have chosen this struggle for a couple who didn't care as much?

As all the women sat on chairs in a circle to watch the mom-to-be open the cute gifts of little onesies and toys, I counted the number of presents left to open and thought I could just manage to make it through. But then there was a lull in the conversation.

A woman across the circle locked eyes with me, then in her booming voice asked what I'd been dreading, "So, Deb, the question that always comes up at these gatherings... [pregnant pause] when are you going to start a family?"

A wave of inadequacy and shame washed over me as all conversation stopped. I began to sweat. Cornered, with all eyes on me, I glared at the woman, suddenly so angry at her cluelessness. I blurted out, "I know that question always comes up. That's why I often avoid these gatherings."

She raised her eyebrows at my response, clearly believing my non-answer was rude and she deserved details. Relief washed over me when she backed off and turned to the woman on her left. I recognized how oblivious she still was though when a few seconds later, she asked the same intrusive question of her. "How about you? Any family plans?"

I'm usually a patient person. I had thought my defenses were up. What had happened to my expectation that I was ready to respond well if someone asked a painful question? The searing emotional pain that shot through me at her question shocked me. So did the way I floundered and failed to filter my response. I caught a couple of sympathetic glances from other women but stayed quiet for the rest of the time. I left the shower as soon as it was politely possible. I cried all the way home.

This was only one painful moment, on one day, during many months and years of infertility.

I realized after that shower I needed to work through some of my grief and shame before I'd be able to trust my responses to others who didn't understand the pain of infertility. Yes, this woman had crossed a boundary, but I needed to practice how to respond by speaking the truth in love. I needed to develop some practiced answers so I wasn't thrown off balance. I needed to learn to guard my heart better in these types of groups. And as I took time to work through some of the pain, I decided it would be a good idea to avoid situations that triggered me toward anger or focused me again on my lack of children.

For a time, I stopped going to baby showers. I stopped going to church on Mother's Day and Father's Day. I stopped working in the church nursery. I gave myself permission to take a break from events that tempted me to focus on what I couldn't have—pregnancy or having babies.

The Bible didn't say I needed to go to baby showers, but it did say I shouldn't hurt someone with my anger. So, I took some time to heal and learn new coping tools for responding to others while grieving. (I did send gift cards with nice notes to the moms-to-be for the next season of baby showers.)

Daily Stress

The stress of infertility can be enormous. Along with the general grieving process comes the emotional stress of the constant cycle of hope and despair. On the good days, there may only be a mild tug in our hearts. But on the bad days, the pain may feel uncontrollable, making it difficult to function at all. In dealing with this roller coaster of emotional stress as well as the physical stress of medical testing and treatment, we may find we don't have much energy left over to deal with the rest of life.

In studies, the levels of stress that accompany infertility can be quite high. The authors of *Overcoming Infertility* share, "With the exception of a life-threatening illness, infertility is probably the most difficult and protracted medical problem a couple will have to face."[57]

Infertility brings day-to-day stresses that compare to living with a chronic illness such as dealing with a schedule of doctor's appointments and medication, uncomfortable or painful medical procedures or surgeries, side effects of drugs, needing emotional energy to work through fears and grief, and adjusting to a different reality than we'd planned. As in the case of chronic illness, we may keep hoping for a miracle turnaround, which may happen, but isn't something we can count on. This hope-grief cycle can eventually lead to both physical and emotional exhaustion.

The stress an infertile couple carries can also be likened to the stress a military family who is devastated by a loved one gone missing in action may experience. These different groups can both grieve while simultaneously holding out hope, sometimes for years.

It's easy to believe we should try to compartmentalize our infertility to keep our life more balanced, but infertility affects so many areas of life. It's one thing to anticipate a problem going to a baby shower, but emotional pain can also surprise us out of the blue, blindsiding us.

I recently broke my big toe. When I went into urgent care to have it x-rayed, the technician turned to me in the waiting room and asked, "Is there any chance you might be pregnant?" I couldn't believe it. I'd broken my toe! And the answer wasn't a simple yes or no. I was on the second half of my cycle when it was always a (small) possibility. Now I felt I had to explain my infertility history.

What made it worse was a man in his fifties now stood next to the technician, waiting to talk to her. I glanced at him to see if he would go away, but he didn't. I gathered my courage and explained to her that though I didn't know for sure, it was unlikely I was pregnant because I'd been diagnosed with infertility. But no, I hadn't been using birth control.

The technician said I needed to get a pregnancy test before they could take the x-ray. I responded that I'd just ovulated, so a pregnancy test wouldn't be accurate yet. (I avoided making eye contact with the man who still stood two feet away, though by now he was acting as if he'd rather be hiking through lava than listening to this conversation.)

I had to wait three days until I could get a pregnancy test before urgent care would x-ray my toe. No, I wasn't pregnant. Yes, the toe I'd been painfully hobbling on was severely broken. I couldn't believe even a broken toe could expose my infertility.

Emotional Exhaustion

One of the inconceivable things about infertility is how it wears us down emotionally month after month because the stress isn't being alleviated. For two weeks after ovulation every month, we try to follow the rules for pregnant women because we hope we might be sharing our bodies with a baby.

If that's not enough, we're constantly hearing or reading about the dangers of eating or drinking specific things during pregnancy. Some things pregnant women are told to avoid or use sparingly are coffee—because it contains caffeine, x-rays, all medications unless approved by a doctor, vaccinations, excessive heat from hot tubs, saunas, hot baths, alcohol, tobacco, and certain sports. I've even read books that say to avoid pesticides, certain household cleaners, and shellfish. No wonder we feel a little crazy at times if we need to act like we're pregnant while being infertile.

Trying to avoid pregnancy-related thoughts by ignoring them might work for a bit. But it's difficult because each infertile woman runs into face-to-face reminders all the time. On a sample day, she decides she won't think about having a baby all day:

- It's her day off, so she thinks a little gardening this morning sounds good. She picks up the insecticide and notices a warning for pregnant women on the label.
- She decides instead to go in and watch some TV. But up pops a commercial for a pregnancy test, followed by a commercial for a new baby doll.

- Maybe she'll catch up on social media instead. Then a friend's pregnancy announcement comes up in her feed.
- So she's off to her dentist appointment. As she sits down in the chair, the dental assistant tells her she's due for x-rays this visit. "Could you be pregnant? she asks.
- At least in the afternoon, she's planned a trip with friends to an amusement park for some much-needed fun. While standing in line she sees the posted warnings for pregnant women for certain rides. And a sweet-faced child in line asks, "Where are *your* babies?"
- That evening, she attends a social gathering for work, hoping the interesting conversations will distract her. Then someone raises a questioning eyebrow when she refuses an alcoholic drink. And where did all these pregnant women come from? She sees pregnant women everywhere that she's never noticed at work.
- Back home, a headache creeps in. But when she goes to take medicine for it, she struggles to get the bottle open because of the totally unnecessary childproof cap.
- As an ultimate distraction, she decides to do a little work on her taxes before heading to bed. Then she comes to the question on the form that asks, "Do you have any children?"

It takes some strong emotional resources to navigate through these stumbling blocks in the typical day of an infertile person.

Physical Exhaustion

And it's not just emotional exhaustion, because cumulative physical exhaustion can play a part too. The time it takes to pursue medical testing and treatment for infertility can compare to taking on a part-time job on top of an already busy life. The tests, appointments, drugs, procedures, and surgeries, along with feeling we've donated our body to science, can wear us out.

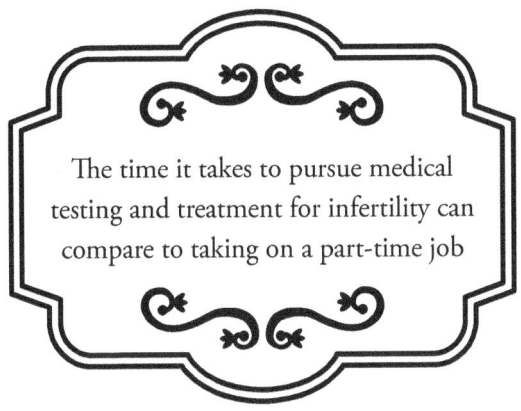

The time it takes to pursue medical testing and treatment for infertility can compare to taking on a part-time job

No wonder we're overwhelmed.

Ways of Coping

Coping Suggestions

Coping means maintaining your life and continuing to function as best you can while processing your grief. You don't have control over much on this journey, so it also means choosing to be kind to yourself while you travel this road. Here are some suggestions. Feel free to add more as you find ideas that work specifically for you.

- **Keep a journal.** One of my journals started as a pregnancy journal, but when the pregnancy ended in miscarriage, it became a place to write about the confusion and grief.
- **Talk kindly to yourself.** Become aware of the tapes or automatic responses that play in your mind. Choose to talk to yourself like you'd talk to a loved friend if she were experiencing what you're going through. Investigate God's grace, then speak it to yourself.
- **Do research.** Finding out information about your infertility issue can give you some sense of control. Write down questions as they come up, then research the answers.

- **Choose to move.** Get outside. Do something that brings you joy or used to bring you joy. Walk if you don't have the energy to do anything else.
- **Eat nutritious food.** Don't do this only because you might get pregnant but because you are worth taking care of.
- **Pick a consolation prize.** When your period comes, do something you wouldn't do if you were pregnant: go splurge and get another latte, take a long hot bubble bath, have a glass of wine, order shellfish at a restaurant, go waterskiing, indoor skydiving or even hang gliding.
- **Allow yourself to laugh.** If you can learn to laugh at yourself and see the funny side of these horrible experiences, you'll have developed a wonderful coping skill. Laughter can be a great stress reliever, even if it's from dark humor. I learned to joke at infertility meetings, "With all the time I've spent with my feet in stirrups, you'd think I'd be an accomplished horsewoman by now." If it's ovulation day and you only have fifteen minutes to have sex during a lunch hour before one of you leaves on a business trip, you've got two choices. Either you become uptight, or you learn to laugh.

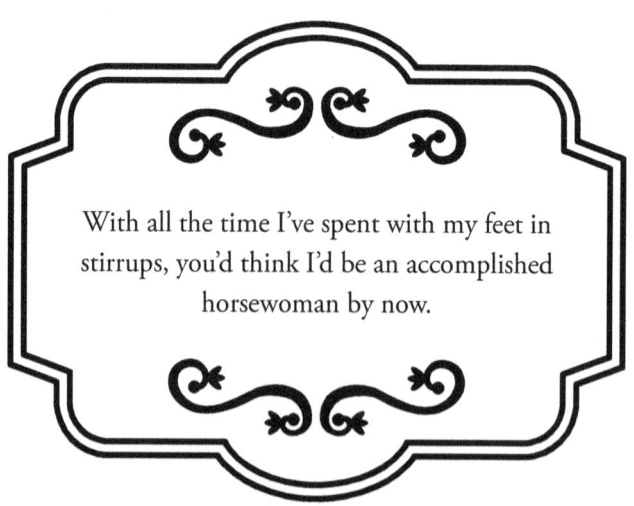

With all the time I've spent with my feet in stirrups, you'd think I'd be an accomplished horsewoman by now.

- **Don't let others determine what you need or make them guess your needs.** Tell your doctor, husband, family, or friends what you need, but also be aware they may not be able to give you everything you'd like. They're only human.
- **Remove yourself from stress when needed.** Your high-stress times are not the times to be hard on yourself. You won't always be able to meet everyone's high expectations. You're only human also.
- **Find someone to talk to who can gently support you.** It may be your husband, a good friend, or a counselor. It may also be a group of infertile women or couples who get together in-person or online for community support.
- **If you can't find a person, find a book.** A book can also be a great support, so look for a book to read about infertility, loss, your relationship with God, a current area of struggle, or simply spend some time off in a fictional world.
- **Ask for prayer from your friends, family, or pastor.**
- **Meditate on Bible truths that promise God cares about you.**
- **Try to notice God working in other areas of your life.** This isn't advice to *look on the bright side*, but an invitation to truly discover where God is caring for you in other ways while you're on hold in the childbearing area. Ask God to show you how he's loving you in other ways.
- **Change what you can.** Looking back at our first few years of infertility, I see we also had a lot of other stressors during that time. I had a very difficult job. Mike was struggling through grad school. We moved five times in one year. We had crazy landlords and bug infestations. And that's not counting the water flooding from broken pipes in our living room. Some of these stressors couldn't be avoided, but some could.

- **Stay aware of events that may affect your mood.** One infertile friend chose to deal with her cycle of hope and grief by being aware of her cycle and never accepting an invitation to a child-oriented function until she'd checked her calendar. If the event was scheduled for day sixteen of her cycle when she should have just ovulated, she would accept. But if the event was scheduled for two days after she expected her period, she declined.

Coping with Holidays and Special Events

Holidays can be especially trying whether we're grieving infertility or the loss of a baby. Even in the most supportive families, we may become distressed by nosy relatives, comparisons, unfulfilled expectations, a symbol of another year gone by, or the drawn-out child-focused and family-focused celebrations.

First Samuel 1:1–18 describes how painful family celebrations can be. Year after year Hannah went to the Jewish feast where her infertility was exposed. She was teased to the point of tears. Feasting was a part of the celebration, but Hannah couldn't eat.

Her husband, Elkanah, didn't understand. He asked her, "Why do you weep and why do you not eat and why is your heart sad? Am I not better to you than ten sons?" v. 8, NASB. In other words, "Buck up, Hannah, and eat something! You still have me!"

Did this make Hannah forget her pain? No. In verse 10 we read she's now *greatly distressed* and weeping bitterly.

Eli the priest didn't understand either. Eli thought she was drunk. Hannah was honest with Eli about her overwhelming concern and how she was provoked to the point of shaking and tears. It wasn't until Eli joined her in praying for God to answer her prayer for a child that her sorrow lessened and peace came to her.

Then Hannah "went her way and ate, and her face was no longer sad" (v. 18). She could only move on once she knew her pain was understood. Then she regained hope. But this came after years of suffering through celebrations.

Mother's Day and Christmas are two of the celebrations that are most difficult for infertile women today.

Mother's Day

I sat about four rows from the back of our church trying to regain control of my tears. I wondered if it would be less distracting to the other worshipers to open my purse and rustle around for another tissue or get up and go to the restroom. Rustling for the tissue won out this time because I realized I'd have to walk past the people sitting behind me, showing them my tear-streaked face. I was so ashamed that once again I was crying over not having a baby.

Mother's Day at church was especially hard. It was heart-wrenching to hear about what a gift and blessing children are, how the children of a woman who fears the Lord will rise up and call her blessed (Proverbs 31), and the reminders of the great mothers in the Bible.

I thought back to one church we attended. Ushers gave carnations to all the mothers, who were then asked to stand up during the service to acknowledge the great work they were doing for the Lord in raising their children well. I stayed seated.

During another service, a pastor chose this holiday to admonish young couples from the pulpit for following society's wrong values. He told the congregation that if we valued making money over having children, our priorities were off. Many people didn't know we were trying to have a child. Was I being admonished too?

I felt isolated, branded as inferior, stamped as someone who didn't value what God values.

Visiting after the service was just as brutal. Either I felt the sting of someone's insensitivity or saw pity in people's eyes. I resolved to stay away from church on Mother's Day until the hurt lessened. This was a tough decision for me. It usually meant I stayed home by myself because Mike was involved in teaching or running the services. I even stayed home one year when he preached the morning sermon. I knew he wasn't going to touch on motherhood, but I didn't know what to expect from the other parts of the service or people attending.

I worried I'd look like a failure as a Christian for staying home. I imagined people saying, *it's too bad she isn't able to get past her selfish desires to rejoice with the rest of us. If only she were more spiritually mature.* I struggled with not being able to live a *victorious Christian life.* My inability to explain our situation to others added to my pain and confusion.

Is avoiding the situation a valid way to cope?
Mother's Day is one of the hardest holidays for infertile women or women who've lost a baby. I didn't choose to stay home from church on Mother's Day because I wanted to diminish the recognition of other mothers. (Motherhood is a difficult role that should be supported. Besides, I owe my life to my wonderful mother!) The reasons were hard to articulate, but I'll try.

First, I realized listening to the virtues of motherhood being extolled encouraged me to sin at this point. It caused me to take my eyes off what God was doing in my life right now and shift them back to my barrenness. If I'd gained some peace in the previous months because I'd let God's love for me soak in despite him not giving me a child, on Mother's Day that ground I'd gained was lost again. And I sank back into depression.

The second reason was that I felt I was a distraction. My aching for my missing child was so great, I built up strong walls against the emotional pain to function through each week.

At church though, it was often difficult for me to keep those walls up because part of worship's purpose is to help us let down our barriers to become intimate with God. Singing has always been a part of worship that touches my emotions. When I sang in church, my love for God welled up, along with my conflicting struggle to understand why I felt abandoned by Him. Worship exposed my raw insides. Inevitably, I'd start crying.

Then I'd worry my crying was a distraction to others who were celebrating. I didn't want to diminish the joy of this holiday for others. I wanted them to have the happy celebration they deserved.

I wasn't about to quit church altogether. I knew I benefited from this corporate connection to God in so many ways. Skipping Mother's Day for a while helped me stay connected to my church.

If we're in pain, so are others

One benefit that developed from feeling such pain on Mother's Day though, was that it opened my eyes to others struggling to find joy on this holiday. I started noticing how many are processing grief or pain on Mother's Day. One woman's mother had died the previous year. A single woman wondered if she'd ever have the chance to become a wife and mother. Another mother's child was in rebellion. And another mother had placed her baby for adoption. One had had an abortion. Another grew up with an abusive mother.

These women don't fit the joyful celebration of Mother's Day either. If you find others who struggle on Mother's Day, try sending them a card to let them know you care. Or plan to get together with an infertile friend to encourage her that she isn't alone in her struggle.

Christmas

People often feel stressed by the complex events, traditions, and family interactions that typically surround Christmas. Adding infertility or a recent loss can be overwhelming. I'd always been a person who loved Christmas and everything surrounding it. (I even had to sneak a bit of Christmas music in July because I couldn't seem to live without it for the eleven months between Decembers.) I loved getting the tree, hanging and filling Christmas stockings, making fudge, and pausing to wonder at the miracle of God coming to live among us.

But it became depressing to deal with the focus on children and family while hurting from infertility. I tried to focus strictly on the spiritual celebration, but so much focused on a pregnant Mary and baby Jesus.

I felt guilty and sad to be unable to celebrate and worship wholeheartedly in the traditional way. But the pregnancy and baby focuses were such reminders of what God was withholding from me. As an infertile friend once said, "I know God could make me pregnant if he chose to. He didn't even need a husband for Mary!"

The Christmas celebration felt so intertwined with celebrating God's gift of Christ coming as a baby. I couldn't seem to get past the baby focus in carols about *the newborn King, Holy Infant so tender and mild, this is the night of our dear Savior's birth,* and *for unto us a Child is born,* to feel worshipful or positive.

It took years, but I learned to refocus my worship of God during Christmas so I could celebrate again. As in many other areas of my life, I had to rethink Christmas because of infertility.

Is Christmas only about pregnant Mary and baby Jesus?

Christmas is about God showing his miraculous love for us. Here are some ways I learned to focus on other areas of God's many-faceted love for us during Christmastime:

- Instead of focusing on Jesus as a baby, I learned to focus on the rest of his life as an adult and his teaching. The whole reason Christ came was to give us hope and a way to have a relationship with him.
- I learned to concentrate on Christmas enabling us to become adopted children of God. This turned my attention away from the birth process and more toward the redemptive aspects of adoption.

- I looked for and found two Christmas carols with a spiritual emphasis that didn't focus on Jesus as a baby, "Joy to the World" and "O Come, O Come Emmanuel." I felt relieved to know I could sing these carols wholeheartedly and allow myself to feel what I was singing without worrying that the image of a baby would pop up in the words.
- An advent wreath helped me to remember and focus on the long time the world waited for a Messiah to come. Lighting one candle during each of the four weeks before Christmas helped me to realize that the Israelites waited for many years without any sign of fulfillment. They waited and wondered just like me.

Christmas traditions

Christmas can be a great time to celebrate as a couple and create traditions that bond the two of you. Talk with your spouse about what you each enjoy about Christmas and what hurts. Be creative in thinking of nontraditional things to do that you'd both enjoy. Don't put off starting traditions until you have children. Consider doing things during Christmas that would be difficult to do with young children, such as having an elegant dinner or traveling. Or give yourself permission to enjoy fun, child-like traditions without children, such as wearing matching pajamas or socks, filling each other's Christmas stockings, buying keepsake ornaments for each other, making Christmas cookies together, or creating a special Christmas breakfast.

What if an old family tradition is too painful? Are you obligated to continue it? Can you identify the parts that are more difficult right now and avoid those? If you expect a family tradition will be painful for you this year, try to see if family members would be willing to try something new. Asking to alter a family tradition can risk possibly offending family members because extended family traditions are often tied to deeper meaning and family history.

If the tradition is still meaningful to others in your family, then encourage them to continue it, but allow yourself to minimize your participation. Show that you care for your family in other ways such as sending letters or going out of your way to make plans to visit them at times other than the holidays.

If times of opening gifts are the most painful for you because you can't handle all your small nieces and nephews for days on end, maybe you can minimize some of the time you're together with extended family. You could arrange instead to open presents by yourselves, then get together just for Christmas dinner rather than spending all morning immersed in exchanging gifts. Another possibility is to try scheduling most of your time with your extended family in the afternoon (during nap time) or the evening when the babies might be asleep.

If lessening your time with family doesn't work for you, don't be afraid to kindly say no to events you find too painful to bear. Sometimes by passing up one event you can build up some emotional buffer room to help you cope with the next one.

For those who've lost a baby, it's all right to skip some painful traditions and rituals. Tell people you're grieving, so would like to do things differently this year. It's also acceptable to spend time with fewer people. Don't expect holidays to be the same as in the past. It takes time to adjust to our new normal.

Don't expect holidays to be the same as in the past. It takes time to adjust to our new normal.

With our new sensitivity, we may be more aware of other people who are lonely or hurting at Christmas. Maybe there's another childless couple, a child who needs extra attention, a single person, a college student away from home, or an elderly person who also feels left out. Take time to send a note or ask them over. Buying clothes for a needy family's children one year also helped remind me having children doesn't mean the end of all problems.

Whatever we do to cope with the holidays, we can reassure our family and friends we care about them and our intense pain won't last forever. Then we'll be able to choose the things that won't re-injure our hurt. It's okay to guard our hearts from those who don't understand. It's okay to make different choices due to our current emotional limitations.

Your Personal Journey

1. Which area of your infertility causes you the most stress right now? What other stressors do you have in your life right now? Which stressors could you change?
2. What triggers you to feel anger, depression, or sadness?
3. What two ways you will choose to be kind to yourself in the next month?
4. What holiday traditions would you like to start with your spouse? How might you modify some existing holiday rituals to make them better this year?

11

Sharing Support—Your Spouse

*Many men grow up to see a conversation as a contest—
either to achieve the upper hand or to protect themselves
from other people pushing them around.
For many women, however, a conversation is a way to seek
and give confirmation and support.[58]*
—Deborah Tannen

*A key lesson I've learned in living through six years of
infertility and two adoption processes is that my wife
is really different from me. We have very
different personalities and comfort levels with situations.
All of that produces the likelihood we're going to
respond differently to things that are important to us.*
—Steve S.

About three years into our infertility journey, we found ourselves at a crossroads. One path led toward adoption, the other continued along *the medical path that would hopefully end at a biological child. We each wanted to go in a different direction to build our family.*

I'd had enough of being poked and prodded, so was quite ready to turn toward adoption. I felt so wrung-out emotionally, I cried at the mere thought of going back to the doctor. I was ready to stop the roller coaster of office visits, surgeries, and fertility meds. Plotting my daily temperature and filling my calendar with more doctor's visits only felt like reminders of my failure to conceive. I was ready to be a parent through adoption and was concerned that once we got approved by an adoption agency, we still might have years to wait.

Mike, on the other hand, felt more strongly about having a biological child, so he wanted to continue on the medical path until we'd exhausted all medical options. Part of his reluctance to pursue adoption stemmed from some heart-wrenching stories we'd heard about babies being taken from adopting parents after a birth parent changed their mind in a private adoption. Neither of us felt we would handle that well. He also didn't like what he perceived as competition with other couples to adopt a healthy newborn baby. In addition, his family heritage placed a strong priority on biological bloodlines.

So, we did the only thing we could. We camped out beside the proverbial fork in the road and took a break for a few months.

One reason this decision was so agonizing was that we had always worked together as a united front against infertility, but now the struggle had shifted. I started to see Mike's viewpoint as blocking my chances to become a mother through adoption. He began to view my desire to adopt as giving up on the biological child he hoped for.

I felt myself withdrawing because I could no longer go to Mike for comfort. I thought, can't he see how desperately I want a child? How can he deny me this? Why can't he view adoption with the same joy I do, as a symbol of Christ adopting us?

He wondered, why is she pushing so hard to start the adoption process now? Can't she see the possibilities and benefits of having a biological child?

It took hours, days, weeks, and months of talking to work through this issue. It encompassed thinking through our deep values, planning for other life goals, and figuring out realistic expectations for each possible route.

I finally realized Mike wasn't against adoption. It simply felt safer to him to go the medical route. And Mike finally realized how afraid I was that I'd never become a mom. He also began to understand how hard the medical testing and treatments were on me. Another thing I realized was that I had processed more of my grief at not being able to have a biological child than Mike had.

He had been busy focusing on other life goals while I was eyebrow-deep into methods of creating a family. I had faced and grieved the loss of a biological child more deeply each month, so I had processed the loss sooner than he had. We needed multiple discussions to understand first ourselves, then each other, to arrive at a mutual conclusion.

When we worked to understand the depth and scope of each other's feelings, we were finally able to agree on a compromise. Mike agreed to put our name on an adoption agency's waiting list (which at the time had an estimated three-to-five-year wait). And I agreed to continue with infertility testing and treatments while we waited for an adoption to come through.

We both had to work extremely hard to find words to express ourselves and understand each other's underlying feelings. Our reasons were deeper than the initial objections we each presented. Only when we uncovered these deep-rooted desires could we each compromise a little to fulfill both of our goals, Mike's for a definite answer on the possibility of a biological child, and mine to have a child to raise before I grew too old and ran out of energy to raise one.

This enormous obstacle taught Mike and me again how different we were from each other. At times in this process, we felt our differences separated us by a great chasm neither of us could cross.

Different Reactions of Men and Women

Infertility can cause prolonged stress in a marriage. If you're feeling the stress, know you're not alone.

While it's not fair to generalize because each person is unique, there is some benefit in realizing men and women often react differently to infertility.[59] The differences that show up during the stress of infertility can first strain a marriage relationship before growth is seen. Not only is each spouse affected by infertility, but the marriage relationship itself is redefined.

Understanding and supporting each other while facing infertility often takes lots of time and communication. The resulting strain can potentially worsen depending on how we handle it. Even in the best of marriage relationships, the number of life-changing decisions infertility introduces can be stressful.

- Do both of us have an equally strong desire to have children?
- Do we agree on the best way to build our family?
- Do we cope with stress the same way (ex., talk it out vs. retreat)?
- Do we cope with conflict the same way?

Opposites often attract, so many spouses have personalities that are wildly different from their partner's. Surprise! One spouse wants to research the problem and create a battle plan, the other wants to wait and see what happens. One is pessimistic about the outcome, the other is perpetually hopeful the answer is around the next corner. Discovering and accepting our differences, learning to function together through grief, and working together toward life goals are important relationship work for those with infertility.

One night we invited husbands to share at one of our infertility support group meetings. It was a few years into our infertility when Mike described his feelings about our differences. He said:

> Though I'm an emotional driver and often get angry when I'm driving on the freeway, I haven't gotten very emotional about our infertility. I've always figured our problem was just timing, and eventually it would work.
> Then we started realizing the medical problems involved. Deb began to hurt emotionally and get frustrated. All the while, I focused on grad school and my career. I hurt with her, but what I remember most was the nuisance of sex being scheduled for us. I was confident we would get pregnant eventually, but it was okay with me if it didn't happen right away.
> I wasn't despairing, Deb was despairing. There were times when I saw her hurting and I'd ask, "What do you want me to do? How can I help?" It's such a helpless feeling.
> I think I maintained a high confidence level about having children because I didn't have the same emotional investment as Deb. Many men don't seem to get the same level of satisfaction from having babies. I've also been more detached from the whole medical process. It's been easier for me to say we'll keep going because she's the one who has to keep doing the bulk of the tests and treatments.
> Also, I saw it more as a challenge. Until we'd gone through every single test the doctors offered, I wasn't going to admit defeat.

Whether by conditioning or genetics, men and women often approach problems from different viewpoints. [60] [61] These differences are offered here for discussion, though your personal experience will be uniquely yours.

Here are some general examples of how men may react differently than women:

- Men often don't see infertility as a threat to their identity, even when they have the reproductive impairment.
- Men often experience infertility indirectly through the effect it has on their wives.
- Men may discuss problems with fewer people, leaning more on their wives for sole emotional support.
- Men may find it more difficult to talk about their feelings.
- If a problem is shared with men, they often focus on finding a solution and acting to fix the problem.

Meanwhile, many women approach issues such as infertility with these types of responses:

- Women often experience infertility as a blow to their identity, regardless of whether a reproductive impairment is found in their body.
- Women have a greater need to share their burdens and find it easier to ask for help.
- Women find it difficult to separate other parts of their lives from their infertility problems.
- Women tend to express their feelings more easily.
- Women don't necessarily expect an answer or solution when discussing an issue. They appreciate the comfort and support that being listened to gives them.

Know the Foe

When we don't understand differences in our spouse, we often try to win our spouse over to our *right* way of thinking. Communication is good, but how it's done is critical. Multiple talks or even intense discussions (read, *ahem*, arguments) are natural when trying to work through deep issues such as:

- feelings that are difficult to put into words,
- life goals,
- what we each perceive as God's calling for our life,
- the best medical tests, treatments, and timing,
- the best adoption path and timing,
- and how a child would change our place in our culture.

When we're working through these issues, we need to remember not to confuse attacking the infertility problem with attacking others, including our spouse. Here are some guidelines from the Bible about working out differences:

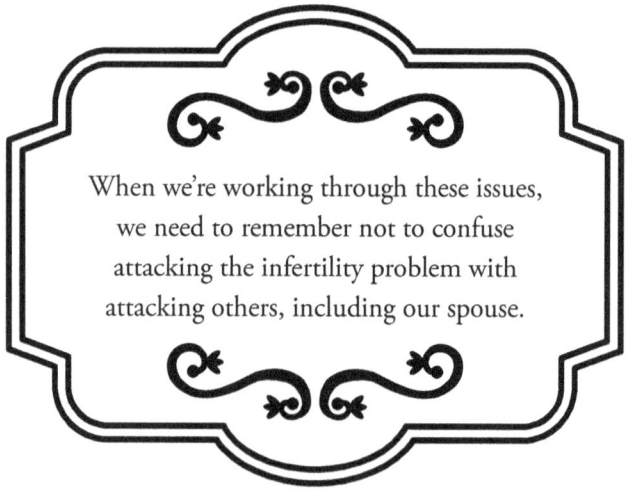

> When we're working through these issues, we need to remember not to confuse attacking the infertility problem with attacking others, including our spouse.

- "Let everyone be quick to hear, slow to speak, and slow to anger" James 1:19 NASB. It's better to first try to work at fully hearing what the other person is saying and meaning, setting any anger we feel aside.

- "If you are angry, don't sin by nursing your grudge. Don't let the sun go down with you still angry—get over it quickly." Ephesians 4:26. Stopping to remember that the foe is the problem, not each other is important. With each issue that arises, we can work to resolve them rather than withdrawing from each other.
- "Put them all aside: anger, wrath...and abusive speech" Colossians 3:8 NASB. As we talk things out, it's essential to remember not to say anything abusive toward each other that we'll regret later, avoiding blaming, name-calling, or loaded words.

Working through the grief of infertility is difficult for individuals and couples to endure, but continuing to reach out, learning more about each other, and caring for each other's needs can bring deeper intimacy to marriages.

From the Male Perspective

When the Problem is Sperm

If the medical problem lies in an issue within the wife's body, men tend to be more pragmatic about infertility. When the medical problem lies within the husband's body though, men often respond more emotionally than the typical male response.

The husband is then the one who may need to take fertility drugs, have a varicocele procedure, or wear a cooling device to cool his scrotum for better sperm production. These actions affect the private areas of his body as well as his psyche. Because the ability to father a child is sometimes wrongly connected with sexual performance, he may also feel his masculinity and sexuality are being questioned.

Ted felt this when doctors found problems with his sperm. He said:

> When I was thirteen, I had one of my testicles removed. It was up in my abdomen. The doctor had to remove it because he thought it was cancerous. It was hard on my pride and ego. My wife felt uncomfortable even bringing it up to me, but we wondered if that was possibly causing our problem. We wanted to find out, so I took every test I could.
> We found out that half of my sperm were dysfunctional.
> I wondered, did some of my defective sperm get into my wife's eggs and cause our children to miscarry? Maybe I didn't produce the right chromosomes. Maybe I didn't have the right mechanical parts within myself to give my wife a child. I felt like a failure. I struggled with feeling I was to blame for our infertility and miscarriage problems. I questioned my masculinity too. I felt inadequate when my virility came under question.

Handling Embarrassment

Men also have to deal with the embarrassment of having to deliver sperm on a schedule for fertility testing. Delivering sperm samples makes most men uncomfortable because of its connection to sexual stimulation. Something very private is suddenly public.

As Ted confirmed, delivering sperm samples has its embarrassing side. He said:

> I was taking a sperm sample to the hospital for a test. As I walked from my car, of course, I ran into someone I knew. There I stood holding my little bag as my friend kept talking. It was so cold outside. I was tense thinking, *these little guys are going to freeze*. I had to quickly think of a believable reason to leave before he asked what I had in my lunch bag.

Men Grieve

Some men feel restricted in how they can express their grief over infertility. Differences in the ways men and women express emotion are taught by our family of origin and culture. Women are given more permission in our culture to cry and talk. Sometimes men feel forced into playing the role of the strong protector when they don't feel strong. Richard discovered this after his wife's second miscarriage. He said:

> The instant I knew we were pregnant with each baby, it was like a big explosion of excitement and joy. Instantly I loved our baby with a forever love!
>
> I'll always love the ones we lost. Every time we had a miscarriage, I thought it would be easier if somebody would instead take my arm or leg so I could have a child. There was a baby I loved, someone who was living just a short while ago, and the D&C procedure that was done after the baby's heart stopped beating, pulled it all apart.
>
> My wife became very withdrawn and hid from her family and friends, but I had to go back to work. The sadness hit so deep I couldn't sleep. It was blacker than black. When you're that low, there's not much anybody can do or say. But I had learned from past experiences how to hide some of that emotion and continue to operate. My wife needed me to be the strong statue of love, tenderness, faith, and hope.
>
> But I wanted someone to lean on also.

Dealing with Infertility Indirectly

One study found when men were affected by infertility, they tended to respond indirectly to it. The men chose objects or activities to fill the void of childlessness. Some chose to *lavish parental affection and pride* on a non-human object (such as improving a house), others became immersed in bodybuilding, personal health, or macho sexuality, while still others got involved in activities that included other people's children (such as coaching a Little League team or leading a church youth group).

This study also found the men who reached out to other children were much more likely to eventually have a child or adopt. These men also rated their marital happiness as higher later on. So, it's important to recognize indirect ways of dealing with infertility.[62]

What's a Husband to Do?

Even though husbands can experience an incredible sense of loss and grief over infertility, they still may not feel it as intensely as their wives. This can create another dilemma for husbands.

Steve learned to understand his wife's grief about childlessness by relating it to other grief in his life. He said:

> I have a sperm motility problem and my wife has endometriosis, which is a killer combination for fertilizing things. It wasn't a huge emotional thing for me to be able to replicate my particular gene pool because adoption was always an option for me. Since it wasn't such a big problem for me, I think that set up and intensified the conflict between my wife and myself.
>
> We both agree about wanting kids, but my wife needs children much more than I do. I mean, I think children are a great concept, but I don't need them to fill an emotional need. She has about 15,000 pounds of concern about kids, and I've got maybe 25 pounds.
>
> The year that changed my attitude and helped me recognize, accept, and even value Vicky's differences was the

year we found out that my father's cancer was terminal. He literally wasted away before my eyes and died. Also, that year I was laid off from work, Vicky lost her job, and we found out we absolutely, positively could not have babies.

I was grieving for my father...I had an intense love for him. I cried almost every day for sixteen months. Vicky loved my dad and felt concerned about me, but she didn't feel it as intensely as I did. It finally occurred to me there was a good reason for that. It was simply a matter of relation. She didn't stand in the same close relation I did to my father.

That's a real difference between me and my wife. I don't stand in the same place in infertility that she does. I don't have the capacity to bear life in my body. I don't have a monthly reminder of that capacity. I haven't lived with the expectation from the time I was a small child that I'd someday bear life and rear children.

Our different reaction to infertility doesn't mean I don't care enough about her, it simply means I don't share in the same experience she does. That was a real turning point. It took some bitter, bitter life experiences to teach me that. But it was a valuable lesson that cemented our relationship and marriage.

Potential suggestions for husbands

- Ask your wife how she would like you to support her.
- Listen, and make eye contact while talking, then hold and hug your wife.
- Share your pain and other feelings about infertility with your wife.
- Pray with your wife and for your wife (Genesis 25:21).

- Become knowledgeable about infertility, grief, or adoption to become more involved in the process. (Read about infertility. Go together to the doctor's appointments. Offer to take a turn recording the temperature chart or other medical tracking. Research adoption agencies.)
- Give your wife time and space to grieve the pain of infertility differently than you. It can be difficult to watch someone you love hurt so intensely, but your wife will heal more quickly if you acknowledge her pain and let her know it's okay for her to express her honest feelings.

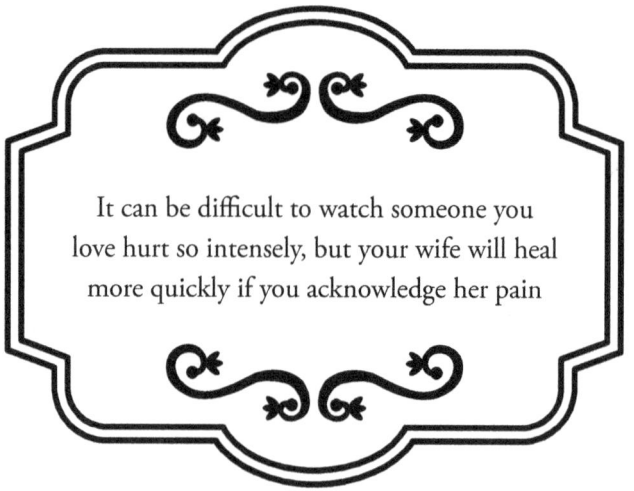

It can be difficult to watch someone you love hurt so intensely, but your wife will heal more quickly if you acknowledge her pain

- Work to discover ways you can work as a team to protect each other when the subject of babies comes up at gatherings.
- Tell your wife you love her, and specific things you appreciate about her.
- Create a special day to celebrate your wife, such as the Saturday before Mother's Day.

- Plan together how you'll handle painful days, such as Mother's Day or Baby Dedication Sundays.
- If you feel frustrated about the amount of time you're spending talking about infertility, try the 20-minute rule. Set aside a certain amount of time each day (ex., 20 min.) when you talk about infertility and promise to listen to each other carefully. Then agree not to mention it again that day (with exceptions for big events like medical procedure days).
- Talk with your wife about related losses you're both experiencing or realizing because of your inability to have children now.
- If you find yourself struggling with the emotional effects of male or female infertility, you might be helped by talking to other men who've been in the same situation. If you don't know anyone to contact, the organization RESOLVE can often help (resolve.org).

What's a Wife to Do?

Dana first thought her husband's easier acceptance of their infertility meant he didn't care. She said:

> My husband was very sweet and supportive of me and my sorrow over our being infertile. He cried with me when the doctor gave us the discouraging news. But he wasn't devastated. He could live without children and go on with his life. I had a hard time with his ability to *get over it* when I felt I'd *never* get over it. My desire for children was such a part of me it reached to my soul.
>
> He was afraid I was being consumed by my desire for a family. I thought he didn't care enough. We had many

conversations, discussions, and arguments over having children and have come to understand our differences. Our marriage is stronger after going through infertility and adoption together, but only because of God's grace and our perseverance at communication.

Potential suggestions for wives

- Ask your husband how he would like you to support him.
- Share your hurt with your husband but let him know you aren't asking him to fix it.
- Pray for and with your husband.
- Husbands sometimes complain they feel their wife only sees them as a sperm delivery service. Respect your husband's feelings and physical well-being in scheduling sex. Schedule times to let him know you value him just for himself.
- If the side effects of taking fertility drugs or other medical treatments are taking their toll on your marriage, be willing to take a break from treatment.
- Learn to laugh together at the ridiculous side of some infertility tests and treatments.
- If you feel frustrated about the amount of time you're spending talking about infertility, try the 20-minute rule. Set aside a certain amount of time each day (ex., 20 min.) when you talk about infertility and promise to listen to each other carefully. Then agree not to mention it again that day (with exceptions for big events like medical procedure days).
- If you need to talk about infertility more than your husband wants to, find other people to discuss it with—other infertile women, a counselor, a pastor, or an online group.

- Tell your husband you love him and specific things you appreciate about him. Create a special day to celebrate him, such as the Saturday before Father's Day.
- Let your husband know specifically what would help you.

Keeping Intimacy Alive

Needing to schedule your sex life is often stressful. Mary and her husband had the usual resentment toward scheduled sex. She said:

> After a while, I resented that it had become my job to tell my husband when I was ovulating and it was the right time to have sex for conception to happen. He always seemed surprised. I felt I was inconveniencing him by ovulating now. I interpreted his surprise as a lack of caring.
>
> Although he also wanted children, I think he felt pressured that he was being called to a command performance.
>
> We decided to post the temperature chart on our headboard where we could both see it and anticipate the *big O* day. That helped him to anticipate when ovulation day was approaching. He saw it was the chart, not me, choosing the time.

Some husbands also find the pressure to perform sexually can hinder their sexual arousal. Being intimate means sharing your innermost self with another, being closely personal, and private. In the beginning, this intimacy may only be discussed between spouses.

When medical testing and treatments are introduced due to infertility, the sexual part of intimacy is inspected, analyzed, scheduled, and discussed in meetings with medical professionals. Often this may feel quite uncomfortable, though good medical professionals often do a great job of easing some of this awkwardness.

Some couples might even begin to link their failure to conceive or their miscarriage(s) to the act of intercourse, so something once so full of joy now becomes linked with sorrow or failure. Infertility can dramatically stress a couple's sex life if they don't take precautions to balance their attempts to procreate with prioritizing their intimacy.

Infertility can dramatically stress a couple's sex life

It's fine to have sex at ovulation time even if you both agree it isn't the best romantic timing. Sex during infertility is one area where humor is imperative. But if you sense an unequal desire to have sex around ovulation time, be sensitive to the underlying reasons. Talk about them before you get into the bedroom so sex doesn't become a point of conflict.

To refocus your sex life on the intimacy it's meant to nourish, try to remember what sex was like before infertility. The emotions and physical feelings of sex are intertwined, so try to recapture those feelings. Put creative energy toward aiming for a variety of ways to be affectionate, such as holding hands, hugging, and other intimate contact.

While intercourse is needed to conceive, remember the act of sex is a gift you give to each other. Your relationship can be damaged if the gift is demanded without regard for your spouse's feelings.

To build intimacy, Pastor Gary Vanderet suggested focusing on this joy of giving to each other. He said:

> God has given us the ability to give the gift of love to another person, and it's the joy of that giving that creates the ecstasy of sexual love. Now to do this, to ensure your mate's sexual fulfillment, you need to talk, to understand, to listen, to care about another's needs.[63]

Along with talking, choosing to express love can eventually bring greater feelings of love and intimacy. Consciously making the effort to do one thing each day to show each other your love will help you focus on your marriage and reaffirm the priority of your relationship.

Specific ways to compensate for lost intimacy

For some couples, although infertility scheduling has been an unwelcome intruder on their sex life, they've also found it's given them an added incentive to keep their sex life strong, consistent, and a priority. Some specific ways to compensate for lost intimacy, especially during medical testing and treatments, are:

- Plan for the husband to be present during procedures such as intrauterine insemination (IUI). Plan a romantic time to be together afterward.
- Plan for a special time together after a particularly stressful cycle, a procedure, or a date you'll receive test or treatment results—either to grieve or to celebrate together.
- Take time to remember to really look at your spouse and be thankful for the good qualities you see.
- Plan dates with your spouse to have fun and remember what you like about each other.
- Take a vacation from treatment to focus on each other.

- Vary who does the initiating and how you initiate sex around ovulation time.
- Pray for each other.

Not Feeling the Same, but Understanding

When we don't react to problems the same way as our spouses, how can we grow in appreciation for them? We can think through our feelings, so when we speak, we speak the truth with love. And we can listen well, giving our partners a safe place to share their pain and fears. Then we work through the sorrow and learn to appreciate our differences. If we both fell into despair at the same time, what a catastrophe that would be. As we grow in our ability to listen to, share our compassion for, and trust each other, our appreciation for our differences enables real intimacy to grow.

Our spouse might not have the same level of pain over the same issues, but we can work at understanding each other's feelings and give space to respond differently. Experiencing different feelings than our spouse doesn't make either of us inferior. We can learn to accept that we don't have to suffer the same depth of grief to want children. As Ted once put it, "I finally understood my wife didn't want me to cry all the time, but she needed me to tell her it was okay if she needed to."

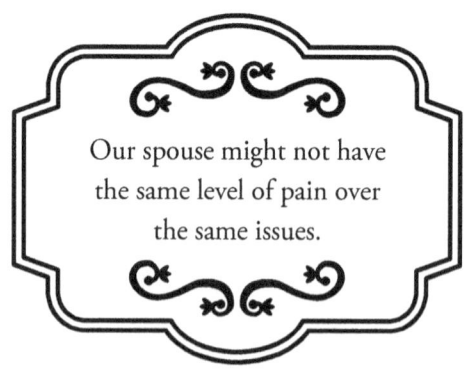

Our spouse might not have the same level of pain over the same issues.

When we finally understand we'll grieve differently, we can stop standing with our hands on our hips thinking, *you should feel the way I feel.* Instead, we can focus on supporting each other and coming to an agreement with our spouse on major infertility decisions.

Infertility puts pressure on both individuals and marriages. Taking good care of ourselves and our primary relationships is vital during infertility. Whether our dream children arrive or not, we'll still want a strong, supportive relationship with our spouse.

Your Personal Journey

1. Read Philippians 2:1–4. Write down specific ways you can support your mate within your marriage to:

- encourage
- console
- show affection for
- show compassion for
- be united with
- maintain love with
- and consider his or her interests along with your own.

12
Finding Support—Friends, Family, and Church

Each man can interpret another's experience
only by his own.
—Henry David Thoreau

I hope that among those of us who may have
never known such pain, failure, or grief,
an enlargement of heart may occur.
—Jack Hayford[64]

Let love and kindness be the motivation behind all that you do....
I urge you to honor and support them.
1 Corinthians 16: 14, 16

On the third Mother's Day into our infertility journey, we arrived at my parent's house for dinner. Both my mom and dad hugged us as we came in, concern and kindness shining in their eyes. They knew what a difficult day I'd already endured. After praying as an extended family for God to bless our mothers, we gathered in the kitchen for the buffet.

My uncle (who didn't know about our difficulties in having children) then loudly announced, "Since this is Mother's Day, all the mothers should help themselves first."

Out of the nine people gathered, I was the only female who wasn't a mother. I froze in place, feeling two feet tall. Already barely keeping tears in check, I now felt flayed open. My uncle's words exposed what felt like my glaring failure for all to see. Those few words squashed my tenuous hold on my value and identity as a whole woman.

I love my sweet mom who tried to diffuse the situation. I could see on her face she understood my pain. "Come on, honey, you too," whispered my mom as she reached for my hand.

"Oh no, not you there! I said mothers only," my uncle accused as he stepped between us and barred my way to the table.

I caught my breath as intense pain scorched through me. Mike quickly navigated me toward the back bedroom, where I sobbed. I was tired of living on the edge of tears for so long. I knew my insensitive uncle wasn't deliberately trying to hurt me. But I also knew he could have honored the mothers in another way without having to exclude me. I wanted to rise above the situation, shrug it off and go on with the dinner. I felt like a failure because I couldn't.

I finally got myself under control, splashed some water on my face, and went out to join the others to honor my mom. I hoped they wouldn't ask about my swollen, red eyes. They didn't ask.

It was another hard, hard Mother's Day I was simply thankful to survive. Afterward, I celebrated that it wouldn't come again for another year.

This holiday sticks in my memory as a prime example of how difficult it can be to know when and who to tell about our struggle to have children. I was glad I'd previously told my mom and dad, or I wouldn't have had their support.

I wasn't yet ready to tell my uncle, who was visiting from another state. My relationship with him wasn't close enough to share my intimate struggles. I also didn't know if he would be supportive or would respond with callous words. I had enough painful emotions to deal with right then without taking a chance I'd need to defend myself to someone who didn't understand the deep ache of infertility.

I've written this chapter for family, friends, and church leaders who care about infertile couples or those who've lost a baby during pregnancy. I've chosen to duplicate some information in this chapter so those wanting to help can quickly read the one section that applies to their friend, family, or church member without needing to search several other sections as well. Thank you for caring about and wanting to offer support to those who are facing these struggles.

I also hope it helps those who grieve. May it clarify and help you choose possible support options you might find helpful.

A Couple May Not Be Childless by Choice

Because many of the feelings and even medical treatments overlap, for the sake of simplicity I often use the general term *infertility* to refer both to technical infertility and the loss of a baby. (I also address the issue of pregnancy loss specifically in chapter 14.)

Friends and family members first need to realize couples without children may not be that way by choice. They may be hurting. Other couples may be following God's leading to not have children (but that's a different book). Either way, they've probably thought about their lack of children without needing suggestions to do so. This simple awareness can go far in reducing insensitive comments to couples. Sometimes friends and family members may not even realize what they say to an infertile couple can be hurtful.

Friends and family members first need to realize couples without children may not be that way by choice.

People who are infertile or who have lost a baby during pregnancy often have the same need for understanding and support as those who've had an older family member or close friend die. Our society and church cultures have established rituals of support to grieve the deaths of older family members, such as a funeral or memorial service. The difference with infertile couples or those who've lost a baby during pregnancy is they often have a less public grief. With infertility or miscarriage, the ways to support those grieving aren't as established, so sometimes friends and family don't know how to help.

Paul's grandfather unintentionally caused him and his wife a stab of pain every time they visited him. "My ninety-one-year-old grandfather asks when we're going to have children every time we see him, and we see him once a week. He has no concept of our problem whatsoever. Subconsciously, that's pressure."

Vicky felt the same hurt from her mom. She said:

> My mother's hobby is grandbabies. My sisters started having babies, so I didn't tell my mom about our problem for

a long time. When I visited, she'd pick up her cat and remark, "Well, this is my grandbaby until I get one."

I'm not the type of person to speak up and say, *that hurt my feelings*. I just fall apart in the car on the way home. Finally, I told my mom about what we were going through and how hard it was.

She seemed to dismiss my pain. She only said, "Oh, honey, just pray about it."

I'd already been praying so hard and for so long!

Finally, my mom has come around to see how much it hurts. But it's been so difficult for me to have my mother of all people not understand.

Offering Practical Support

Infertility—Helpful vs. Hurtful

If you have trouble relating to an infertile friend or family member's struggle, you can imagine how you might feel if the life of your child was taken away. Those struggling with infertility can experience similar intense feelings of grief.

When you don't know, but your friend may be infertile

These gentle suggestions may offer your friend comfort and support. She may find some offers of support more helpful than others. Recognize the uniqueness of her experience.

Supportive words to share

Questions about starting a family can feel too personal to come from strangers or acquaintances. If someone comments on their struggle or loss, take their lead and approach this tender area cautiously. If you've developed enough of a relationship to genuinely care, you might ask:

- *Would you like to have children someday?*
  This can be a more open-ended way to bring up the subject of children, allowing the couple to be as vague as they want to be in their reply. Be sensitive if they don't seem to want to share or change the subject.
- Be aware to include topics in conversation that women without children can relate to also.

Hurtful words

- *When are you going to have kids?*
- *Don't you have kids yet?*
  These questions imply the couple is making poor choices by not having children yet. Most people ask these questions casually without recognizing the deep pain they can cause to those whose attempts to bear children have failed.
- *Are you pregnant?*
  This question is sometimes asked while looking at a woman's stomach. Someone once asked me this question when I wore a flowy dress to work. And you can bet I never wore that dress again. Ever. It's awkward and difficult to recover from asking this question when the answer is no, since it can imply that the woman is overweight enough to look pregnant.
- *Did I tell you about how cute so-and-so's baby is? (for the fifth time)*
- *We all know what labor pain is like…*
  Conversations that include these types of questions or assumptions can hurt when there's constant talk about babies, pregnancy, or birth. These conversations can feel isolating to those struggling to create a family, especially when they go on for hours without asking about the interests of those without children too.

When your friend shares she's struggling with infertility
Infertility is a loss worthy of mourning. It will mean a lot to them that you recognize their loss. I've listened to enough hurting people to know it can mean a great deal to them when someone lets them know they care.

Unless you disagree with a choice an infertile couple makes on a clear moral issue, try to offer uncritical support. Even if you have a moral disagreement, consider doing some biblical and medical research to ensure it's a real moral issue, not just a personal choice, before gently sharing your concern.

Here are some supportive vs. hurtful questions and comments women have said they've received after they shared about their infertility.

Supportive words to share

- *I'm sorry.*
- *I'm here and want to listen if you want to talk about it.*
  Allowing your infertile friend or family member to talk about his or her sadness, hopelessness, or anger won't make it worse.
- *I'd like to do something. What can I do to help you?*
- *I promise to never give you fertility advice.*
- *What do you need right now?*
- *Would you like me to pray with you? How can I pray for you?*
  Then dedicate yourself to pray for and with your hurting friend. Let her hear you pray for her. This may not yet be the time to share biblical truth. Wait until she understands that you see her pain. She might appreciate hearing you pray for her comfort and any specific requests she's mentioned.
- *How are your medical tests going?*
- *How are you feeling?*
- *How are you doing through all of this?*

- *What is this like for you?*
- *Is there something you'd like to do together to give you a break for a while?*
- *I'd love to support you in your journey. Would you like me to ask about how your testing/treatment/adoption is coming, or would you prefer to let me know when something changes?*
- *I wish I could give you reasons why things like this happen.*
  You can admit you don't have all the answers. You don't need to give your infertile friend definitive reasoning for why problems exist in the world. What they need most right now is support rather than logic.
- *I think you would make wonderful parents.*
  This statement depends on how it's said, so be cautious. I felt comforted when a friend said I'd make a great mom because her intent was to reassure me that I wasn't lacking. This same statement could also be used to pressure a couple or discount their desire to choose a path other than parenthood.
- *Ask how they'd like to be notified about someone else's pregnancy or an upcoming baby shower?*
  Offer them a choice on how and when they'd prefer to receive potentially painful news. They may ask to be told privately ahead of time before it's announced publicly online, at a family gathering, or at church.

Supportive actions

Expressions of caring are also wonderful ways to show support.

- Give a hug, make a meal, offer to drive to doctor's appointments. Read about infertility to understand better.
- Send a card, email, or note. One problem for those wanting to support those who aren't able to conceive is the lack of a

specific event to send a card, email, or note. A good time to send a note might be before a medical test or a big adoption interview to let them know you're praying. Another good time can be after they receive bad news from a medical test or treatment or when an adoption falls through and you can offer sympathy. We can also listen for God nudging us to encourage the infertile couple in their struggle.

- Include your infertile friend in your plans even if your plans include other mothers, but give your friend an out when they've had enough. When they're included, try to limit your conversations about how wonderful/terrible your children are or pregnancies were.
- Choose to get together with a childless person without your children sometimes.
- Offer to research support groups, Christian counselors familiar with infertility, or supportive pastors.
- Tangibly encourage an infertility support group. A friend of one of our group members made dessert for our infertility support group meeting. Another member's friend offered money for postage and supplies to show she cared.
- Understand if your friend doesn't attend a baby shower, a family gathering that focuses on children, or a Mother's Day church service.
- Offer to write a letter of recommendation or take pictures for a potential adoption.
- Offer to help with financial needs when a major medical treatment is needed.
- Offer to help with financial needs when a couple chooses to adopt. Many adoption agencies encourage couples to set up an adoption fund account, so you can offer to donate toward the adoption. (This can be a biblical way those who may not be in a position to adopt can still fulfill God's instructions to care for orphans.)

Hurtful words

Trite comments or pat answers can be heard as ignoring or minimizing the couple's grief and can make them feel like you don't care. Proverbs 25:20 says, "Being happy-go-lucky around a person whose heart is heavy is as bad as stealing his jacket in cold weather, or rubbing salt in his wounds."

Some comments imply the couple's infertility is their fault (for example, if they were less stressed, they would be pregnant by now). If someone shared she had a broken arm though, responses like these would seem silly. Similarly, these responses don't make sense for medical problems that cause infertility, such as uterine fibroids, hormonal imbalances, blocked fallopian tubes, or low sperm count.

- *It will happen. Don't worry.*
- *Kids aren't all they're cracked up to be.*
- *Here, take mine. That'll cure you from wanting kids.*
- *At least you have the fun of practicing.*
- *Maybe you weren't meant to have children.*
- *You can always adopt.*
- *Just relax or take a vacation.*
- *You're still young.*
- *I know someone who tried [insert crazy idea]. Maybe you could try that.*
- Any comment that starts with, *Look on the bright side...*
- *Are you pregnant yet?*

  After someone shares their infertile status, asking if they're pregnant can make them feel they've failed again. Instead, ask your friend how they'd want to share their good news if they become pregnant. Most will shout it from the rooftops when they're ready.

- *Are you sure you understand how babies are made? Do you need some help to get your wife pregnant?*

Refrain from jokes at the couple's expense or about something being wrong with an infertile couple's sex life.
- *Why don't you try adopting? Lots of people get pregnant when they try to adopt.*
Offering poor medical advice is hurtful. Some people believe the old wives' tale that if a couple adopts a baby, they'll relax and increase their chances of getting pregnant, but this is incorrect.

First, according to a large study done by Stanford University Infertility Clinic, fertility is not enhanced by adoption.[65] Instead, those who adopt may have a slightly lower statistical chance of becoming pregnant than those who don't adopt. You might know someone who adopted and then became pregnant, but their adoption made their infertility visible. Childless infertile couples who finally become pregnant may not be seen as infertile because they may look like they *timed* their pregnancy.

Second, this statement demeans adopted children as simply a method of getting to the *real* prize of having a biological child. Adopted children are created in the image of God and given the same family status as biological children. They aren't ever a means to another end.

- Don't ask about in public what your friend has told you in private. Keep her confidences. Let her decide what parts of her story she shares with whom.

When your friend shares she's struggling with secondary infertility

Those with secondary infertility (who struggle to have another child) are also hurting. Listen carefully, as she may find some offers of support more helpful than others. Also see the suggestions in the section, "When your friend shares she's struggling with infertility."

Supportive words to share

- *It must be hard to not be able to have another child. I'm sorry.*
- *Can I babysit your child while you go to your fertility appointment?*
- *I'm so sorry. Can I help you in any way?*

Hurtful words

- *Don't you think your child needs a baby brother or sister?*
- *At least you already have one child. Can't you be happy with just him/her?*
- *At least you don't have to deal with sibling rivalry.*
- *Just be patient. It worked once, so it will work again.*
- *At least you know you can get pregnant.*
- *When are you going to have another child? You're running out of time if you want your kids to be close.*

When your friend shares she's experienced a miscarriage or stillbirth

When your friend experiences a miscarriage or stillbirth, these suggestions may offer comfort in her grief. It may be difficult for anyone who hasn't experienced a pregnancy loss to understand the pain it can bring. But you can give your friend who has lost a child the gift of an invitation to talk if you feel comfortable listening without judgment.

Supportive words to share

- *I care about how you feel.*
- *I'm so sorry.*
- *I hurt for you.*
- *I'm here and want to listen if you want to talk.*

- *I'm so sorry for your loss.*
- *Losing a child is a tragedy.*
- *Would you like me to pray with you? How can I pray for you?*
  Then dedicate yourself to pray for and with your hurting friend. Let her hear you pray for her. This may not yet be the time to share biblical truth. Wait until she understands that you see her pain. She might appreciate hearing you pray for her comfort and any specific requests she's mentioned.
- *How are you doing through all of this?*
- *Did you name your baby?*
  Then use the baby's name when you talk about him or her.
- *Your miscarriage wasn't your fault.*
- *I wish I could give you a reason why terrible things happen. I know God hurts with us when we hurt.*
  It's okay to admit you don't have all the answers. Job's friends offered answers that weren't helpful.
- *It must have been hard to have been so intimately connected to your baby when you lost it.*
- Acknowledge the couple's loss. Perhaps share your feelings of grief about the loss of their child.
- If you've had a similar loss, give them priority to speak of their fresh loss first, then they may find comfort from you sharing your loss story.
- Say nothing, but be willing to simply sit quietly with your friend in her pain. Your presence or your gift of tears can offer profound comfort.

Supportive actions

- Give a hug.
- Grief can be exhausting. She might appreciate an offer to make a specific meal, drive her to a doctor's appointment,

or watch her other children while she deals with memorial service arrangements.
- Read about miscarriage or infant loss to understand her experience better.
- Pray for her and her family.
- Attend a memorial service for the baby if invited.
- Call or send a sympathy card.
- Call or send another card on the baby's due date, birthday, or the anniversary of the baby's death.
- Give her a remembrance of the baby such as a piece of jewelry (ex., a baby ring), a flowering plant, a tree to plant in her yard, flowers in a baby vase, or a poem.
- Don't avoid her, even if you don't know exactly what to say or do.
- Include her in events, even those including other mothers, but give her an easy out when she's had enough. Limit your wonderful/terrible child or pregnancy stories.
- Invite her to a non-child-focused event, especially if she doesn't have other living children.
- Be sensitive to her on holidays and events such as Mother's Day, Christmas, baby dedication services, or baby showers.
- Remember, you don't need to feel responsible for fixing her sadness. Simply walk with her as she walks the path of grief. God is the true Healer. If your friend seems stuck and unable to move on to healing, you might gently suggest she can be compassionate to herself by requesting help from a counselor or care ministry.

Hurtful words

- *You're still young. You can always have another.*
  Other children will never replace a unique baby who has died.

- *Aren't you thankful for the child (or children) you already have?*
- *Maybe there was something wrong with the baby. It was probably for the best because everything happens for a reason.*

  These comments are especially painful because malformed babies and deaths are tragedies that weren't in God's original plan. Because of God's love for us, he will turn illness and death around to redeem it for good eventually, but the death of a child in itself is not a blessing.
- *God will work the death of your child for good.*

  This isn't the time for Romans 8:28. This is the time for Proverbs 25:20 instead, "Being happy-go-lucky around a person whose heart is heavy is as bad as stealing his jacket in cold weather, or rubbing salt in his wounds."
- *I hope you feel better soon.* Or *Don't you think you should be over this by now?*

  Allow couples time to grieve. These comments can make them feel they should ignore their grief to make others feel better.
- *At least you never knew the baby.*

  This isn't seen as a blessing to couples who ache to know their baby or who have already spent months bonding.
- Anything said in a joking or trite way might be received as devaluing her child or her grief.

A Helpful Friend

Family and friends may feel they need to walk on eggshells for a while around someone who is infertile or has experienced a pregnancy loss, but remember this time of grieving is for a season. Their pain won't always be so raw. Understand that right now most of their energy may be taken up in simply surviving.

Here's an example of a letter that helped a dear friend after her miscarriage. For someone who hasn't experienced the same type of loss, you could write a letter in a similar tone.

Deanna was devastated after her miscarriage, but she prayed for the first time in a long time after receiving the letter below. Deanna said this letter helped her reconnect with God because it acknowledged her pain and need to grieve. Because Lorry had also experienced a loss, she shared a piece of her story and some specifics that were helpful to her. Lorry offered that she was available to talk but didn't push.

Deanna,

As I sit here in my kitchen thinking of you, your husband, and your child, I find myself in tears. I am sorry your baby died. I would not presume to say I have all the answers for you and Rich, but I can tell you that when I confronted God with all of my hurt and anger, he was able to bring answers and deep healing, even for issues deeper than my son's death....

Be tenacious and truthful in your pursuit of God and his healing words. Know he wants to reveal himself to you. Give yourself the freedom to express your hurt and frustration. He's not looking for a perfect performance to come out of your reaction, but he wants to gently reveal deeper truths to you as you respond to him openly and truthfully. When we walk through long, dark valleys (or are carried) the burden is so heavy. But God is equipping us, building our faith, and calling us ever so sweetly, ever so quietly, ever so lovingly.

Rest in the arms of the One who gives hope, who comforts the weary. Rest in your grief. Hope will wait right next door.

I know the Lord will be faithful to you and Rich. If it would be helpful to chat, please call.

Much love and prayers for healing,
Lorry[66]

Offering Spiritual Help

Be cautious in giving biblical advice, especially if it's said in a way that might cause shame. You can also offer spiritual support by remembering to speak highly of the calling for each woman as an individual before God, not only for those who become mothers.

Listen and Mourn
This is the time to listen well and mourn with those who mourn. Try to identify with the infertile person's pain first. Then communicate your understanding of it. It's easy to quote Romans 8:28, "all things work together for good," but remember Romans 8:26 comes first. "The Spirit also helps our weakness; for we do not know how to pray as we should, but the Spirit himself intercedes for us *with groanings too deep for words*" NASB (emphasis mine).

This isn't the time to question a hurting person's faith, offer simplistic answers, Christian slogans, or even Bible verses that state it will all work out in the end.

Supportive words to share

- *I'm sad with you.*
- *I know God is hurting with you too.*
- *Would you like me to pray with you?*
- *How can I pray for you?*

Hurtful words

- *Maybe it's just not God's will.*
- *It will all work out for good.*

Encourage Honesty with God
Encourage the hurting person to be honest with God. For instance, anger is a natural stage of the grieving process. Encouraging honest and respectful communication with God, even when it includes anger, can allow a grieving person's relationship with God to grow. (God knows anyway.) King David in the Bible is a great example of how to be honest with God.

If someone expresses destructive anger or seems to become stuck in this phase, then consider referring the hurting person to a Christian counselor or care group at your church (Ephesians 4:26).

Supportive words to share

- *You can be honest with God about everything you're feeling.*

Hurtful words

- *You shouldn't get angry.*

Encourage Their Faith in a Loving God
When asked how well-meaning Christians add an emotional burden to those already suffering, Philip Yancey, the author of *Where Is God When It Hurts?* said:

> Many Christians talk a lot about healing, and they're doing it from a positive basis… they're wanting to provide hope. But if the person who is suffering does not find healing, if God does not choose to heal that person, then very often that person feels like a second-class citizen, that there is something wrong with [them] spiritually. [They] don't have enough faith. God has passed [them] by.[67]

Suggesting a couple's lack of faith is causing their infertility or caused their child's death isn't helpful. Ultimately, it remains God's choice alone whether or not to heal each health issue. He may choose not to heal people, even though they have enormous faith (ex., Luke 1:6-7, Hebrews 11:36-39). God's choices and timing often remain a mystery, because he sees a far-bigger picture. Focusing on God's and your love for those hurting or facing any health issues will be more helpful to them.

God's choices and timing often remain a mystery, because he sees a far-bigger picture.

Besides, in another biblical example of healing, Jesus indicates it's the faith of the friends that counts. In Luke 5, a man's friends lowered him through a roof to Jesus in the hope he'd be healed. Jesus said the friends' faith enabled the man to be healed.

May the struggle of your hurting friends allow your faith to grow too as you seek God in ways to support them. (For more on these examples, see chapter 9.)

Supportive words to share

- *I don't have all the answers.*
- *I know God grieves with you.*
- *You are deeply loved by God even when terrible things happen.*

Hurtful words

- *Maybe God isn't giving you a child because you lack faith.*
- *Maybe God is waiting to give you a child until you repent from sin in your life.*
- *Just pray about it.*

A Special Note for Pastors and Church Leaders

Pastors and those in church communities can specifically help couples struggling with infertility.

Families may be more visible or typical in churches though, so some churches can end up focusing almost exclusively on families. While family needs are important, churches also need to help those without children (including singles) or they can begin to feel like second-class citizens, which is contrary to Scripture.

Couples trying unsuccessfully to have children can even begin to feel like outcasts if every sermon contains illustrations of family life with children rather than a variety of illustrations that include the diversity of God's people.

Sermons can value family and speak highly of them without inferring that achieving the status of motherhood or fatherhood is the only way to please God. He doesn't love anyone more if they're able to become parents. God loves, wants a relationship with, and has a good plan for each individual.

One man, Paul, struggled with the child-centered focus in his church. He loved his church but felt isolated because of their emphasis on children. He said:

> Being at our large church became such a painful, painful time, that we dropped out altogether for about six months. Everyone was so focused on having babies.

Sunday mornings became a baby-fest where everyone talked about their babies and children for half of the Bible class time. The teacher would introduce and have each newly pregnant mother stand.

On the class bulletin board, they posted a chart showing how many people had two-year-olds, how many had one-year-olds, how many babies were on the way.

We were left off the chart.

On the other hand, church can also be an immense source of compassion, wisdom, support, and strength for couples struggling to create a family.

Julio felt this support from his church's pastor.

One of the most encouraging things that happened was when I attended a small church. My wife and I started telling people in the congregation that we were infertile and were in the process of trying to adopt.

During the prayer portion of the service, we asked the pastor to pray that the adoption would go through. He prayed a heartfelt prayer for us to be able to adopt. He didn't hint we had a spiritual problem. He prayed fervently for us to the point of tears. He devoutly believed in prayer.

His understanding caught me completely by surprise.

What Can Pastors or Christian Leaders Do?

Be inclusive of grieving couples

- Sit with them in their pain.
- Be sensitive to someone wanting a memorial service. If a couple has miscarried a baby, offer an intimate memorial

service as a remembrance that could help with their grief process and healing.
- Make sermons inclusive. Emphasize the value of each individual in God's eyes in sermon illustrations. Some of the church's current emphasis on marriage and children is a valid reaction to our society, where they are undervalued. But the church can value and support marriage and children, speaking highly of them, without focusing exclusively on them. Families are important, but they aren't the Bible's main emphasis. The two most important things God calls all of us to do are to love him and love others. Everyone can do that.
- Examine your attitudes toward women's roles. Instead of venerating motherhood as a woman's highest calling, encourage infertile women that God values them just the way he created them. Help them find biblical role models who may not be parents.
- Ask a childless couple to write something for your church newsletter or as an insert to your church bulletin to raise awareness of infertility. (This could be anonymous if requested.) Acknowledge with them and your congregation that God is present even when life isn't perfect. Before Mother's Day or Father's Day can be a good time for this.
- If someone is interested in starting an infertility and/or pregnancy loss support group, consider allowing the group to meet at your church.
- Check that the young couples and young family classes don't become so centered on babies, they make an infertile couple not feel comfortable at your church.
- Make room in your church's programming for non-family-oriented ministries.
- Specifically mention childless couples (though not by name!) on Mother's Day, Christmas, and other holidays

that are child-focused. Sometimes if you simply include the idea that many hurting couples long to become parents too, it can make them feel seen and included on those holidays.

Research to Understand

- Take the time to read about infertility and miscarriage to gain compassion for the people in your congregation who struggle in these areas. A list of recommended books on infertility, miscarriage, and stillbirth can be found at: AchingforaChild.com.
- Become aware of the ethical issues involved with infertility treatment so when a couple asks for counseling on these issues, you're aware of some specifics of the medical treatments offered, what the Bible says on the subject, and related principles to help them make decisions.
- Become aware of care groups offered in your area to offer those looking for support. Look for resources on infertility, miscarriage, stillbirth, or grief to have available to offer those requesting counseling.

Reassure

Some couples might be concerned about whether their infertility or baby's death could be a sign of God's displeasure with them. This confusion may come from references to barrenness as a curse in parts of the Old Testament. Help them understand that God's specific plan for Israel was different in many ways than his plan for Christians today. Be prepared to share why a couple's infertility today is a medical issue, not a punishment from God.

Ray S. Anderson, a professor of theology and ministry at Fuller Theological Seminary, once explained it this way:

In the Old Testament, childbearing was considered crucial to the development of Israel as the people of God. The messianic hope of Israel is grounded in the birth of a child, the Messiah.... So, conception was interpreted as a mark of divine favor, and infertility as a sign of divine displeasure or indifference....

With the birth of Jesus, however, we see a radical transformation of this emphasis on childbearing.... The primary metaphor is no longer conception, but adoption. The value of each person is centered on being a child of God, not in having children.

All this does not, of course, remove the frustrations and grief of the infertile couple. But it does remove the stigma and the feeling that infertility is a failure of prayer or a form of divine displeasure.[68]

The Infertile Couple's Choice to Share

If we choose to share our struggle to have children, will we receive support? It's our choice whether to tell others about our infertility. Sharing this with our family, friends, or church can range from uncomfortable to frightening. Infertility is such an intimate subject to talk about because it's related to self-image, sexuality, and life dreams. It would be nice to know how someone will respond before we tell them, but it's a gamble. If a friend can't relate to our struggle with infertility or understand it to the degree we'd hoped, our pain and sense of isolation could increase.

But sharing can be a wonderful way to deepen relationships and stop unintentionally hurtful questions. If we receive a negative reaction when we first share with someone, we can try to remember this is usually the person's inexperience with infertility, not intentional meanness.

Sharing Becomes Easier When the Shame is Gone
For a while, I didn't want to share about my inability to have children or my miscarriages because I saw it as a punishment. Once I understood my struggle was due to true medical problems, I became more confident in sharing these experiences with others.

It was still an intimate subject, though, so I shared selectively with those I felt genuinely cared and could keep the information confidential. I found the pain lessened once I found supportive people with whom I could share and who would pray for me.

Gracious Answers to Insensitive Questions
What do we do if we're caught off guard by questions about our family plans? First, we can decide how well we know the person asking. Then determine the intent of his or her question. Is she being polite and trying to make conversation? Is he simply curious? Or do they truly care?

Then, based on our perception of the person's intent, we're free to vary our answers. We don't need to tell our life stories to every acquaintance. We don't even have to tell it to a family member if we expect they won't understand. But if we're feeling strong that day, we can try to share with and even educate the person about our struggle.

It's also helpful to plan a quick answer that we've practiced. When we're caught off guard by questions about our lack of children, perhaps we can say something like, "We don't know what the future holds for us, but we know God will be with us."

When We Aren't Up to Sharing
Returning a question with another question is another way to turn the focus away from a sensitive question. For instance, if a stranger at a party asks, "Do you have any children?" We could reply, "No, we don't, how about you?"

If it's a person at church who pressures us by asking, "When are you two going to start a family?" We could respond with, "It's in God's hands. How about you? Do you have any areas in your life where you're waiting for the Lord's answer right now?" The key is to have a brief response ready, then turn the conversation by quickly changing the subject.

If we decide not to share, yet someone continues to ask intrusive questions, a simple, "Oh, excuse me, please," then heading off to the restroom or elsewhere will often work.

Finding or Starting a Care Group

Sometimes, finding others who are walking the same road and speaking the same language can be a huge support. Finding a community of those who've faced infertility or who've lost a baby during pregnancy can be a healing balm to our souls. If you're interested in starting or joining a care group, I've compiled a guide to help. You can find it at: AchingforaChild.com.

Forgiveness and understanding

At times the pain of infertility may be so intense, we may have a difficult time forgiving insensitivity from the fertile world. But our goal should be to follow Colossians 3:13, which says, "Be gentle and ready to forgive; never hold grudges. Remember, the Lord forgave you, so you must forgive others."

We need to overlook other's mistakes. As Proverbs 19:11 says, "A wise man restrains his anger and overlooks insults. This is to his credit." (Just think of all the credit we're building up!)

Just as we want to ask for understanding during our infertility, we also need to look behind fumbling words to see the caring intent of our family and friends. Even if we expect the intent was to hurt us, we can still try to respond both kindly and truthfully.

If someone's comment still bothers us after a few days, we can connect with the person again to say, "I appreciate your concern, but this is why I feel differently about my miscarried baby." Or "I used to feel that way before I was infertile, but now I don't any longer, and here's why."

Instead of taking an uninformed comment personally, try to gently educate the person if you're close to them. Some people may not care to be educated though. If this is the case, feel free to limit your time together until you're stronger. Keep in mind that we're all somewhat awkward when responding to others' grief.

May each of our experiences with grief enable us to better comfort others in their pain.

Thank them for their support
If your family, friends, church community, or pastor are supporting you and making your infertility or loss easier to bear, thank God for them. Let them know you're grateful.

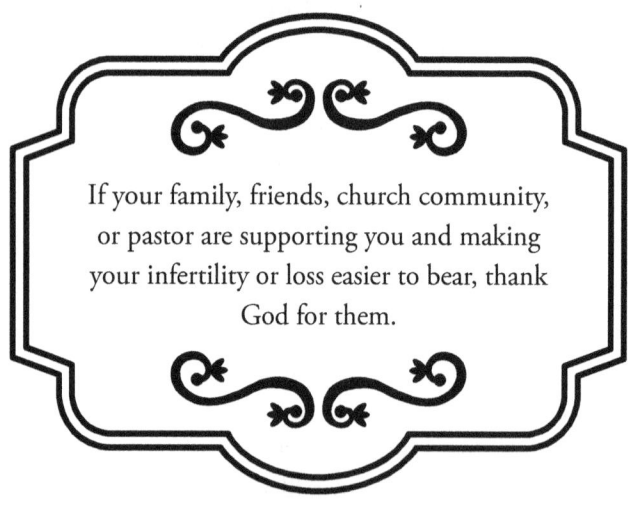

If your family, friends, church community, or pastor are supporting you and making your infertility or loss easier to bear, thank God for them.

Questions for Those Who Want to be Supportive

1. Think about and write down one encouraging thing you'd like to say to your friend who is experiencing infertility or has experienced a pregnancy loss the next time you see her.
2. What is one helpful action you can take to support your friend?

Personal Journey Questions for Those with Infertility

1. What comments or questions about your infertility or loss do you fear you might receive? What hurtful comments or questions have you received?
2. Then think about and write down how you'd like to respond to some of these situations or questions. You may want to respond differently depending on how close your relationship is to the person asking the question. You may also want to consider whether their intent is to support you or if they're interested in learning about the topic.
3. Who has been supportive of you in your infertility? What have they done specifically that has been helpful? How can you thank them? Send someone a note of gratitude today.

Part V

Will We Ever Be Parents?

13

Anxiously Hoping—
The Apprehensive Joy
of a Pregnancy

Hope deferred makes the heart sick;
But when dreams come true at last, there is life and joy.
—*Proverbs 13:2*

Even those who give birth after prolonged infertility
sometimes feel hesitant to celebrate their new family unit
because they have been conditioned to expect loss.
—*Ellen Glazer*[69]

I hesitated to include this chapter about pregnancy because I know that any mention of pregnancy can be painful to those still waiting. I've included this information though, because a large percentage of women who experience infertility, miscarriage, or stillbirth, will go on to have a baby. I also included it because many of these women are surprised when the uncertainty, concerns of another loss, or other emotions absorbed during infertility or loss don't simply disappear when a subsequent pregnancy occurs.

If you aren't ready to read this chapter now, please feel free to skip it and return to it at a later time.

Though Mike and I continued with tests and treatments, by now we'd been earnestly praying and trying for almost six years. Month, after month, after month, nothing had worked.

One month, while taking a break from Clomid, I yet again thought I might be pregnant. My resting temperature stayed up for a few days past the date my period was due. (Yes, I was still charting my resting temperature.) So, I went to the doctor and had (yet another) pregnancy test.

When the words, "You are pregnant," were spoken to me, I was speechless. Miracle of miracles! It was so fun to finally share this news with Mike.

The feelings of shock and surprise lasted for months. My sense of awe and thankfulness to God overwhelmed me. Since I'd learned so much about the conception process and knew the number of things that could go wrong, I was doubly thankful for each test that showed the pregnancy was progressing normally.

Then at ten weeks along, while I was working, I started bleeding. Frightened, I called my fertility doctor. He suggested I go home and rest. By ten o'clock that night the discharge was as heavy as a regular period. Mike and I kept in touch with the doctor, but he said if the miscarriage was inevitable, there was nothing else to do but rest and let it run its course.

We knew we'd lost the baby we'd waited for so long. We couldn't sleep. We could only cry, pray, and hold each other through the night.

The next morning, we dragged ourselves to the doctor's office to see if the miscarriage had been complete or if I'd need a D&C. As the doctor moved the ultrasound wand, I could hardly bring myself to look at the screen. Suddenly Mike said, "What's that?" The doctor grinned and pointed to something flickering on the screen. Then we saw the most beautiful sight ever. For the first time, we saw the beating of our baby's heart.

How the baby survived was another miracle.

I stayed in bed for a couple of weeks as the bleeding gradually tapered off, then stopped. Reluctantly, I left the support of my infertility doctor's office and went to an obstetrician.

During my first appointment at the obstetrician's office, I felt like an imposter. Me? Going to an obstetrician? How absurd. Surely everyone could tell I was infertile and would find out I was only faking a pregnancy because I wanted it so much. I kept expecting the doctor to expose my game. I still resented seeing pregnant women in the waiting room. Even though the ultrasound confirmed again that I was carrying a growing baby, I still felt infertile.

It wasn't until five months into the pregnancy that I finally began to fully believe I was pregnant. I started to hope a baby might even result from this pregnancy.

Then suddenly at six months, I had what felt like gas pains on and off all night that kept me awake. I went to the doctor the next morning to ask for a safe prescription to take for what I thought was bad indigestion.

It was preterm labor.

I was immediately admitted to the hospital. At six months, the baby didn't have a good chance of survival. The doctors tried to stop the labor with intravenous fluids, but it wouldn't stop. Finally, with labor-halting drugs, the labor slowed and stopped.

I spent the rest of the pregnancy with anxiety and joy living side-by-side in my heart as next-door neighbors. High anxiety (over whether the baby would survive today) sat down for daily tea with joy (that the baby had stayed put and grown all through yesterday). I don't know if I could have survived those three more months without God also reassuring me that he would be there to hold me, no matter the outcome.

Finally, only eleven days early, and over six years after we started trying to have a child, our healthy son, Justin, was born. We felt immense relief and overwhelming awe.

Doesn't Pregnancy Erase Infertility?

For many who have experienced long-term infertility or the loss of a baby during pregnancy, those experiences have become an unwanted part of their identity. The anxiety and feelings of a reproductive system that hasn't worked correctly don't go away quickly.

In addition, when those with infertility finally become pregnant, they may now feel separated from their infertile friends, the very friends with whom they'd finally found support. Experiencing something similar to survivor's guilt—the guilt felt when surviving a traumatic event that others don't—they fear telling infertile friends about their pregnancy or even seeing them because they know the hurt being close to a pregnant friend can cause.

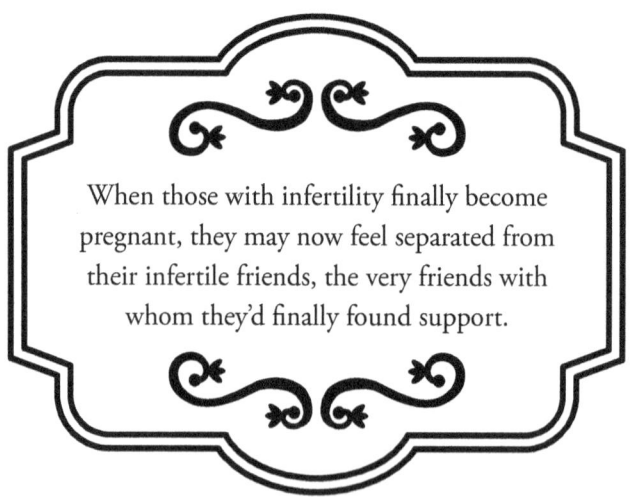

When those with infertility finally become pregnant, they may now feel separated from their infertile friends, the very friends with whom they'd finally found support.

Infertile women may hope once they get pregnant, infertility issues, with all their accompanying struggles, will suddenly evaporate into thin air. For most though, although pregnancy does ease feelings of inadequacy, infertility has changed their knowledge base. The innocence of a typical pregnancy may have been overlaid with concerns because they've learned enough about the reproductive process to realize it doesn't always work smoothly.

Thankfully, the majority of pregnancies for previously infertile couples are uncomplicated. The focus of this chapter is on the ones who might continue to have more difficulty.

Continuing Apprehension

Women who become pregnant after many months or years of being childless or who've experienced pregnancy loss(es) may cope with their fear of another loss by trying to avoid hoping and planning for their new pregnancy. One study looked at how previously infertile couples felt after giving birth. The results showed that among other coping strategies, couples used denial of the pregnancy as one way to cope with their fears about a potential pregnancy loss.[70]

But using denial to deal with the fear of loss can cause difficulty with bonding or not wanting to invest in caring for the pregnancy. Using other coping mechanisms, such as sharing your fears, is a healthier choice.

For those who've lost one or more babies during pregnancy, a new pregnancy may trigger vivid memories of previous losses. Carole experienced this when she found out she was pregnant again after three previous pregnancy losses. Carole said:

> I feel like crying all the time. I thought I had put the pain of my earlier miscarriages behind me, but getting pregnant has brought all the sadness back. I don't feel any hope for this pregnancy.

Having another baby after miscarriage will not erase the pain of losing a child. Each child is irreplaceable.

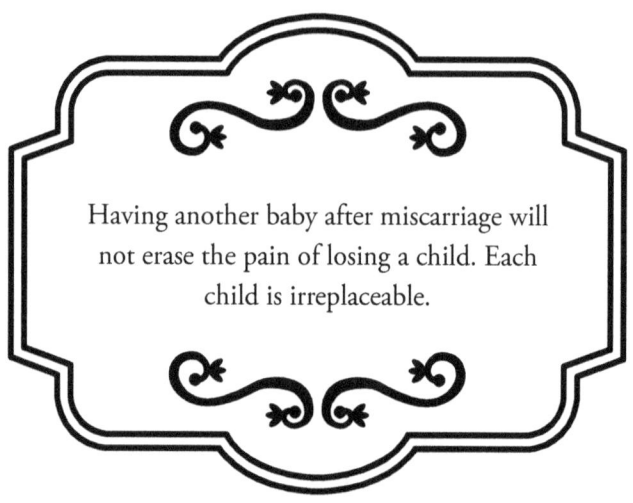

Having another baby after miscarriage will not erase the pain of losing a child. Each child is irreplaceable.

Coping with a High-Risk Pregnancy

First, I want to say again that most pregnancies for women who were previously infertile or who have miscarried are reassuringly smooth.

Those who have experienced infertility or pregnancy loss do have an increased chance though for a high-risk pregnancy over a typical pregnant woman. There are several reasons for this. One reason is the increased risk that comes with carrying and delivering multiples following ART procedures.

Previous fertility surgeries can also increase the chances of a subsequent high-risk pregnancy. Surgeries on the uterus to remove fibroids or to correct a malformation can cause scarring that may increase the risk of miscarriage or preterm labor.

General health or hormonal issues that contributed to infertility and continue during a pregnancy, may also affect the ease with which a pregnancy is carried. [71]

A woman may also be identified as high risk for her pregnancy if she has previously had two or three miscarriages, a stillbirth (if there's reason to believe it could happen again), or a preterm birth.

Finding Medical Support

When Virginia found out she was pregnant again after reoccurring miscarriages, she wanted to find a supportive obstetrician who would give her some extra TLC (tender loving care) for the anxiety she felt with this new pregnancy. She also wanted a knowledgeable specialist with the most up-to-date information on treating miscarriages. She didn't want a doctor who only called her miscarriages *bad luck* as her last doctor had done.

When Deanna discovered she was having triplets after previous miscarriages, she looked for a maternal-fetal specialist who would carefully monitor and support her high-risk pregnancy. As Deanna shared:

> I needed a home monitoring machine to monitor for contractions. I took vitamins and gelatin capsules to strengthen my amniotic sac. Later, when I went into preterm labor, I took medication to control that too. When those medicines stopped working, I still had to spend time in the hospital.

If you've been identified as having a high-risk pregnancy, you may be able to find an obstetrician with experience in high-risk pregnancies or a Perinatologist (a doctor who specializes in maternal/fetal medicine). Look for a doctor who is open to you sharing your concerns and fears and who will take the time to give you extra reassurance if you need it.

Finding Spiritual Support

It may be difficult to share the news of your pregnancy with anyone, but share it with those you feel will support you and pray for you.

One woman in my church asked her Sunday school children to be my prayer support group while I struggled to maintain my high-risk pregnancy. She gave me a wonderful gift in that request. I've saved several crayon drawings and letters from these children who prayed. I saved them in the hope I could later show my child.

One of the letters is from the mother of a seven-year-old boy, who said:

> My son has been praying desperately for weeks to be able to have a puppy. But after hearing about your baby who might come too early, he changed his prayer last night. This time he prayed, "God, you know that puppy I really, really want? Well, I don't need a puppy if you would please just let Deb's baby be born okay instead."

What a selfless prayer! My heart melted when I read that letter. Prayer and God's timing in answering remains a great mystery to me. I don't know why some prayers are answered right away and some aren't. But we're told to pray and ask for prayer. I'm so grateful for these children who sincerely prayed as well as our family, friends, and church family who did the same. These sincere prayers for my child's safety were a balm to my soul.

Finding Other Support

Discuss your fears and or concerns with your spouse, doctor, counselor, friend, or care group. Give yourself extra grace during this time. Read about what's typical for pregnancy and call your doctor if you have questions about how your pregnancy is going.

Also find ways to best take care of yourself and the baby during the pregnancy. Look for ways to support yourself physically (including nutritionally), emotionally, and spiritually.

Your Personal Journey

1. Are there any other issues (besides childlessness) you're hoping getting pregnant will solve? What are they?
2. What fears, if any, do you have about pregnancy?
3. What promises from God can you hold on to during this time? (Luke 12:7 is a good one to start.)

14

Grieving the Empty Cradle—Miscarriage and Stillbirth

When young children, some newly minted,
are recalled by their maker, away from the coziness of home,
does heaven bewilder them? Where are the teddy bears?
Are there puppies and kittens? Will an angel sing them to sleep?
Comfort, dear Lord, those who have lost little ones,
and hold them in the hollow of your hand.
—Margaret B. Spiess[72]

Out of my deep anguish and pain I prayed,
and God, you helped me as a father.
Psalm 118:5 TPT

After two long years of trying to get pregnant again, the pregnancy test stick had finally turned pink! Other than a little spotting, everything looked fine. I was now nine weeks along, so I'd known and treasured this miracle for weeks. I'd been in that morning to have my first ultrasound. The gestational sac looked good. The nurse hadn't been able to see the baby's heartbeat, but she assured me that was common. It was probably too early to detect it yet. I felt confident everything was fine.

I had no idea anything was wrong when I answered my phone later that afternoon. With one call, my world tilted crazily. The nurse from my doctor's office said:

"I'm afraid I have bad news for you. Your blood test results show the baby stopped growing.... I'm sorry."

The shock held me together until I hung up the phone. Then overwhelming, wracking sobs came from deep within me.

My baby isn't alive?... My baby has died?

Just then, Justin, who was two and a half by then, pushed open the bedroom door, his eyes wide with fright. "What's wrong, Mommy?"

Since I couldn't hide my grief, I chose to tell him. I sat on the rocking chair and helped him climb into my lap. I held him tightly. It took me a while to get the words out. I remembered his joy—how he danced around the bedroom when we first told him he was going to have a baby brother or sister. Tearfully, I choked out, "You know our baby that's inside Mommy's tummy? Well, the nurse just called and told me the baby got very sick and died."

Justin looked away and let out a woeful, "Ohhhhh."

He looked as confused as I felt. I rocked with him and asked him to sing "Jesus Loves Me" with me. Listening to him sing, "Little ones to him belong, they are weak, but he is strong" touched me deeply. While my world crashed around me, I realized anew what a miracle it was he was ever born.

But that didn't stop the grief of losing this child.

I thought the lessons I'd learned through my many years of infertility would protect me from the new grief of miscarriage. I was wrong.

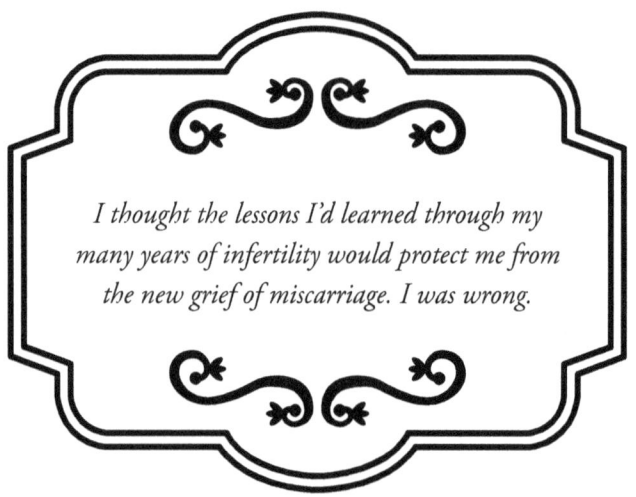

I thought the lessons I'd learned through my many years of infertility would protect me from the new grief of miscarriage. I was wrong.

This new heartache was different. It took a few weeks after the miscarriage for it to really hit. Although I thought about losing the baby and felt sad, I still functioned normally for a while.

Then the numbness wore off. I tried to handle the feelings of grief that hit me like waves. I was so tired of hurting from infertility, tired of being the one who struggled. I wanted to be strong.

Not even Mike grieved over this baby's death as I did. People who cared about me wanted me to recover quickly and suggested I focus on thankfulness for the child I had.

I decided I just needed a thicker skin. Maybe if I tried to think positively, the sadness would diminish, maybe evaporate altogether. So, I chose to be strong and act as if it didn't hurt.

Meanwhile, Mike thought I was recovering well. He thought since our baby was with God, it was okay. He wanted to focus on hope for the future.

When a friend found out that the baby she'd miscarried was a girl, I mentioned to Mike, "I wish we'd known what the sex of our baby was." He didn't see the pain behind the statement and voiced his frustration that I'd brought it up.

Two months after the miscarriage, we drove away on a planned vacation. I thought I'd been doing a good job of ignoring my feelings of grief, but I was quiet. Without the distraction of our busy schedules, Mike was soon frustrated at my distance.

I later realized deeper grief probably hit when my hormone levels dropped. I'd built up a wall to hold in my emotions so I could function, but that wall distanced me from other emotions too. It was as if I knew how a person should act, so I ate meals and looked at scenery by rote, but I spent most of my energy guarding against the grief. Keeping the pain buried took a lot of effort. As I began to acknowledge the sadness I'd buried, I also acknowledged I'd begun to harbor hurt feelings against Mike. Why wasn't he suffering like me? Didn't he care about losing our baby?

I finally couldn't avoid or hide my heartache any longer. My protective walls collapsed, and I ended up crying in the car the whole way up the coast of California. What we both came to realize was that I needed to mourn the loss of our baby.

Differences in the Loss Timeline

The grief of miscarriage or stillbirth is different than that from the inability to have a child because the grief of a pregnancy loss is focused on one event in time—the death of a unique child. The heartbreaking fact is that pregnancy loss is not a rare occurrence, since as many as one in five pregnancies miscarry.[73]

Women who get pregnant but miscarry are sometimes seen as more fortunate by those who have never been able to conceive. Vicky once expressed this feeling to our infertility group, "I would never want to experience the losses you who have miscarried have gone through, but I feel like less of a woman because I've never been able to get pregnant." But those who've lost a wanted baby during pregnancy don't perceive themselves as fortunate.

Women can suffer the grief of miscarriage quite early when they go through IVF treatment. They're told when life has begun—their eggs have fertilized and begun dividing. So, when their embryos don't implant after they're transferred, they can grieve at these new lives ending.

At the other end of the pregnancy-loss timeline are women who carry a pregnancy full term. If their baby is stillborn (which happens in fewer than 1% of third-trimester pregnancies), they also grieve the life of their baby with whom they've bonded for months.

Each one grieves differently. For those who have struggled to have a family before becoming pregnant, losing a child can encompass an even greater sadness.

The Physical Side of Losing a Baby During Pregnancy

The physical symptoms preceding and accompanying a pregnancy loss can be frightening. The details of this type of loss aren't discussed much, especially with someone pregnant, so unexpected symptoms can add to the fear.

A *miscarriage* is the death of a baby before the twentieth week of pregnancy. The chance of losing a baby decreases as the baby grows. Seeing the baby's heartbeat on an ultrasound is a promising milestone of reduced risk. Most pregnancy losses happen before this.

The physical symptoms can include moderate to severe cramping that dilates the cervix and attempts to expel the fetus. The cramping is accompanied by moderate to heavy bleeding, often passing large blood clots, and eventually passing the fetus.

In some miscarriages, the baby doesn't pass or doesn't pass completely. If women's physical symptoms aren't severe and they're strong enough emotionally, some fertility specialists advise miscarrying women to wait a few days to see if their body will miscarry the baby on its own. This is because adhesions or a weakened cervix from a Dilation and Curettage (D&C) can possibly contribute to future infertility.[74] Yet, waiting too long can also raise the risk of infection or other problems. If the baby doesn't pass completely, a D&C will need to be done.

A *stillbirth* is the death of a baby after the twentieth week of pregnancy. By this time the pregnancy has begun to *show* and the mother can often feel the baby's kicks. A stillbirth is much more public because it's harder to hide and can involve more explaining to outsiders.

Many of these women speak of the horror of needing to go through a typical delivery, knowing their baby has already died. Thankfully, many hospitals and professional medical organizations now provide training to their medical staff to help them deal more sensitively with women who lose a baby during pregnancy.

Carole's account illustrates some of the physical experiences of both miscarriage and stillbirth. She said:

> The first time I got pregnant, I was pregnant for three months. That's a long time to bond and plan. I spotted, then started cramping and bleeding. I went to the hospital emergency room where the doctor did a suction D&C. It was very painful and traumatic. I was depressed for about a year afterward.
>
> Two years later we got pregnant again. This time I didn't allow myself to bond or believe. During the fourth month, I started to believe the baby would live. After all, most miscarriages happen in the first three months.
>
> I remember feeling the wonder of it all—a baby was growing inside me. I saw an ultrasound of the baby and started feeling her kicking. I had to wear maternity clothes, so people at work started noticing.
>
> At six months, while my husband and I were taking our last vacation alone together, my body started feeling different. The pressure seemed lower down. I denied anything could be wrong because I'd had no problems, no spotting,

the ultrasound was fine, and I could feel the baby kicking. But soon I couldn't suppress my anxiety any longer. We called the nurse, then started for home. I started timing my contractions in the truck, then we had to stop for bleeding and diarrhea.

By the time we got to the hospital, I was past the point of no return. As the baby was being delivered, I remember the doctor telling me the baby was no longer alive. A nurse asked if I wanted to see the baby. I said no, but later changed my mind and asked to see her. She was beautiful. Little fingers, little toes, all perfectly formed. A beautiful face with eyelashes. It was so unreal, like a bad dream. When I went home, I was afraid to be left alone.

Three weeks later, the morning of my first day back to work, my milk came in. I'd taken the pills to dry up my milk, but they didn't work. I had to go buy nursing pads. My leaking breasts were a constant reminder of my loss.

Then two years later, I had a good pregnancy, and I finally had my son. I'm so thankful for the gift he is to us.

When my son was four, I got pregnant again. At my first checkup, the doctor said the baby's size was one to two weeks behind, based on the conception date I had told him. I asked for an ultrasound that afternoon. The growth of the fetus was four weeks behind schedule, but I knew when I'd gotten pregnant.

I felt very sad knowing I was pregnant, but the baby inside me wasn't alive. I had to wait a week until I started cramping and bleeding. I miscarried at ten weeks. I still kept cramping and bleeding, so I had to go in for a D&C. They assured me it wouldn't be as painful as the first one, but it was. [Carole's doctor didn't use any anesthetic with her D&C's.]

As I lay on the table alone, I felt the pain, fear, and loss welling up. The D&C did turn the bleeding off like a switch. I was grateful for the care of a doctor and modern medicine. I thought a hundred years ago I might have bled to death from this.

Emotionally, I felt as if I'd fallen into a black hole. I cried for this child I wouldn't have and for the uncertainty of whether I would ever have another child. I didn't think I could live through the pain.

I still yearn to hold a baby in my arms and call it mine. Yet, there is no assurance there will ever be another. We haven't decided whether we will try again.

[Carole eventually did become pregnant again and carried a healthy baby girl to term.]

Women may experience many physical symptoms other than abdominal pain after a pregnancy loss. They may experience aching arms and aching breasts with lactation (milk coming in). They may also experience headaches and postpartum depression as hormone levels rapidly decrease, difficulty sleeping, profound tiredness or fatigue, and a still rounded body that can't fit into normal clothes.

Some women may even experience *phantom* kicking and movement, as Beth did. She said:

> I've read about people who lose a leg or arm and still feel the phantom limb itching. I feel phantom kicking. I feel a bump from the inside and suddenly think, *oh, that was the baby*. Then I realize again my womb is empty.

Why Do Miscarriages Happen?

Surprisingly little is known about why babies die in the womb. This can be especially agonizing if you experience repeated losses. For a long time, doctors believed miscarriages were the body's way of expelling babies with whom something was already wrong. In most miscarriages though, there's no known cause.

Many factors can play a role in the death of a baby in utero. The most common causes of miscarriage are birth defects or chromosomal abnormalities (from eggs or sperm), immunological issues, endocrine issues (ex., polycystic ovarian syndrome, luteal phase defect, diabetes, thyroid disorders, low hCG or progesterone levels), uterine malformations, poor maternal health (ex., certain autoimmune disorders or poorly treated blood pressure), lifestyle factors (ex., alcohol or high caffeine use of over 7 cups a day), or infections.[75]

Feel free to ask any questions you may have from your infertility specialist, gynecologist, or obstetrician. No question is trivial when it concerns your child's life. Your doctor can also test a miscarried baby to determine the cause of the miscarriage in the hope of preventing a reoccurrence. For parents who are struggling emotionally, this may be difficult. If the doctor asks you to save the expelled fetus for testing, feel free to ask specifically what the testing might reveal.

What Can be Done?

Those who experience a miscarriage are often left wondering what they can do to help a future pregnancy. In some cases, treatment may be recommended to adjust hormone levels, treat infections or endocrine disorders. Surgery may be needed if the problem is a structural issue. Psychological support and counseling have also been shown to be crucial during treatment for recurrent miscarriage.[76]

Many women have voiced that if they're blessed with another pregnancy, they'll trust their intuition more and won't hesitate to call their doctor if they feel something unusual. They'll also feel more comfortable asking for an ultrasound to check on the baby if they need reassurance that everything's okay.

The Emotional Side of Losing a Baby During Pregnancy

Couples who lose a baby during pregnancy, may not only feel their loss, but as parents, they can also experience their child's loss. They may mourn that their child never heard their love songs sung, never felt the enfolding hug of their arms, or never saw how they would be celebrated. They've lost a part of themselves and an irreplaceable person's life at the same time.

Even some of the medical terms used to discuss pregnancy loss can cause emotional pain. What was a baby just a moment ago may now be referred to as a miscarriage, a spontaneous abortion, or as fetal tissue.

Often the tragedy of pregnancy loss comes as a shock. "I felt like I was living on a different plane of reality," explained Jackie. "I'm sure some of my emotions were hormone-related, but I was a basket case."

Many people will experience this same shock later in life at the death of a parent, sibling, or spouse. But since miscarriage happens to couples in their relatively young, childbearing years, it can be their first encounter with death. If they were lucky enough to have had a fairly uneventful childhood, they often haven't yet formed many coping mechanisms to deal with tragic circumstances. Youthful optimism may suddenly be replaced with the knowledge that devastating circumstances can happen to them.

If a couple has invested themselves emotionally (and financially), in an adoption attempt that falls through, they can also experience much of this same emotional grief of losing a child they're bonded with.

Many grief emotions overlap those of infertility. I've addressed these in chapter 8. In pregnancy loss, the grief can be compounded by the physical symptoms discussed earlier. In addition, the grief of pregnancy loss can often include preoccupation with the baby, fantasies about the baby, and feelings of responsibility for the baby's death.

Volatile Emotions

Virginia realized that her constantly changing emotions made it difficult to communicate with people after her miscarriage. Virginia said:

> The way people treat me varies from perfect to appalling, but then how does anyone know the right thing to say? Even two months later, my mood can change at the drop of a hat so something said this morning that was fine will make me cry this afternoon.
>
> The best support I've had comes from those more willing to listen than to talk, who sincerely hug and don't offer platitudes. I'm so ashamed of some of the dumb things I've said and done to others in their low times. But for this reason, I don't blame anyone for what they say or do to me.

Early Bonding

The depth of grieving isn't respective to the gestational age of the baby either. Huge hormonal fluctuations happen at the beginning of pregnancy. These hormones stimulate changes in the mother to protect the baby, such as an aversion to smells and foods, and promote bonding.

With planned pregnancies, parents may have dreamed about the baby even before conception. With earlier pregnancy testing and ultrasounds now available, the attachment between mother and child can form even earlier. Parents may have already spent time early on in the pregnancy anticipating the baby's hair color, whether it's a boy or girl, its personality, or how old the baby will be on the first Christmas.

Lara Freidenfelds, in *The Myth of the Perfect Pregnancy: A History of Miscarriage in America*, explains:

> Two months into pregnancy, at a stage when women in the not-so-distant past would have been just beginning to trust their suspicions and intuitions that they might be pregnant, and waiting cautiously for the confirmation provided by a second missed menstrual period, women in America today have often already spent weeks celebrating, caring for, and growing attached to their expected children.[77]

It makes sense that women who have spent months or years working toward becoming pregnant or dreaming of their future child may form an attachment earlier in their pregnancy. Bonding may also begin at different times for each pregnancy, depending on other co-existing factors too.

Your depth of grieving may depend more on how important the relationship with your baby was to you. If others don't understand your need to grieve, try to realize their lack of understanding may be due to their lack of experience with this type of death and their inability to *see* it or experience it firsthand. Look for support from someone who understands your need to grieve.

Need for Others to Validate the Baby

When a pregnancy finally happens, but then the baby is lost, the swing of emotions can be enormous. The new mom has gone from feeling empty to feeling full of life. The bounce back to barren can be too excruciating to describe.

Yet others may not understand the need to grieve the loss of a baby who wasn't known outside the mother's body. The couple may look for validation of their real loss, but the loss may not feel as real to others since they haven't experienced the separate life of the baby in the same intimate way. A deep bond with the baby may have formed though. Rest assured that the baby was real, and you've experienced the death of a unique and treasured individual when a pregnancy loss occurs.

Even in the Christian community though, you may be surprised at the lack of response when others hear of your baby's death. The Catholic church tends to encourage a more compassionate response than many Protestant churches. Even Christians who strongly protest abortion can sometimes fail to recognize and support couples who grieve the life of their babies lost through miscarriage or stillbirth.

Christians who strongly protest abortion can sometimes fail to recognize and support couples who grieve the life of their babies lost through miscarriage or stillbirth.

Platitudes such as *maybe there was something wrong with the baby, so it was better it died* are hard to hear. See chapter 5 for comfort on the reality of your baby's life in the womb.

Give grace for this lack of understanding when you can. I must admit that before my miscarriage, when I knew a woman had miscarried, I thought about her hurting physically. I didn't think about her grieving, not until I experienced it. I just didn't know.

Guilt
Even when the facts say the loss had nothing to do with any actions of the mother, women may need to work through unrealistic feelings of responsibility for their baby's death.

After her miscarriage, Beth had terrible nightmares that reflected her internal struggle. She said:

> I keep waking up sobbing from horrible, devastating, dreams of babies dying and blood everywhere. I've also dreamed of stabbing my husband and daughter, that I somehow have to kill them, though I desperately want them to live. The dream ends with my friends reassuring me it was something I had to do, and it was for the best.
>
> I must keep dreaming this because it has something to do with accepting the miscarriage, but still wanting to fight against it with every ounce of my being. I guess I'm also still feeling responsible for my baby's death and fear if my baby could die, so could the rest of my family.
>
> Maybe I'm working out the inconceivable knowledge that neither my brain nor heart had any control over my body. If I couldn't trust my own body to take care of a baby I wanted so badly, what would stop it from harming more of the family I loved? I'm living in a body that betrayed me by not protecting my baby. I'm pretty calm on the outside, but I have this raging battle going on in my mind.

How Long Does Grieving Take?
I didn't fully understand the subtle pressure to finish grieving quickly until my infertility care group read through the book *Life after Loss*. The author, Bob Deits, writes of the naiveté of many people who have not yet experienced grief. He says, "Many polls and studies have asked the public, 'How long should it take to mourn the death of a loved one?' The most common answer: we should be

finished grieving between forty-eight hours and two weeks after the death!"[78]

That's astounding. Bob wrote that those who had experienced grief didn't feel this way though. He summarized that normal, intense grieving, with its many ups and downs, may be expected to last 18 months to 2 years, and beyond that range also falls within the time limits of typical grief.

Even though I'd resolved my anger at God and recognized he loved me, that didn't stop my intense grief over my baby who had died. At the same time though, I felt the reality of heaven and the hope that my answers awaited there. If you find yourself grieving deeply, know that's natural. Your time and intensity of grief will be unique, but hold on to hope that joy will come again.

Music seemed to reach my grieving soul and offer me hope. I was touched when I heard this song by Wayne Watson. It expressed not only the grief and confusion I felt but also the hope of anticipating heaven when we'll find the answers:

Home Free

> I'm trying hard not to think you unkind
> But Heavenly Father, if you know my heart
> Surely you can read my mind
> Good people underneath a sea of grief
> Some get up and walk away
> Some will find ultimate relief
>
> Home free—eventually
> At the ultimate healing
> We will be home free...
>
> Out in the corridors we pray for life
> A mother for her baby

A husband for his wife
Sometimes the good die young
It's sad but true
And while we pray for one more heartbeat
The real comfort is with you [79]

Remembrances and Ceremonies

I realized that my grief simply meant my baby's life mattered. So I looked for a way to honor and remember our baby. Mike suggested we name the baby. Then we decided to take an afternoon, go into the hills in back of our apartment, and have a private memorial service. I chose a small box and placed inside it a little blue and white sleeping outfit I'd bought, our baby's first ultrasound picture, and a letter I wrote to our baby.

We picked a beautiful spot next to the creek. I read the letter I'd written to our baby. Then with small shovels, we dug a hole and buried the small box. We sat on a nearby log and prayed together in this peaceful, quiet place. We prayed for our baby and the healing of our grief. As we listened to the wind rustling the leaves, the soft music of the creek, and felt the warm sun on our faces, I finally began to feel my emotions calm. The grief didn't seem as raw as it did before.

Because of that wonderful afternoon, I'm able to remember that peaceful place when I remember our baby, rather than the pain, blood, and horror of the miscarriage itself. This is the letter I wrote to our child:

Dear Aaron (or Erin),

> I loved you from the moment I first knew about you. I began to love you even earlier than with your older brother because the first time I was pregnant, I couldn't allow my-

self to believe I would actually have a baby. But I let myself relax and fall in love with you right away because his presence helped me believe I might hold you in a few months. When I daydreamed, your image was clearer to me because I imagined you'd look like your brother.

I'm sorry. I don't know why you died, but I did my best to take care of you. I wish I had some answers. There's no way my finite mind can make sense of this. All I know is this world is imperfect.

I can't wait until I can see you again in heaven. Will you be a little baby then or full-grown? You were too small for us to know if you were a girl or boy. Will we recognize each other's souls?

I hope your great-grandma is gently rocking you and singing you her favorite Scottish lullaby. You'll always be part of our family here. When people ask how many children we have, I'll answer *one*, but will silently think about you and respond inside, *we have another one waiting in heaven*.

I'll always love you, my little one, gone too soon. I hope this incredible pain of missing you eases. I feel so torn between wanting to go to heaven to see you and staying here. It isn't that I want to die, I just want to visit and make sure you're all right. My arms ache to hold you. To rock you. To kiss your soft head. To smell your sweet baby scent. To tell you I love you. But I can't.

So, let's both hold on to God until we're finally together again.

Love,
Your Mommy

When my deep sadness returned on the baby's actual due date, we went back to this beautiful place to remember. Since our baby was due close to Christmas, we also bought a little tree ornament of an angel and wrote the baby's due date on it. Each year we're comforted by this remembrance of the child who spent such a short time with us.

Memorial Ideas to Say Goodbye and Remember

Ceremonies and rituals have always been an important way to help us celebrate life or mourn its passing. Don't worry your baby wasn't *big enough* to warrant a farewell ritual. Regardless of gestational age, your baby was someone whom God thought was important enough to call into existence.

- Photographs. If you want to have studio photographs taken of your stillborn baby, ask for recommendations from your hospital staff or search online for "photographer stillborn babies." Photographers who specialize in these types of photographs are usually sensitive, compassionate, and want to provide photos as a memorial for your family.[80]
- Burial. If you experienced your pregnancy loss at a hospital and want to attend the baby's burial, ask the hospital staff about their miscarriage or stillbirth burial policies. You may be able to attend the burial or other options may be available to you under your local and state regulations.

    Burial cradles and urns are available to purchase for a dignified burial of even those babies under twenty weeks gestation. To purchase a burial cradle or urn for a miscarried baby, search online for "miscarriage burial cradle" or "miscarriage burial urn."

    Couples may also choose to have their baby cremated. Some then bury the ashes under a flowering bush planted in remembrance of their baby.
- Memorial service. A memorial service can be held at any time. If you would be comforted by a private or public me-

morial service, feel free to plan a service that will help you say goodbye to your baby. Use it to express your feelings and what your baby meant to you.

Invite close family and friends if you want to include them. Having family and friends present at the ceremony is helpful because those who attend are less likely to forget the baby. They're also more likely to be available to the parents throughout the bereavement period.

- Write a letter, poem, or story. Write about and for the baby expressing your hopes and love, disbelief, anger, disillusionment, and despair.
- Save mementos of the pregnancy. You can save such items as a favorite maternity top, ultrasound pictures, or pictures of the mother while pregnant,
- Save mementos of the birth. The baby's hospital identification bands, footprints, crib card, lock of hair, the baby's blanket, or clothing the baby was dressed in can serve as mementos.
- Plant a tree or flowering bush.[81]
- Buy a piece of jewelry with the baby's birthstone in it.
- Buy a Christmas ornament to hang each year in remembrance of your baby.
- Frame a poem or special scripture to hang on the wall of your home.
- Choose a special day to remember your baby every year. You could plan a picnic in a pretty spot on the baby's due date each year, give to a charity, go out to dinner, or visit the baby's grave. You may want to change what you do from year to year, but you'll know the day is set aside as special.

Remain honest with yourself and choose something that honors your baby's life. Discuss what will work best with your spouse.

Spring Will Come

Eventually, you may become so involved in life, you forget to remember this pain at times. Don't feel guilty for forgetting or not being able to feel the emotions as deeply. This isn't forgetting your child. It's just that the scales have tipped back again in the direction of celebrating life, such as it is.

Picture yourself as a broken seed that is buried in the dark for a while. Your grief and quiet waiting don't mean all life is over. Though you can't imagine it now, spring will eventually come to your heart. Out of the winter of your grief, new hope will be born.

Your Personal Journey

1. Read the words or sing the hymn, "It Is Well with My Soul," written by Horatio G. Spafford. (Search "lyrics it is well with my soul.) Mr. Spafford was a successful attorney and the father of five when a series of disasters struck. His only son died, and his ample real estate investments burned down. Then while the rest of his family was on a ship crossing the Atlantic, the ship sank. All four of his daughters drowned. Only his wife survived. As he traveled on another ship to join his wife, he passed over the place where his daughters had died. There he wrote the song that begins:

   When peace, like a river attendeth my way,
   when sorrows like sea billows roll,
   Whatever my lot, Thou hast taught me to say,
   It is well with my soul.

2. If you've experienced the loss of a baby, reread the section, "Memorial Ideas to Say Goodbye and Remember." Write a letter to the child you lost or consider if one of the other

ways would help you express your grief and discuss it with your spouse. (Choosing a special way to honor a baby who died can even be done years later.
3. Underline Song of Songs 2:11 in your Bible to help you hold on to hope for your future:
"The season has changed,
the bondage of your barren winter has ended,
and the season of hiding is over and gone.
The rains have soaked the earth
and left it bright with blossoming flowers."

15
Adopting—A New Path

When one door of happiness closes, another opens;
but we often look so long at the closed door
that we do not see the one which has been opened for us.
—Helen Keller[82]

In adoption, the labor is longer.
And it is an emotional labor, not physical.
—Vicky

I waited patiently for God to help me;
then he listened and heard my cry.
He lifted me... and set my feet on a hard,
firm path and steadied me....
He has given me a new song to sing.
—Psalm 40:1–3

When a woman at church heard we were infertile, she responded flippantly, "Well, you can always adopt." I was hurt by her lack of *understanding for the frustration of infertility.* I also knew she didn't have any idea about the amount of work or the cost involved in adopting a child.

Before Mike and I were married, we (naively) decided we would have two children, then adopt a third. So, adoption was always in the back of our minds. About three years into our infertility, we decided to put our names on an adoption waiting list while we continued with medical treatment.

We checked out a private agency in our area, but they wanted $3,000 upfront with no guarantee of a child ever being placed. So, we signed with our county's Department of Social Services, even though they estimated the wait would be three to five years.

Instead of years, the social worker called us six weeks later. Because half of Mike's heritage is Japanese, our ethnic background matched a Caucasian/Japanese baby who would be born soon and placed for adoption. The social worker asked if we wanted to start the home-study process. We jumped at the chance and began filling out heaps of paperwork. Then we attended meetings where the county workers analyzed our childhoods, marriage, family relationships, income, housing, and prospective parenting skills.

We passed! Just two months later, after fast-tracking our paperwork, we were set.

Finding a couple who matched the baby's racial heritage was not only important to the county, but also to the birth mother. We became more excited as the possibility became more certain. We were the only waiting couple in the county who fit the ethnic background for this baby.

We kept asking when the baby was due, but the birth mother had a different social worker, so we struggled to receive clear communication. Our social worker kept responding that she wasn't sure when the baby was due. She said she'd at least give us twenty-four hours' notice of the baby's arrival.

We waited in this limbo of knowing we'd only have 24-hours-notice before our baby arrived. We waited in this state for Five. Long. Months. Each day, we wondered if this might be the day we'd receive the call to pick up our baby.

Then we found out the birth mother was carrying twins!

We were overjoyed. We prayed for the birth mom and babies every day. We wondered how we should prepare, but we couldn't yet bear to keep car seats, Moses baskets, and baby paraphernalia in our home. So, we arranged to borrow them from friends at a moment's notice. We couldn't stop ourselves from choosing names and buying sets of outfits though. We bought a set for every conceivable combination—two boys, two girls, or a boy and a girl. We waited and jumped every time the phone rang. Only months later did we find out the birth mom was only two months along when she first contacted the county (which is highly unusual).

Finally, the call came. The birth mother had given birth at a nearby hospital. One girl and one boy! Our social worker gave us permission to go peek at them in the hospital nursery, though nothing would be final for a day or two. The waiting was finally over!

Or so we thought.

We continued to wait for the word that we could pick up the babies. After several days and many phone calls, I got a different call.

The birth mother had changed her mind.

Our dreams and hearts were crushed. Again.

After a few weeks, I finally gathered the strength to return the new baby outfits that I couldn't help buying to prepare for these babies. I dragged myself to the store. I almost had to leave when the saleswoman smiled at me and asked, "Reason for return?" I don't even recall what I choked out in response as I fought off tears.

I still pray for God's protection and guidance for those babies and pray they'll grow up with family who loves them.

We went back to our childless lives and more waiting.

A year or so later, we signed up with two lawyers to add the option of independent adoption, which was often quicker. (Each lawyer had connections with different pregnant women.) We filled out more forms, paid additional fees, and wrote "Dear Birth Mother" letters. Nothing happened for another full year.

Then I became pregnant and was able to give birth to our son. We celebrated and enjoyed him.

Soon, we were struggling with secondary infertility. When our son was in preschool, we stepped back on the adoption path and tried to adopt a baby from Romania. We signed up with an international agency, paid the initial payment, then learned that instead of the expected cost we were originally told, the cost had now tripled. That was beyond our means.

At the same time, we learned couples were having problems bringing their Romanian babies back into the country because the adoption laws of Romania and the U.S. didn't match. Although we prayed for God to provide additional adoption finances. The way didn't open up for us. Soon after, the country of Romania closed its doors to international adoption. We didn't know how long this would last. God had closed another door.

In all, we committed to five different adoptions, only to have them all fall through.

Adoption is its own kind of roller coaster.

It wasn't until ten years after our son was born that we were able to adopt our baby daughter from China. God was in this. I believe we were meant to adopt our specific daughter. If one of the other adoptions had worked out though, we may not have pursued her adoption. The whole process was part of God's plan for our daughter to find us and for us to find her, but the process sure wasn't simple.

Is Adoption the Easy Way to Build a Family?

Adoption is one of the most beautiful and loving ways to build a family. A couple with love in their hearts finds a child who needs that love, and they become a family. This mirrors the picture of what God has done in adopting us, so he becomes our Father, and we become his children. It's also a positive answer to the problem of abortion or children unable to be cared for by their birth parents.

I've included our experience of unfulfilled attempts at adoption not to discourage those of you pursuing adoption, but to suggest adoption isn't the easy fix for infertility that some people portray it to be. The blood, sweat, and tears of the emotional labor in adoption is hard work. This isn't understood by many in our society. This can lead to some insensitive comments, such as, "Oh, you adopted. You got a baby the easy way."

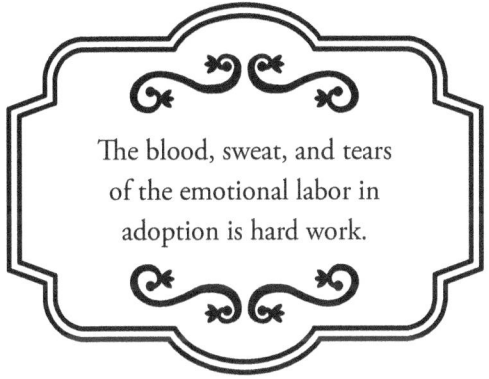

The blood, sweat, and tears of the emotional labor in adoption is hard work.

If they only knew.

I believe couples who are willing to make the sacrifices in both cost and effort to go the adoption route will most often end up with a baby. However, adoption requires focused perseverance and may offer its own heartache along the way.

If you're willing to investigate the type of adoption you want to pursue, try to locate a child, complete a home study, attend required counseling, complete and file the legal paperwork, and possibly travel to the baby's birth site, adoption can be a rewarding way to build your family. Adoption is as much a miracle as giving birth.

The strong desire for a child has motivated many couples to build beautiful families through adoption. These families see adoption as a special blessing and a gift to all involved.

This poem, written by a twelve-year-old son to his adoptive mother, shows this:

Real Women
I've been blessed with two real women in my life.
They never knew each other.
One I don't remember, the other I call *mother*.
One chose life for me and not abortion.
The other teaches me the Christian way.
One gave me my heritage, the other gave me my name.
One planted the seed of life, and the other will walk me through it.
One provided me with talents, the other teaches and encourages me to use them.
One gave me up for adoption because she loved me.
The other had been praying for a child, and God led her straight to me.
One I know as Megan, the other I know as Mom.[83]

What Adoption Is Not

Adoption is not a psychological or physical cure for infertility. People have told adoptive parents, "If you adopt, then you'll probably relax and get pregnant." This isn't only incorrect, but this thinking can be harmful to an adopted child if they're seen as a means to a biological child. Children who are adopted into families need to be seen as unique and special human beings in their own right. They may enter the family differently from biological children but they're equally precious in God's sight.

Vicky learned adoption didn't erase all her old emotions of infertility. She said:

> I had expected adopting would take away all the sadness I felt from infertility. But it still hurts when women share their birth stories even though I have a precious, beautiful daughter.
>
> It hurts when my daughter says, "Mommy, why didn't I grow in your tummy?" I have to say it makes me sad too. I wouldn't want to have a different child, but I would have liked Megan to have come from me.

Infertility brings many losses, the loss of the experience of conceiving a child together who is a combination of both husband and wife, missing out on the experience of pregnancy and giving birth, the loss of control, the loss of self-esteem, and the loss of being a parent to a child. Adoption only *cures* one of these losses—becoming a parent to a child.

Before moving on to adoption, it's important to face and resolve some of your sadness about infertility. This doesn't mean you need to exhaust all medical avenues before choosing adoption, but you should realize an adopted child won't heal all your wounds.

Making the Decision

Sometimes the decision to adopt is made more abruptly because a major medical problem is discovered fairly early in infertility testing. Although the grief can be more intense at discovering the door to a biological child has firmly closed, it may make the decision to adopt clearer.

Rosie and Gordon knew Gordon might have trouble becoming a father because he'd had chemotherapy for cancer earlier in his adulthood. When his sperm count tested low, Rosie thought the doctor would simply give Gordon something to raise it. But instead, the doctor told Gordon his sperm count was so low, he should think of adopting if he wanted children. The doctor sent Gordon home with an adoption agency's name scrawled on a slip of paper.

The shock was hard on both Rosie and Gordon. Using donor sperm wasn't an option with which they felt comfortable, especially Gordon. So, they started looking toward adoption.

More often, the decision to adopt is made gradually as the door to a biological child slowly closes. Couples need to decide whether the door to a biological child has closed *enough*, though the door may never completely shut until their childbearing years are over.

When Vicky and Steve realized testing and treatments were dragging on too long and what they wanted most was to raise a child, they turned their focus toward adopting.

> There comes a time as you're going through infertility, the clock starts ticking, and you realize you don't have much time left. Your medical options start running out, or you can't afford them, or you don't feel morally that you can go one more step medically to get a baby.
>
> Adoption usually isn't a decision where people wake up in the morning and say, okay, let's adopt. It's more of a gradual awakening to, well, maybe we could do that. Do we really want to be childless forever? Is this an option we want to pursue?
>
> We decided we wanted to have a child more than Vicky wanted to be pregnant. We'd been emotionally and physically wrung out by two years of infertility tests and surgeries. We decided we were ready for children, not more

tests. We quit all the medical procedures and sought a child through adoption.

Because adoption usually takes a great deal of effort, both husband and wife need to be motivated and committed to it. If you're having trouble deciding if adoption is for you, consider the following with your spouse:

- Are we ready to love a child who wasn't born to us?
- Do we have the emotional energy, finances, and other resources we need to adopt a child?
- What appeals to us about building our family this way? (For example, we would help a child who needs a home, or we would be able to stop medical treatments.)
- What doesn't appeal to us about building our family this way? (For example, we wouldn't be able to ensure the baby receives healthy nourishment during the pregnancy or the birth mother could change her mind.)
- Are we still young enough to parent a child?
- Is now the right time for us to pursue this?
- How will our friends and family react? How will we deal with that? (Just as we receive a variety of reactions when we share about our infertility, some families may support our desire to adopt, while others may not.)
- What do we believe God wants us to do regarding adoption now?

The decision comes down to, *do we want to be parents? Do we want to raise and nurture a child? Do we want to contribute to the physical, emotional, and spiritual growth of a child? Do we want this even if we can't experience a pregnancy, the baby doesn't carry our genes, and might not look like us?*

After discussing these questions, you'll know better if you're ready to adopt.

Adoption Options

Once you decide to pursue adoption, one option is simply to tell everyone you know that you're ready to adopt, then wait. Sometimes this alone can connect you to a baby, as it did to Julie and Russell. Julie said:

> Family was so important to us because we'd both lost ours.
>
> Off and on for four long years, the disappointment of the unfulfilled dream of having a child began to chip away at our faith. Amazingly though, after each month's letdown, we'd somehow manage to hold onto a glimmer of hope.
>
> This past October, the night we returned from vacation, our friend told us her aunt knew of a thirty-four-year-old woman who was pregnant and wanted to place her baby for adoption. Oh, and by the way, she's due anytime! Are you interested? On faith, we went for it!
>
> We found out this baby about to be born was truly a miracle. Last March—at the same time one of our pastors prayed for God to bless us with a child—the birth mother was frantically trying to borrow money for an abortion but to no avail. A few weeks later, she started bleeding and nearly miscarried. Then the bleeding stopped. God had spared our baby's life for a special purpose.
>
> One month later, after we took a four-hour, midnight ride to the birth mother's city, our precious little boy was born. Miracles truly can happen.

Although it gives us hope to hear of babies who practically knock on couple's doors (after four years), most will need to be more active in their search for a child to adopt. If you choose adoption as a route to build your family, talk to others who've recently adopted and ask how they did it. Also, read some blogs and books devoted to adoption and the process.

Below are brief overviews of the different routes currently available for adoption in the U.S. Other countries often have their own variations of these routes. I have friends and acquaintances who've successfully adopted through each of these different routes. All of them have positives and negatives, so choose whatever path suits you best.

Agency Adoptions

An *agency* is an organization that's licensed to place a child in an adoptive home and help with the process.

Public agencies

A *public agency*, such as the Department of Social Services, is supported by tax money. Public agencies usually deal with domestic adoptions and foster parenting/adoption programs. Their children are usually available for adoption because the birth parent's rights are in the process of being legally terminated or because parents have chosen to relinquish the children. These children are often older (grade school), have special needs, or belong to sibling groups.

The foster/adoption program is for children who have a limited chance of returning to live with their birth parents. The children are placed in a fost/adopt home before they're legally free to be adopted.

Molly and Tony successfully adopted two children through a public agency. They found the county agency flexible and supportive. After years of frustration and disappointment, Molly had become pregnant once but miscarried the baby, so they looked to adoption to build their family. Molly said:

A woman at work had adopted through the county. She planted the seed in my mind. About a year later, a woman whom I had told of my infertility gave me the card of a social worker at the county to call.

We had tried many other doors. In one week, we had interviews with two women looking for parents for their unborn babies. When we weren't chosen, we felt rejected. The loss of these opportunities was hard to bear.

We interviewed so many adoption counselors and agencies. None of the doors opened.

So, we called the county and went to the first meeting.

I've never been a real baby person, so we told them we were willing to adopt siblings under the age of eight. After all our years of infertility, we were ready to get on with having our family.

We went through the home-study process and became licensed as foster parents. The day our application/home study process was finished (three and a half months later) we got the call that they'd found a match for us.

They showed us pictures of David (age seven) and Brian (age five), with lots of records, court reports, and information about their birth parents. They were already legally free to be adopted and were living in a foster home. We just knew it was right and God's plan for us. Two weeks later we met our sons.

Eight months later we were in court finalizing the adoption. They're both such sweet-tempered boys. They're in counseling to help them talk about and deal with their past. David was old enough to remember his birth parents. We talk about their past in normal conversation because we have the records and know their history is a part of them.

I loved David and Brian before we met them, not because of some fantasy, but because the Lord confirmed it.

The joy of the moment overflowed and fear melted away. They are our sons.

This Christmas, we'll be putting bows on each other—Tony, Brian, David, and me—and giving thanks for each one.

Benefits. If the adoption is a straight adoption, the children have already been relinquished. The cost is the lowest of any adoption options.

Drawbacks. Public agencies don't place many babies, so the wait for an infant can be many years. They may be more concerned than most private agencies with matching ethnic backgrounds. Most adoptions through a county agency are done through foster/adopt programs.

The Department of Social Services' main goal in the foster/adoption program is to give every chance for the children to be reunited with their birth parents first. Visitations between the child and the birth parents, as the birth parents are given time to show if they can meet parenting standards, are a part of this program. Only if and when the parental rights are terminated will the child be free to be adopted.

The fost/adopt program lessens the trauma children can experience when they're shuffled around to various foster homes before being placed in an adoptive home. But for couples who've already dealt with loss, the uncertainty of fostering a child not yet free for adoption can feel emotionally risky too. Broadening your perspective to learn about what foster parenting entails can be helpful when adopting from a public agency.

Private agencies

Private agencies are licensed by each state to perform adoptions but are funded by private money. They're similar to the public agencies in that they perform a home study before the placement of a child.

Private agencies usually offer help in finding a child to adopt. Many private agencies are open to working with a birth mother to choose the adoptive parents she wants to place her baby with.

Linda and Tim are currently waiting to adopt a child through a private agency. They chose the route of a private agency because it offered guidance through the adoption process, counseling, a set fee, and help in locating a child. Another factor was the more favorable laws in their state for adoptive parents when adoption is done through an agency versus an independent adoption.

They've just completed a year of meetings, paperwork, and their home study. They expect to have a child placed in their home within a year.

Benefits. Laws often allow the relinquishment of birth parent's parental rights more quickly with private agencies than with independent adoptions. The relinquishment is final once the birth mother releases her child to the agency. More infants are placed through private agencies than through county agencies.

Drawbacks. Each agency has its own set of criteria that may or may not work in your favor. The cost is usually a fixed amount (of several thousand dollars) although some agencies will offer a sliding scale.

Private Adoption (Independent Adoption)

A private adoption is a legal agreement made directly between the birth parents and the adoptive couple. Laws vary from state to state but in most cases, an attorney coordinates the transfer of the baby from the birth mother to the adopting couple. The attorney also completes and files the legal documentation.

In this type of adoption, the couple usually searches for the child through networking, sending out search/resumé letters, or advertising. The birth mother is often involved in choosing the couple to adopt her baby. Instead of paying an agency fee, the adoptive couple usually pays the attorney as well as reimburses the birth mother for specific medical costs, living expenses, and counseling.

The legal forms to complete an independent adoption can be filed without an attorney in very simple adoptions. But if there's any chance a problem might develop with the birth parents or if there's any question about the exact legal forms that need to be filed or when, then it's safer to hire a lawyer. Even if you file the legal forms yourself, you'll still need to have a home study completed by a public or private agency or adoption social worker.

Some organizations or individuals act as adoption facilitators in private adoptions. They may help connect babies and adoptive parents, give advice, and assist in writing *Dear Birth Mother* letters. Facilitators may save you money by assisting you at a lower hourly rate than an attorney or they can be costlier.

Vicky tells how she and her husband, Steve, chose the independent adoption route. Vicky said:

> We were pretty devastated by the time we decided to adopt and weren't strong emotionally, so it was hard. We chose independent adoption because our county had two hundred people waiting for a healthy child at the time. They had children with serious problems available, but we didn't feel strong enough to take one of those children.
>
> We researched to get every address we could, related to adoption, then sent away for information and applications. One place that sent us information was a resource center that assisted with independent adoption, so we chose to use them. They shared ideas with us on how to get the word out that we were looking to adopt.
>
> Then we waited for five months.
>
> In December, we got a call from a young woman who said shyly, "Hi...are you still interested in adopting a

baby?" We met with her. And five months later, which was a long time to wait, she gave birth to a little girl.

When our daughter was born, we got to the hospital at midnight and said, "We're here to see our baby!" The nurse knew nothing about it, so we had to go home without seeing the baby. I cried. I thought, this is it, we're not going to get her.

The next day, during regular visiting hours, we walked into the hospital room. Our birth mother, Diane, said, "Oh, there are the parents." Then she handed Megan to me.

I got to hold Diane's hands and look in her face and say, "Thank you for this gift."

Then she kissed Megan goodbye and said, "I'll love you forever, my little daughter."

Then we went home.

Two weeks later Diane called and said she wanted to see the baby. I thought she'd changed her mind and was going to take Megan. I sat rocking in the chair, crying, "God, please don't let her take our baby, please." This is the hard part of independent adoption.

Diane came in, looked at her, and said, "She's cute. Where's her room?"

We showed her the nursery. We talked a while and she left. She just wanted to make sure Megan had a nice place to live.

Six months later we signed the papers, and she was our kid.

We send Diane letters occasionally telling her how beautiful Megan is, and she contacts us occasionally. God was so gracious to give us a beautiful baby daughter. And I'm so glad I can tell Megan the last thing Diane told her as she kissed her goodbye at the hospital. She won't have to wonder if her birth mother loved her.

Benefits. Most domestic adoptions are done privately, so more babies are available through private adoption. Adoptions done independently can often take less time than agency adoptions. The couple only needs to fit the birth mother's criteria. Couples may be able to attend the baby's birth.

Drawbacks. In many American states, the birth mother has a longer time period to change her mind in an independent adoption. So there's more uncertainty about the outcome during the child's early placement in your home. You may become more involved with the birth mother, which can have both benefits and drawbacks.

The cost varies widely, depending on the expenses of the birth mother and the attorney's fees. This option can be more expensive than an agency adoption.

There is more potential for dishonesty on a birth mother's part, so the news stories we hear about birthparent scams are usually associated with independent adoptions. If the birth mother changes her mind about placing the child or is dishonest in her requests for payments, the adopting parents have no recourse to recover the money they've paid.

International/Cross-Cultural Adoption

An *international adoption* is usually done through a licensed agency in your country that cooperates with an agency in the child's native country. Agencies often specialize in working with specific countries. A home study is generally required before placement. Each country has its own rules and restrictions for adoptions regarding parental age, travel to the country, and length of stay needed in the country. Adopting the child in your home country is a separate legal step after you return with the child.

In a variation of this called adopt abroad, you can use a lawyer or private party to help you find a child in another country, then travel to that country to complete the adoption there. A home study is still required by an agency in your home country.

If you choose to adopt a child from a different ethnic background, but the child is born in the United States, this is called a *cross-cultural domestic adoption*. This can either be done privately or through an agency.

Laura explained the process she and Jim went through to adopt internationally.

> We worked with a clearinghouse that directed us to an agency in Pennsylvania. This agency had contacts in Chile. When our home study with the agency was done, we had to get approval from immigration and give some financial information showing we could support a child.
>
> We got our referral for our daughter about eight months after we first applied at the agency. She was four days old. Once we got the referral, there were lots of other documents the country of Chile wanted us to fill out.
>
> We got all that done and then waited for four more months.
>
> I flew by myself to Chile and stayed two days. [The required stay may have changed.]
>
> I didn't even have to make an appearance in a Chilean court. The Chilean government gave the mother some time, then she appeared in court to relinquish the child. Then the court made us the baby's legal guardians before we could even see her.
>
> My emotions felt frozen until I got the final stamp of approval. Then I started to cry. I called my husband, Jim, and told him she was beautiful. She had these huge deep-brown eyes.

I brought our daughter home about a year after we started the process.

Benefits. Often other countries have more liberal age restrictions or allow single-parent adoptions. The waiting time can be minimal. If you choose a well-known agency, with good connections in the child's native country, and a good track record of adoptions from that country, your chances of the adoption completing are quite high.

Drawbacks. You need to feel comfortable that your child will probably not look like you. You may be asked about how your family originated throughout your child's life. If you see this as a chance to share the benefits of building families through international or cross-cultural adoption, and you can share with your child how you value his or her cultural heritage, this may be a good adoption route for you.

The cost of adopting internationally is often higher than most domestic adoptions. Some countries are not well regulated, so delays can occur in these countries. Children from countries with less-adequate medical care may have health issues that haven't been recognized before the adoption.

Special-Needs Adoptions

Children with *special needs* are adopted through both public or private agencies. These children are usually more difficult to place, so they may be more readily available for adoption. They often have physical health issues, cognitive issues, or mental health issues. They may be age ten or older or be of minority heritage. They may also belong to a sibling group of three or more.

If you want to adopt an older child or a child with special needs, take time to research the unique needs they may have throughout life, so you're better prepared to help them.

Benefits. Financial subsidies are often available to help with ongoing medical or counseling costs. Adoptive parents may also feel they're helping a child in dire need.

Drawbacks. These children may often need additional help throughout their lives, including extra time and expense for medical appointments, counseling, schooling alternatives, or surgeries. Often, adoptive parents may need training to develop expertise in caring for them. The agency can help locate specific training if needed.

One adoptive father of a special-needs child suggests, "Couples need to be certain the Lord wants them to adopt a child with special needs. So, make this a prayerful decision."

The added daily and life-long costs involved in raising a child with special needs are greater than with a typical child. Research to ensure you're able to parent a child with special needs for the long term. Remember also, that as with parents who have a child with special needs born to them, if you choose to adopt a child with special needs, God will help you grow as parents to meet the child's needs as well.

Open or Closed Adoption

Another aspect of the decision about which path to take in adoption involves how much openness you want with the birth parents and for how long. Many domestic adoptions have moved toward openness. In a completely open adoption, the birth mother may live with the adoptive couple before the birth, then the birth mother and father spend time with the child as the child grows.

In a completely closed adoption, no information is shared between the birth parents and the adoptive parents. Some international adoptions are closed adoptions because of laws in the child's native county. Placing children for adoption is illegal in some countries, so birthparents must relinquish their children anonymously.

Most adoptions fall somewhere in the middle of these extremes. In a middle-of-the-road case, the birth and adoptive parents may meet once before the birth to exchange non-identifying information such as first names and medical information. Then the adoptive parents may send letters and pictures occasionally through an intermediary for the first few years of the child's life. Sometimes an agreement is made that the child can meet the birth parents when s/he turns 21.

Discuss with your spouse where you feel comfortable on the closed-to-open adoption continuum.

The Home Study

Most couples come to adoption feeling battle-weary after already having endured the stress of infertility. The idea of being analyzed by strangers to see if they'd make good parents adds pressure and may resurrect feelings of inadequacy or anger.

Instead of seeing a home study as a test to pass, try to see the questions as discussion topics for you and your spouse. Although it's stressful, try to view the process as a way to prepare yourselves for parenting.

Adoption Costs

Adoption costs vary drastically. The cost of adopting requires sacrifice for most couples. For some couples, the cost of adopting is prohibitive.

While many medical costs of infertility may be covered by medical insurance, adopting couples may have no assistance for adoption expenses which can run tens of thousands of dollars. In addition, while infertility expenses may be spread over months or years, the cost of adopting a child may need to be paid within a short time period.

Finding Help with Adoption Costs

Dr. Alan McNickle, a former theology professor at Moody Bible Institute, has adopted two children. He suggests one way churches can show their support for couples seeking adoption is to view it as a ministry and help financially.

> If people feel before God that they need children, it seems appropriate to share their financial situation with their friends and church to allow other believers to minister with them. This is just like other social problems where people lose jobs and the last people to hear about it are their friends. They may be too embarrassed to share their needs because of pride. Financial advisor, Larry Burkett, said people who are in need are often not aware of the money that's available if they would let their needs be known. Often, they are afraid to ask because they might be embarrassed if the adoption fell through.
>
> Also, sometimes mission organizations have contacts in other countries for children waiting to be adopted. Those children could be helped [if the couple allows others to help them financially with their adoption].

In addition, Dr. McNickle suggests that couples can simplify their lifestyle to help save more money for adoption and warns against materialism in our society. He says, "We have to decide what our goals are and what we need as far as our lifestyle goes.... It's a matter of what we want to do with our life. A consistent biblical worldview demands we make choices for eternity, not simply to satisfy personal, creature comforts."

Other options that may help with adoption costs:

- Fundraise with a GoFundMe account (gofundme.com) or with the help of an organization such as Show Hope (showhope.org).
- Ask if your company reimburses employees for specific adoption expenses. If not, petition them to do so. In fair-

ness to employees, many companies will reimburse adoption expenses to an amount equal to the typical cost of giving birth.
- Check if an adoption tax credit will be offered this year.
- Look for an agency that offers a sliding-fee scale.
- Ask adoptive parents you know how they funded their adoption.
- Search, "how to raise funds for adoption."

Nursing an Adopted Baby

Part of the sorrow of being unable to carry a child can be the inability to nurse a child. Our bodies are amazing though, and a woman can often produce milk simply with the stimulation of a baby suckling. If you're interested in nursing your adopted child, this can be done. Most women can produce some milk and some women can even produce a full milk supply. Your local La Leche League can supply the special equipment to feed your baby supplemental formula as you're nursing him or her.

Search "nursing adopted baby" for more information.

As one mom commented about nursing her adopted newborn, "You get all the hassles of bottle feeding with all the hassles of nursing, but for me, it's been worth it."

Even if you're unable to produce a full milk supply, the baby can bond with mom, receive some immunities from the colostrum, and benefit from the enhanced jaw and speech development that nursing provides.

Researching Adoption

If you're considering adoption, do all you can to find out more about it. Investigate agencies—many of them have informational meetings. Talk to a variety of people about their experiences with adoption. Ask those who've recently adopted and those who adopted decades ago.

Ask agencies or attorneys how many families they've helped finalize adoptions for, the type of children (infants, school-age, special needs), and a breakdown of their fees (some have sliding scales).

Start or join an in-person adoption care group with others hoping to adopt or join one online. (For information on starting or joining a care group, see: AchingforaChild.com.)

If you decide to pursue a child through adoption, may God speed you toward finding your child.

Your Personal Journey

1. Do you see adoption as an option for you? Why or why not?
2. If you were able to choose a child through adoption, what would be important to know about the child you'd want to adopt?
3. Which type of adoption seems the most attractive to you? Why?
4. If you aren't ready to move toward adoption, is there a deciding factor in the future when you'd be ready to consider it?

16

Parenting After Infertility or Miscarriage

A spring day in December is always more precious than one in May.
—Irwin Philip Sobel

Be very careful never to forget what you have seen God doing for you. May his miracles have a deep and permanent effect upon our lives! Tell your children ... about the glorious miracles he did.
—Deuteronomy 4:9

If your infertility path results in a child through either birth or adoption, your struggle may inspire you to value the miracle of that child even more. Most fertile couples cherish their children, but those children are like an elegantly planted garden, planned, cultivated, and beautiful. The child of an infertile couple, however, is like a single, brilliant red wildflower vibrantly blooming in the middle of a barren, lifeless desert.

Vicky felt this sense of wonder about the daughter she adopted six years earlier. She said, "I'm still amazed our childless household now has a child's toys lying around and the joy a child brings. I thank God for that."

Joys and Benefits

Couples who become parents after infertility have developed an immense capacity for feeling joy at the sight of their child. They don't take their child for granted or view them as a burden. They have the pleasure of being able to tell their child he or she was very much wanted. They would have valued their child's life if it had come easily, but the time of waiting deepened their appreciation for this personal miracle.

Through our efforts to have children, we realize what a miracle it is that babies are ever born. Children are an expression of grace. They are freely given, but not deserved or owed to us. They are gifts. Infertile people understand that well.

Rich, whose wife had multiple miscarriages and whose triplets were originally given only a slim chance to live, says he's still in awe about finally being a dad. Rich said:

> There's nothing like having little ones running through your house. The children are almost eighteen months old now, and I still can't believe I'm a daddy. When I walk through the door and see three pairs of arms reaching out, saying, "Daddy!" it was worth every struggle, every pain. When you hug them, you hug them that much tighter, when you kiss them, you kiss them that much more tenderly. It's better than I ever dreamed it would be.

Infertile couples have also had more time to think through parenting issues beforehand, so they may be more aligned on child-raising issues. They've had time as a couple to develop trust, interdependence, and skills in working as a team, all of which can help in parenting. Always aware that they might have a baby next year, they've had time to listen, watch closely, and discuss what they've seen with others' child-rearing practices. Because their friends' children may be older, they can watch their parenting choices and see what seems to work and what doesn't.

One of the particular joys infertile parents share is how their changed priorities affect their parenting. Carole, who experienced two miscarriages and a stillbirth, found she was able to reevaluate what was important when her son was born. Carole said:

> I didn't worry about cleaning. I just took the time I needed to rock my baby. Because of my previous losses, I don't think I ever really bonded with Ben until after he was born.
>
> Maybe it all felt so magical and new because I hadn't bonded with him during my pregnancy. I wanted to hold him and not let go. Even now, five years later, the wonder and joy of having him fill up my heart pretty much every day. I feel so thankful for the beautiful gift God has given me.

Often, parents who first went through infertility are willing to let the less important things in life slide while savoring moments with their child. Remembering their time without a child can sometimes help lessen times of typical parenting frustration.

Challenges

Although parenting a child after infertility is an incredible joy, it also offers some challenges. When a child comes, does the specter of infertility fade into a bad dream? It can to a degree, but the trauma can also still affect parents' lives. The degree of permanent change often depends on how and how deeply we were affected.

Unrealistic Expectations about Our Parenting

Just as we can idealize a pregnancy, we can also idealize parenthood. We may subconsciously expect parenthood to heal our past hurts and erase the feelings we experienced while infertile. But having a child doesn't automatically erase the feelings that being infertile brought up. Just as everyone needs to do, we'll need to continue to go to God for healing for the rest of our lives. Because God is our healer, and our child is not our healer.

Couples may also expect, again unrealistically, if they ever had a baby, they would never yell at their child. Their child would also never rebel against them because she would sense the incredible love they have for her. But struggling to become parents doesn't make anyone into perfect parents or promise them perfect children. It's important not to feel guilty when parenting overwhelms you at times. No child will be perfect no matter how much they're loved. Look at Adam and Eve—they were offered the perfect life with the most perfect Father, yet they still rebelled.

Awareness of the Fragility of Life

The booklet *Your Next Baby* shares a quote from a mom in Louisville who had a previous baby die. She said, "Every night I whisper in his ear, 'Always know I love you, and please, don't forget to breathe.'"[84]

Infertile parents may often feel aware of the fragility of their child's life. They've learned life isn't always fair, and they aren't immune to tragedy. They may worry they could lose their child or may feel unaccustomed to happiness and fear this blessing won't last.

Being aware your child is special, combined with feelings of parental responsibility, can bring an intensity to parenthood that may lead to overprotectiveness. Being protective as a parent is good. Being overprotective means becoming so concerned for the safety of your child, you isolate or inhibit her from experiences that are good for her growth and development. It's holding on too tightly because we still don't trust God.

After God finally gave Abraham a son, he tested him. God wanted to make sure Abraham wasn't turning his focus to the gift instead of continuing to trust him (Genesis 22:1–19). God knew how important Isaac was to Abraham, but he wanted Isaac to be a catalyst for a stronger relationship between Abraham and himself.

And can you imagine how Hannah felt? After struggling for so long without a child, after she weaned him, she followed God's nudging and gave Samuel to her priest to raise (1 Samuel 1). Hannah had learned God was in control and she could trust him. Because of the choices she made, her child lived a life full of connection to God, faith, and leadership.

If we're tempted to try to hold on too tightly to our children because they were so hard to come by, it's comforting to read that after Hannah gave Samuel to God, he grew up surrounded by the presence of the Lord (1 Samuel 2:21). If we make the daily choices to point our children to God and trust him, we don't need to worry. Our children will grow up surrounded by God's presence. If we're able to have a child after infertility or miscarriage, remembering that God loves our child even more than we do can ease our anxiety over his or her safety.

If we're able to have a child after infertility or miscarriage, remembering that God loves our child even more than we do can ease our anxiety over his or her safety.

Continued Differences

Carole had a difficult time adjusting to the isolation motherhood brought. Carole shared:

> I love children and I wanted children, but after my son was born, it was a real adjustment. I no longer worked and was home all day. All of my friends had been from work, so I was lonely. No other moms lived anywhere in my neighborhood. No one was home but retired people.
> And they didn't want to babysit—ever.

Infertile parents can feel isolated because their closest friends may remain infertile. These friends don't want to spend time with a new baby even if it's yours. Or perhaps we didn't keep up friendships with people who had children because we were protecting ourselves.

Maybe we thought once we'd had a child, we'd slide seamlessly into the *mom's club*. This transition may be more difficult for many infertile women though. For instance, if an infertile woman eventually has a multiple birth, that still stands out as different. Strangers approach moms of multiples in stores to ask, "Did you take fertility drugs?" (This was my friend's reality.)

If you've adopted a child, you still won't have a story about giving birth to share. If you adopted a transracial child, you may not fit the typical family image (but you may find a strong camaraderie with others who have similar adoption stories or uniquely created families as well). You may not slip as easily into the typical mom role as you expected.

Rosie felt this yearning to just be a regular mom. Rosie said:

> We were walking our daughter Cici one night in her stroller when a couple walked by her and admired her. The woman said she just found out she was pregnant, and she wanted to know my obstetrician. It made me sad to say I never had an obstetrician. Why do I still have to feel different?

Infertility changes us. We're similar, yet still can feel different from other parents. Being the ones left out for so long can make us more aware of never wanting to exclude others. Hopefully, we can step closer to resting in God's total acceptance of us rather than needing acceptance from others. We can also learn to reach out to others who may feel different.

Uncertainty

If couples used high-tech methods to conceive or became parents through adoption, they may wonder at times, *did we push too hard to become parents? Do others know better how to care for this child?*

Whole books have been written about raising adopted children and how adoptive parents need to come to a point of feeling complete entitlement, or the right, to raise their child. Again, it's a process as parents get to know their child. They don't need to have all the parenting skills down by the time their child turns two months old.

Childless couples may also feel unsure about their ability to be good parents if they've avoided being around children because it was too painful. By the time they have a child, all their friends and family members may already have older children. Now the new parents are often on the receiving end of advice, sometimes phrased as, *sure, your child seems happy now, but just you wait until…*

If you feel insecure being a novice parent, by all means, listen to the advice. It may be wise, worthwhile advice. Take what makes sense and discard the rest. But also remember God has given *you* your child to raise. For some reason, God's plan most often involves giving children to people with little or no parenting experience. Maybe it's so parents will keep going to him for help.

More or Fewer Children Than We'd Planned

A history of infertility may have a direct effect on how many children we end up with. Some couples end up with fewer children than they wanted, and others may end up with more than they're prepared to raise.

Rich said this when he shared about parenting multiples:

> The only thing that hurts is you can't hold all three of them in your arms at the same time. And you long to. It's also hard to discipline them. In raising triplets, there are times you have to sit back and bite your lip because they're just exploring and grabbing like all eighteen-month-old children.
>
> Financially we make it month to month. Sometimes I feel like we do it with mirrors. It has certainly rearranged our priorities. It's an incredible financial burden, and I don't see us coming out of it anytime soon. But it's worth it.

Deanna had to learn to respond to the insensitive comments people make around her triplets. She said:

> When people see me with the triplets, some of them say, "I'm sure glad it's you and not me."
> I've learned to reply, "Well, I'm glad it's me too."
> Or I also hear, "Wow, you sure have your hands full!"
> It's a joy to answer, "Yes, and it's so much better than when they were empty."

Learning to persevere through struggles is a valuable skill for parenting. Yet, infertile couples who become parents will stumble through most of the same pitfalls other parents do. Infertility doesn't allow them to bypass the challenges of parenting (although personally, I think that would only be fair). No parents or children are perfect.

Your Personal Journey

1. How do you believe parenthood will change your life?
2. Do you anticipate any specific challenges in parenting?
3. While you wait for children, are there ways to help lessen the struggles you expect parenthood will bring? (For example, if it isn't too painful, consider discussing parenting styles with your spouse or spending some time with others' children.) Give yourself permission to prepare for eventual parenting.

17
Living In-Between—Secondary Infertility

*Another Christmas morning,
And my family is still not complete.
Not enough stockings on the mantel,
Not enough toys under the tree.
Too few little hands helping make cookies
Why can't I just be grateful for the child I have,
At this sacred time of year?
Because it's another Christmas morning
Without my baby.
And I miss him
—Marty Heiberg* [85]

*Like arrows in the hand of a warrior,
So are the children of one's youth.
Blessed is the man whose quiver is full of them.
—Psalm 127:4–5 NASB*

I hesitated to include this chapter because the pain of secondary infertility can be confusing to those hurting with primary infertility. But I also wanted to support the many women enduring the real struggle of secondary infertility. If you aren't ready to read this chapter, please feel free to skip it and return at a later time.

We only waited ten months before starting to try for our second child. Since we had hoped to have three children by the time our first was finally born, we didn't want to lose more time. Since my reproductive system had only worked correctly once in almost six years of trying, we also didn't want to miss the one time it might work again in the next six years. But soon we were dealing with secondary infertility.

I assumed since we already had one miracle child, we wouldn't feel emotional pain while trying for another child. I soon discovered I was wrong.

The lessons I learned the first time helped—I entered this journey with less tunnel vision, more patience, and felt God's love for me much more than the first time. I'd also developed some coping skills from the first prolonged battle.

But, as the years passed, I again experienced the intense yearning for another child. Along with it came frustration and a sense of injustice that we had to work so hard for another child when children came naturally for most.

During this time, I wrote this poem in my journal:

Faltering Steps

Lord, I hate to bother you again.
I know you have blessed me beyond my dreams,
but your first blessing was so wonderful,
I can hardly wait for another.
I thought my body was healed.

> *What has happened?*
> *Here come some of my old feelings of worthlessness returning.*
> *Please help me remember all the lessons you've taught me.*
> *Help me remember your love and hold on to you.*

Are There Different Sizes of Quivers?

Looking at Psalm 127:4–5, I began to wonder if there are different sizes of quivers. When is a quiver full? Some couples feel their family is complete with one child. Others plan for six children to *fill* their household. To them, one child is just the beginning of their family. So if they experience infertility after having one, they live with a sense that their other children are missing.

Those going through secondary infertility may look at a photo of their small family and wonder if their family will ever be *complete*. At the park, they watch their child play and wonder when their brother or sister will arrive to sit on the other end of the teeter-totter. They only know their quiver has more room but they're missing the child or children to fill it.

"When most couples think of having a family, they think of having two or more children," says Marianne Carter, a licensed marriage and family counselor who works with infertile couples in California. "A lot of parents feel strongly about wanting that balance."

An example of this comes from a man, Jeff, in the book *Healing the Infertile Family*. He says:

> I've always been an iffy sort of person when it comes to family life. The only constraint I ever put on it was that if I ever had kids I would have more than one. I was an only child and as I grew up I always said to myself, "Boy, I never want to live in a family like this." I used to talk to walls because there wasn't another kid there.[86]

Many reasons can make up your idea of the perfect-sized family. You may have as many reasons for wanting an ideal family size as wanting a child in the first place. For instance,

- you may have had a favorite brother or sister with whom you had a special relationship (ex., you shared confidences with them that you would have never shared with your parents),
- you might have been an only child and felt lonely, or
- you might have wonderful memories of a house full of people—all connected to you—gathered for special holidays, such as around the tree at Christmas.

Secondary Infertility Defined

A couple with secondary infertility wants but is unable to conceive or carry a child to term following the birth of one or more children. This includes those struggling to have a second child, third, fourth, or more. Couples who have adopted a child and want to adopt other children to *complete* their family may also struggle with secondary infertility.

Some couples with secondary infertility experienced trouble conceiving the first time, so they have an inkling they might have trouble the next time. Hopefully, these couples have been able to develop some coping tools from the first time around that will help them through infertility again. The downside for these couples is they start the process more worn down from what they've already gone through.

Other couples who became pregnant easily the first time are often shocked to find out they can't conceive again. For couples who are new to infertility, the shock, confusion, and initial grieving can add further stress.

Secondary infertility is more common than most people realize. Of all the women who have had a baby, close to ten percent will later experience secondary infertility, according to fertility specialist Dr. David Adamson, "If approximately ten percent of women have secondary infertility, that means 400,000 couples who have a baby this year are going to later experience infertility." (There are now close to 4 million children born in the U.S. per year.)

Feelings of helplessness and hopelessness affect couples with secondary infertility. Marianne Carter wrote, "It touches the core issues for everyone: their goals, expectations, womanhood or manhood, body image, sexuality, their reason for being and for living. That's why it's so difficult and devastating for almost everyone."

Sara, for instance, had no trouble conceiving her daughter during her first marriage. Then, after a divorce, when her daughter was eight, she married her husband, Paul. Suddenly, she couldn't wait to have a baby with him. When a year passed without a pregnancy, she saw her gynecologist. He discovered Sara's fallopian tubes were severely scarred, most likely caused by an infection sometime after she had her daughter. He told her that her chances of becoming pregnant without some high-tech help were slim. She was amazed at how difficult secondary infertility was for her.

> For the first time in my life, I didn't know how to control the emotions I felt. I couldn't understand why my emotions were so strong when I already had a child. I finally realized it was because I had no control in this situation where I longed for another child.

Although couples with secondary infertility already have a child, they also have a concrete idea of the dream they can't achieve. Dr. William Brown, past chairman of OB/GYN at The Good Samaritan Hospital of Santa Clara Valley, spoke about how knowing the joys of parenthood can add to a couple's sadness, "My patients who have children at home and are experiencing infertility have a clear picture of what they're missing. It's a personalized feeling of loss."

Medical Explanations

How could someone who has been able to have a child not be able to have another? Doesn't one child *prove* fertility? These questions make sense until you realize a problem with fertility can happen at any time. Other than a congenital problem that caused sterility from birth, just about any of the reasons listed in chapter 4 can also cause secondary infertility. Perhaps after the last child, the husband or wife was exposed to toxic chemicals, an infection, injury, or surgery. Or a medical problem, such as endometriosis, fibroids, or diabetes may have progressed to the point it now affects their fertility.

Age is also an important factor. The passage of time since the last pregnancy can compound a problem, since becoming pregnant gets harder to achieve with advancing maternal age. As age increases, the chances of conceiving decrease while the potential for miscarriage increases.[87]

Additionally, a complication with a woman's previous pregnancy such as placental abruption, cesarean section, or retained placenta could require an operation or medical procedure that caused scarring. An infection after delivery could also damage a woman's uterus or scar her fallopian tubes.

A hierarchy of pain?

Couples experiencing infertility after having a child, often find discussing it even more difficult than for those experiencing primary infertility. One concern is that others might view their secondary infertility as insignificant. So they don't share because they expect little understanding or support if they talk about their struggle.

To the misinformed who imagine a hierarchy of pain, secondary infertility may seem to be at the bottom of the list. At the top of the list is the woman suffering from primary infertility. Beneath her is the woman who has miscarried (at least she got pregnant). And at the bottom is the woman who has secondary infertility (at least she has a child).

Pain is pain. No one benefits when any time is spent trying to justify whose pain is worse.

Infertility is painful. Your pain is significant, no matter how many children you may already have. Yours is the pain you see all day long. Any pain comparisons are ridiculous. The yearning is still there, the control or choice isn't.

In Bob Deits's book, *Life after Loss*, he asks the questions:

> Which grief experience is the worst? Is it more difficult on the widow if her husband suddenly and unexpectedly drops dead of a heart attack? Or is it worse if he dies an inch at a time from cancer? Is it worse to lose a spouse to death or divorce? Is the death of a child the worst of all losses?
>
> The truth is, these are irrelevant questions. There is only one very worst kind of grief, and that is yours.[88]

Some Unique Problems of Secondary Infertility

Couples with secondary infertility experience a unique set of problems trying to balance taking care of the child they have while also pursuing having another child.

Scheduling Medical Treatment

Mei had a preschooler at home and shared with our group how difficult she was finding the IVF process this second time around. She said,

> You know, the Pergonal shots and blood tests are just as painful as they were the first time. But this time, on top of everything else, I also need to find a team of trusted

sitters for my daughter during my many medical appointments. And I sometimes only have a day's notice of a new appointment when it's dependent on other progress made, like how my eggs are developing. I can't expect friends to stop their lives for me. This is the fourth month I've asked for their help.

Women undergoing medical treatment for secondary infertility often have many doctor's appointments per month, for which timing is critical and dependent on their cycle day, so they may only have short notice. These women must depend on others for something as personal as continuing their fertility treatment and caring for their child.

This pull between caring for my child and choosing medical treatment again to have another almost gave me whiplash. It became graphically clear to me the week I started Pergonal treatment:

Mike scheduled leave from work to join me for this next doctor's appointment. I was having an ultrasound to check my ovaries. He would learn how to give me injections of Pergonal. I had coordinated all the moving pieces surrounding the appointment like an air-traffic controller.

Just before we needed to leave, I brushed my hand over our two-year-old son, Justin's, forehead and discovered it was hot. I took his temp and found he had a 101-degree fever. First, I canceled the babysitter. Then we discussed rescheduling the appointment. But we couldn't reschedule it because our insurance was changing. We were about to lose our infertility coverage because of a job change. It was this month or maybe never. We talked about how often our son ran a fever when he was teething. Could that be it? We decided to give him medicine to reduce the fever and take him with us.

I tried to keep Justin low profile while we waited at the office and was glad when he fell asleep. After my ovaries were checked, we sat in a small room and watched the instructional video on how to give Pergonal shots. Because the wait and appointment took so long though, the next time I felt Justin's forehead, the medicine had worn off. He felt so hot it scared me.

I panicked and dashed out to the receptionist to ask for a thermometer. Mike immediately called me back. I spun around to see Justin, throwing up all over both of them. We rushed him through the waiting area and into the hall bathroom outside the office. We did our best to clean him up, then Mike took him out to the car, while I stopped back at the office to collect my purse.

The nurse wanted to give both of us further instructions, but I told her we had to go. I desperately wanted to take Justin home to deal with his high fever. At the same time, I knew we only had insurance coverage for this month of Pergonal. At $3,000 per cycle, we couldn't afford to pay for it out-of-pocket later.

So, the nurse quickly gathered my Pergonal and syringes while I wiped up more mess, paid the bill, and apologized profusely. I left knowing we might not have gotten enough instruction for Mike to give me the Pergonal shots. So, I understood in leaving that we could be losing out on one of our best chances to ever get pregnant again. Meanwhile, Justin recovered quickly from his fever once we got home.

We had to call the doctor on the phone that night for more instructions about the shots, but after several aborted attempts, because I was shaking in nervous fits of laughter and wouldn't present a still target, Mike was able to give me the first of what would turn out to be many shots. I must admit, I didn't have much faith in his ability since he always avoids needles or shots like the plague. But he came through like a champ.

We were thankful we didn't have to skip our best medical option for a pregnancy that was covered by insurance. But we felt so pulled to be in two places at the same time, both needing to take care of our sick son and attending the fertility appointment.

Balancing Finances

Medical treatment may also be more difficult because of additional financial needs for those with secondary infertility. A childless couple is often willing to make financial sacrifices for a future child. When a child is already in the picture though, those with secondary infertility may feel a greater need to balance current financial stability as well.

If a couple already dealt with primary infertility, they may have spent much of their savings on the first rounds of fertility treatments. The couple may be operating on a reduced income as well if one parent has cut back on hours or has chosen to stay home with their first child.

Balancing the Existing Child's Needs

"The parents want a sibling for the child," says Marianne Carter. "Some feel if they can't have another child, then they are putting their child at a disadvantage." In a paradox to this, the parents may also feel guilty about not focusing totally on their first child because so much time and emotional energy are being spent on pursuing another baby.

Because a child's world centers on himself, he also may begin to wonder if he's causing the problem. "Did having me make you so you can't have any more babies?" Or she may feel threatened by the thought of another baby, "Why do you want another baby so badly? Aren't I enough?"

Balancing your desire for another baby with the needs of your current child is a difficult battle for those with secondary infertility. The more intense the medical testing and treatment or adoption search, the harder it can be to maintain this balance.

I've struggled in walking this fine line. Since part of my infertility problem is irregular ovulation, I've taken many cycles of Clomid and Pergonal. With Clomid, I become very tired and emotional. I must cut way back on my schedule to keep my head above water when I take it. While some women have few side effects, for me, I imagine it's similar to severe PMS all month long. While taking Clomid, I cry at everything from McDonald's commercials on television to graphs showing the number of women unable to receive prenatal care. This is not my normal state, and these symptoms go away once I stop taking Clomid.

During primary infertility, I knew my husband or adult coworkers could handle and understand any times I might be extra-emotional. With my young son though, when I try with a Herculean effort to be patient and fail, I wonder if I might be doing damage to his growing little psyche. I feel torn. How can I justify taking Clomid to have another baby, when it stops me from being the best mom to the son I have? But, how can I not do everything within my power to work at getting pregnant when it took so long to get there the first time?

Difficulty in Finding Support

Lost camaraderie and survivor's guilt around those with primary infertility

At one meeting, a woman experiencing secondary infertility told about her profound sense of isolation. She said, "I feel like the shunned of the shunned."

It's difficult when you feel isolated from those with whom you've connected and finally found support. If the people you've learned to rely on can no longer accept you as *one of them,* you need to start over in finding support.

Women with secondary infertility remember the pain when they talk to friends who are experiencing primary infertility. They may feel guilty for having a child. Their child can seem a barrier between them. They can feel that asking for another miracle makes them look greedy. They've already had their miracle. They may even feel guilty around women who have adopted a child if they were able to experience a birth.

Yet those with secondary infertility also feel a similar frustration as those with primary infertility when they see friends easily becoming pregnant again and again. Couples with secondary infertility can suffer when their reproductive ability evaporates. They know their body isn't working correctly. They still struggle through the same tests and treatments. They live with infertility every day.

Infertile couples need to support each other. Those with secondary infertility need to be ultra-sensitive to a childless couple's pain, always guarding their talk about their child. And childless couples need to realize the pain of not being able to conceive or carry a child can still be intense even when a child has been born. It takes special sensitivity on both sides, but both sides can support our infertile sisters.

Infertile couples need to support each other.

Lack of understanding from the fertile world

Most couples with secondary infertility find a total lack of understanding or compassion. The door to support seems firmly shut. Those with secondary infertility sometimes encounter a stigma attached to having an only child, an assumption of selfishness. This is the same stigma that can be directed to childless couples in families, churches, and cultures. Singleton children may be perceived as spoiled, lonely, or unhappy. Others may view the couple as not prioritizing children enough or being *too busy* to give their child a sibling, especially if the couple has not shared about their struggle to have another child.

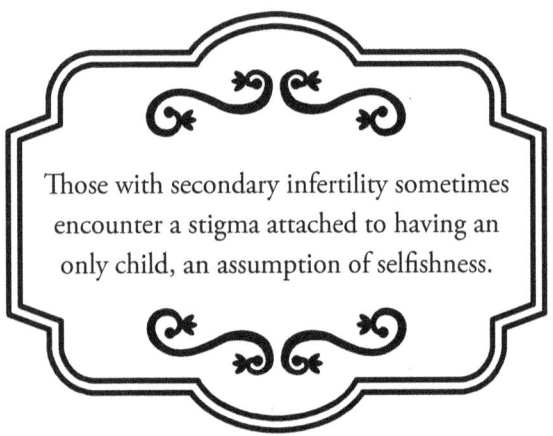

Those with secondary infertility sometimes encounter a stigma attached to having an only child, an assumption of selfishness.

Sara was dumbstruck at the response someone at work gave when she talked about her only child. Sara said:

> A woman I worked with but knew only casually, was waiting for me to finish at the copier. To make idle conversation, she asked, "You got any kids?"
>
> I answered, "Yes, one."
>
> She shook her head and replied, "Only one kid? ... Cheap, cheap, cheap!"

With primary infertility, couples may occasionally be offered sympathy, *I can see how it would be hard to have no children ... but have you thought of: taking a vacation? Eating black bananas? Or standing on your head?* While others may offer unhelpful options, if you look deeper, most times the desire to help is underneath.

With secondary infertility though, couples can receive the same type of intrusive questions only phrased differently. Instead of being asked, *when are you finally going to have children?* they're asked, *when are you finally going to give so-and-so a little brother or sister? Isn't it time? You don't want her growing up to be an only child, do you?*

If people realize the couple with one child is struggling to have another baby, the comments can immediately switch to, *but you already have a beautiful child. Aren't you thankful for the one you have?*

The problem with the lack of understanding from the fertile world is that since you have a child, you need to spend more time with these fertile people who might not understand your struggle. Your child wants to play with their children. You can't choose to retreat from the fertile world as you might while experiencing primary infertility. You're thrown into toddler play-groups or preschool where you're surrounded by women pregnant with their second, third, fourth, or more. They don't relate to the emotional and physical struggle you have in getting pregnant. They either forge ahead enlarging their families on schedule or worry more about not getting pregnant again.

Look for the compassionate exceptions though. I have a friend who wanted a large family, by today's standards, of five children. I could tell she deeply valued having children though she had no trouble conceiving. This friend has been able to empathize with me because she can't imagine what her life would be like without her children. She's been sensitive and supportive throughout my years of secondary infertility. I hope you'll find understanding friends like this as well.

Difficulty in finding others with secondary infertility
Sometimes the fear of how others will respond keeps those with secondary infertility silent. During a recent RESOLVE symposium, I sat on the grass during the lunch break with another woman. When I finally got up the nerve to mention the miracle of my son

after years of infertility, she exclaimed, "Oh, you have a child also? I haven't said anything about having my daughter all morning. I was afraid I was the only one, and I would alienate everyone."

Many women even feel guilty going to a doctor. Infertility specialist, Dr. David Adamson, sees this in his practice. "A lot of women say, 'I feel guilty about being here. I know so many other people deserve a child more because I already have one.'

I just say, "Count your blessings...but let's try to get another blessing."

Concerns about Having an Only Child

If you can't have a second child, you may share some of these concerns of parents with only children:

- You may worry about the many experiences and growth opportunities your child might miss without siblings.
- You may be concerned about your child's loneliness or lack of family connection to others throughout his or her life.
- You may fear your only child might die, leaving you childless again.
- You may be concerned about your only child having the sole burden of caring for you in your old age.
- You may be concerned your only child might be perceived as entitled, lonely, or lacking the best start in life.

Your Child's Reaction

Your child can also add to your frustration if they begin to ask for a sibling. Recently my heart broke when I heard Justin plead in his prayers at night, "Dear God, if it's all right with you, pleeeease let us have another baby."

When Justin is sad or says he wants a brother or sister like his friends, I try to validate his feelings of sadness. I also check my own actions, to make sure I haven't been overexposing him to my infertility trials. I try to share with him what I've learned about God loving us. I reassure him that God is in control and is our friend who can be closer than a brother. I reaffirm to him how happy we are that he was given to us by God.

I realize that maybe God will allow our son's loneliness as an only child to draw Justin to himself, as he has done with me through infertility. As with childlessness, the answer to contentment must be with our view of a caring God, the certainty of his love for us, and the knowledge that he's in control.

Some suggestions for enriching our child's life while they wait for a sibling:

- Work at helping our child create lasting friendships. Often friendships can last a lifetime, and friends can be as close as siblings.
- Provide opportunities for our child to take care of and teach younger children. This can expand his or her intellectual abilities and social development.
- Maintain our sense of perspective about rules and about being overly protective. We can ask ourselves, *what would I do if this child were one of five children?*
- Build our financial resources to ease any burden of caring for us financially when we're older.

Advantages of Another Time Around the Block

The greatest advantage of secondary infertility over primary infertility is obvious. You have a child. You're parents. Not being able to have another child emphasizes your amazement that you ever had a first child. Just as the Israelites set up stones for a memorial to remember when God answered their prayers, you have a living memorial of God's gift to you. Gratefulness has become part of your everyday life. The time spent waiting for your child made you more aware of cherishing every moment you have with them.

Being a Member of the Parent *Club*, If Only on the Fringe

With those experiencing secondary infertility, the gap can be smaller between you and fertile couples. If someone shares a birth story, you may be able to join in and discuss your memories.

The downside is that you'll still remember what it felt like to be excluded. During birth story discussions, I often feel torn. I want to participate, but also feel concerned for anyone present who might be infertile and could be distressed by the topic. It's weird to experience feelings of infertility while sharing a birth story.

Patience

Going through primary infertility may have helped you to develop a long-term view of treatment. Instead of your anticipation level being sky-high each month, you know the score and expect a long haul.

I learned to be more patient with my body's compromised reproductive system the second time around.

Knowledge

If you went through lengthy primary infertility, this time you may be a veteran. You may know the staff at the infertility specialist's office, the language and procedures, where to find a network of support, your way around medical computer searches, and some questions to ask. The process may be a little less intimidating and confusing because you've built up a base of knowledge.

Knowing God Better

God hasn't changed, but you may have. Perhaps during the first struggle, you wrestled through your questions with God. You found that God didn't turn away from you when you were angry, open, and honest. Pursuing God through the years of primary infertility may have helped you develop a deeper, abiding faith that is carrying you through this next time around.

Don't Miss the Good Stuff

The pain of secondary infertility is real. If secondary infertility came as a surprise, you may need to start at the beginning, grounding yourself in your worthiness to God, society, and your family just as you are. As you grieve, you can concentrate on remembering to watch for and thank God for past answers, and enjoying your child, while you face your new infertility struggles.

Sara discovered this one day. She said:

> I went to the Halloween parade at my daughter's school this morning. The kids were all so cute dressed in their costumes, but all I could feel was sadness. I realized my daughter was in the sixth grade, so this would be her last year in elementary school doing cute stuff like this. Next year she would take another step away from her childhood when she went to junior high school. I found myself crying all the way from her school back to work.
>
> At work, I finally realized I was ruining today because I was worrying about tomorrow. I was overwhelmed with sadness because I wondered if I would ever have another child to go through all these delightful stages with. Once I saw my thinking was ruining my time with my daughter, I asked God to help me live in today, delight in my daughter, and leave the future to him.

As Sara learned, our sorrow may not go away, but we can choose where to place the majority of our focus—whether on blessings or heartache. I used to think joy was the absence of sorrow, but now I've realized that they so often exist side-by-side.

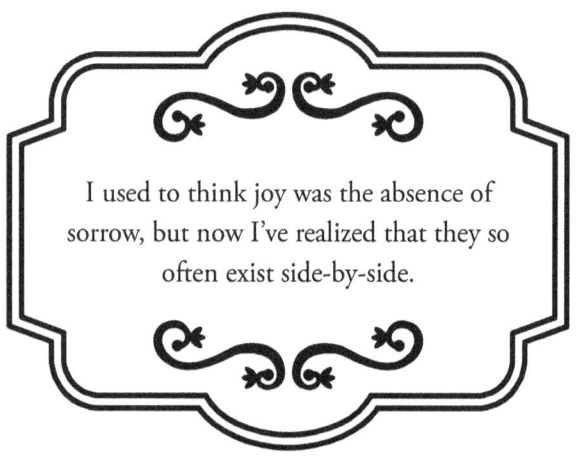

> I used to think joy was the absence of sorrow, but now I've realized that they so often exist side-by-side.

Your Personal Journey

For those dealing with secondary infertility:

1. Try to analyze your reasons for your *ideal* family size. What are the good things about a family that size? Are there other ways to achieve some of those good things?
2. What successes are you having in trying to balance the needs of your current child with having another child? What adjustments might you need to make to have more life balance right now?
3. If you feel guilty about trying to add another child to your family, what's the reason?
4. Have there been times during the excitement of your last pregnancy or while you're with your child that you've been insensitive to childless women? While experiencing second-

ary infertility, how can you choose to be sensitive to women experiencing primary infertility?

For those dealing with primary infertility:

1. Think about how you wish others would relate to your infertility. In what ways can you try to do the same as you relate to those experiencing secondary infertility?

Part VI

Is There Life Beyond Infertility?

18
Using Infertility to Benefit our Lives

Even though the fig trees have no blossoms,
and there are no grapes on the vines...
and the fields lie empty and barren...
yet I will rejoice in the Lord!
I will be joyful in the God of my salvation!
The Sovereign Lord is my strength!
—Habakkuk 3:17–19 NLT

I seldom think about my limitations,
and they never make me sad.
Perhaps there is just a touch of yearning at times,
but it is vague, like a breeze among flowers.
—Helen Keller [89]

Whether we eventually resolve our infertility through having a biological child, adopting a child, or choosing to remain a family of two, this arduous path to creating a family can offer us insights beyond our years. Even if we're still waiting for our infertility to resolve, if we've faced and processed our grief enough, we may eventually be ready to consider some of the silver linings that can surround the dark cloud of infertility. This chapter isn't meant to rush healing, so if you're not yet at this point, feel free to skip it and come back later.

Experiencing infertility and loss changes us. Everyone I've talked to about their infertility journey has said their struggle changed them. As Deanna shared, "We were devastated after losing our babies. Rich said he didn't think he'd ever be that naive again. I don't think I'll ever be the same either. This experience has changed us forever."

We may be changed in both positive and negative ways, so it's good to think about how we've changed. Part of rebuilding after the tsunami of infertility or loss can be inward—allowing God to work in us to restore us, so we can live meaningful lives, aligned with who we want to become. Another part of rebuilding can be outward—incorporating our new experience into our worldview to develop lives of deeper compassion for others. It would be a much greater loss if after surviving nearly unendurable circumstances, we didn't eventually wrestle something positive from the experience.

Part of rebuilding can be outward—incorporating our new experience into our worldview to develop lives of deeper compassion for others.

Recovering Our Balance

How do we know when we're starting to recover and beginning to move on? With most people. this change comes gradually. We may discover when we're listening to someone share their deep pain of infertility, we recognize we're no longer at that same lowest point. While we still may have times of intense sorrow, perhaps the sorrow no longer feels all-consuming or the main focus of our life most of the time. Maybe we find ourselves laughing or singing occasionally as we used to do.

Our tunnel vision starts to widen. We look for and begin to notice God's answers in other circumstances in our lives. We have more energy to concentrate on changing the things we can—improving our jobs, enjoying time with our spouse, and participating in things that bring us joy. And we find the ability to connect with other people again, including fertile couples, friends, and family. Circumstances may not change, but our world enlarges a bit. When these changes begin, we know we've started to recover from the trauma of infertility.

For me, I knew I was regaining my balance when the tenderness of God's love broke through the darkness of my grief.

Cycle of Grief

Discovering our growth and important insights about infertility doesn't erase our need to grieve. We first need to grieve our losses. That's a given. We will know we're beginning to heal when we experience joy in other areas at the same time as our sad feelings about infertility. Eventually, more positive feelings will grow to become the norm again, but this doesn't mean we never feel sad at the thought of not having a child or at having lost our child.

Vicky found that while her pain was slowly replaced with other positive feelings, the sorrow of not being able to create life still returned on occasion. She said, "I've learned all these great things, but even after twelve years, I still find myself crying in church sometimes." The sorrow stops being all-pervasive, but it's normal for the pain or loss to occasionally return.

Getting Stuck

Though processing deep grief can take an enormous amount of energy, at times it may almost feel safer than the unknown of moving beyond it. Maybe we've found a deeper connection with others who grieve. If our grieving helped our relationships grow deeper because we learned to share on a deeper level, we may enjoy the new dimension that came from learning to share from deep heart places. We might fear if we move beyond our grief, our relationships could return to their previous more surface-level sharing.

Grief also carries with it the potential for getting stuck in areas such as our inability to get past our resentment toward God. When we ignore grief or anger and use them as excuses not to grow, bitterness can get a foothold in our lives. If this happens, bitterness can open the door to destructive behaviors in our lives.

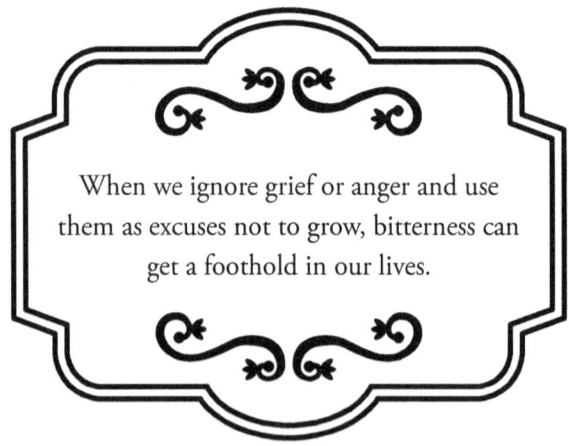

When we ignore grief or anger and use them as excuses not to grow, bitterness can get a foothold in our lives.

Getting unstuck may require a deliberate, conscious effort to refocus on grieving well. We can ask God to guide and change us.

"God I want to *want* a better relationship with you," is a simple prayer that can start the process of allowing God to work in our hearts. If the problem is between us and God, we can spend time reading about who he is in the Bible and talking with others who know him well. We can give ourselves permission to talk with him honestly and listen to his loving heart in prayer.

If you find after a time, you're unable to move past your grief to feel times of joy, look for someone to talk to who can help. This can be a safe caring friend, a care group, a pastor, or a professional Christian counselor.

Learning from Grief

It's an audacious question, but can we look for positive changes from the trauma of infertility or having a child die? Sometimes the silver lining hides for quite a while, but we can still keep our eyes open for it so we don't miss it when it shows up. After many years, here are a few I found.

Realizing What's Important

When we're dealing with issues of life and death, we gain perspective on the rest of life's problems. Many things we used to worry about, we now recognize as less important.

For instance, Rich found he's become less anxious about small problems. "I'm much calmer about things now. I don't get worked up and pull my hair out as quickly as I did before."

Developing Compassion for Others Who Grieve or Are on the Fringes

Many Christians have experienced the feeling of being misunderstood or in the minority when our spiritual beliefs separate us from most in our culture. Being infertile can add another layer to feeling alone because now we're different from most in the Christian community too. But being different often encourages us to analyze and think deeply about life rather than simply going along with the crowd. This can give us a new sense of who we are and what it means to please God over pleasing others.

In the best of all worlds hurting people would come to church, share their hurt, and find loving understanding. But the Church is made of imperfect people. We don't all have the same experiences, so it takes a major effort to try to understand life situations we haven't experienced ourselves. Those with infertility can now consciously connect their own experience of being different and feeling misunderstood to empathize with others who feel different too.

Because we've experienced grief, we're better able to relate to others who are grieving. We're often less afraid to be around those who are grieving. We understand better how to talk with them or just sit with them.

April recognized how her understanding had grown when she was able to feel more compassion for people who experienced loss as well as compassion for herself. She said, "One of the things I lacked as I was growing up was compassion for myself as a child. Through losing my babies and the major struggles we've had starting a business, I've gained a measure of compassion for others and myself that I wasn't able to feel before."

Dave discovered a similar change in himself. He shared, "I used to be impatient with people who struggled with tough circumstances. My basic attitude was 'get over it.' I'm much more patient and feel more empathy for their trials now, even when I don't completely understand them."

Developing Gratitude

It may seem backward but when we lower the bar of our expectations, we often recognize many gifts we and others around us have taken for granted every day. We live life more fully and gratefully because we recognize all of life is a gift, and each blessing in that life is a gift.

After facing the uncertainty of life head-on, we can begin to appreciate more deeply the preciousness of life. This can give us a renewed energy for life and at the same time raise our awareness when others take life for granted. Against the background of knowing tomorrow isn't promised to any of us, while others only recognize that they got what they expected, we recognize more miracles and blessings from God.

Finding Renewed Hope

We may even find our life purpose has been awakened through our struggle. Our values can be refined. We may now recognize more clearly who we want to become.

I remember coming out of my depression after my miscarriage and beginning to really see the world again. As if a fog cleared from my eyes, that spring I was amazed at all the varied shades of green, the vibrant blooming flowers, the brilliant blue of the sky, and the caring people in my life. I was used to accepting certain blessings and people in my life as normal. But after experiencing deep loss, I suddenly recognized these blessings as gifts!

I saw many things again as if for the first time. Some that I'd become calloused to, like the kind touch of a hand, could now move me to tears. Because I'd lost my child, I no longer took the lives of the people around me for granted. I saw each person's life around me as a miracle. I thanked God for clearing away my sense of entitlement to these blessings, creating beauty for our enjoyment, my health and life, and my friends' healthy babies.

Developing Strength to Handle Adversity

We may feel new strength when we realize we've faced one of the deepest fears in almost every culture. And we survived. We can feel a sense of resilience in recovering from a crippling blow. If we've survived the intense pain of infertility or losing a baby, we know we can handle just about anything else. We've gained some tools to cope with catastrophe.

This doesn't mean we won't grieve again, but we recognize a hope and confidence in ourselves that we've found the inner strength to recover from the grief.

Deepening our Relationship with God

Infertility often removes our ability to remain on a surface level with God or ignore him. While others might say they've never thought about how God fits into their lives, those with infertility most likely have at least thought about God by this point. Our simplistic ideas of who God is or what he should be doing are certainly challenged. Similar to the expression *there are no atheists in foxholes*, one hidden gift within the trauma of infertility can be that we've been forced to shed some of the shallowness of an unexamined life.

If we've chosen to investigate, to wrestle with God, to trust our heartache and questions to him, we've been given a chance to develop a stronger, clearer relationship with God. We've been invited to try and test our relationship through our suffering. Hopefully, we're beginning to understand better that God's love doesn't depend on circumstances.

Deep struggles can uncover some of the structures we've propped ourselves up and have been leaning on are counterfeit. When the tsunami of infertility hits, rotten supports are often swept away, allowing us to see God and what matters more clearly. Often, we're better able to separate biblical truth from cultural expectations. God promises that when we're honest with him about our anger, confusion, and hurt, he will draw near to us. We often start to reap benefits from this new, deeper relationship with God.

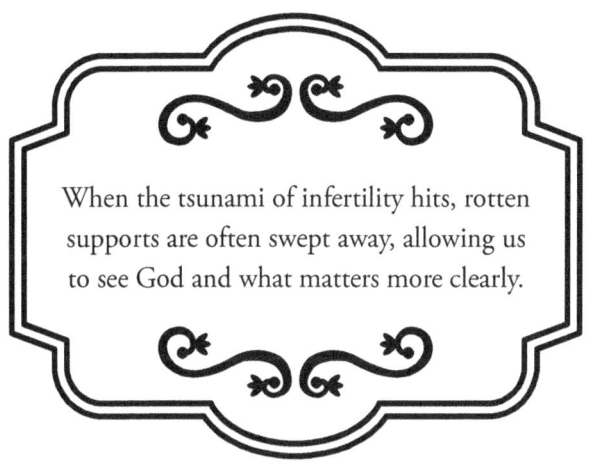

When the tsunami of infertility hits, rotten supports are often swept away, allowing us to see God and what matters more clearly.

A significant part of this richer relationship is the understanding that God is in control and worthy of our trust. Sadly, many people don't recognize this truth and believe they're in control. While some deceive themselves into thinking they're in control until much later in their lives, infertile couples run smack into the concrete truth much earlier than most that God alone is in control. The truth of God's control can initially be scary until it's balanced with his compassionate love. When God's love is embraced as well, God's control can bring comfort and security.

When I stopped feeling responsible for causing every good or bad event that happened to me, I understood infertility wasn't directed against me because of something I'd done. This freed me to recognize with amazement other good, undeserved things that were also being given to me. I experienced the reality of grace.

Strengthening the Relationship with Your Spouse

Many couples have found infertility has helped them learn more about each other too.

Paul and Sara learned how to communicate and love each other better. "At first I didn't want to involve Paul in going through tests and treatments, because I felt the infertility was my issue," said Sara. "I didn't want to bother him or mess up his life. Now I wish I would have included him more."

And Paul responded by saying:

> Once I asked Sara if she wanted me to be there when she went in for surgery. She looked shocked that I would suggest such a thing. I think she was trying not to make a big deal out of it, but being more involved would have helped me too. I had no clue about what was going on.

As with all stressors, how we respond to them can help determine whether we develop a deeper relationship with our spouse. In the same way that surviving hard life issues invites us to deepen our spiritual life, these issues can also invite us into a deeper marriage relationship.

Developing more Honesty in Relationships with Family and Friends

Infertility can also help develop stronger relationships with friends or family. April found it opened up a channel to communicate on a deeper level. She shared:

> The miscarriages have given my mom and me a forum to express sadness. The first time I saw her cry was when I told her I was having my fourth miscarriage. I had only received about three hugs from her in twelve years, but now she hugs me every time I see her.

When we share with our fertile friends or family, some of them don't understand. Others though, will sit and cry with us, hug us, and want to understand. They tell us they can't imagine what going through this is like for us and ask us to share. They choose to grow through our pain too.

Maybe they've had their own pain-filled journey in a different area that we can relate to as well. There's something about sharing with other safe people while in crisis and pain that can develop strong bonds. We expose deep, vulnerable parts of ourselves that we normally keep hidden.

This deep sense of connection can also apply to new infertile friends we meet. Infertile friends who walk beside us on this journey can often become lifelong sisters. I've met some of the wisest, most loving, and nurturing people on this journey. If I'd been given the choice to avoid this very tough path, I wouldn't have had the privilege to connect with many of them. I'm so grateful I've had the chance to get to know amazing people as we've supported each other through traumatic events.

If we notice a positive change, and we want to keep that we've learned through our grief, we can name it and choose to carry it into other areas of our lives. For instance, if we've developed deeper family relationships or friendships, we can voice our hope that we'll continue to share more meaningful issues with the friends who've helped us walk through grief. This can solidify our intentions to keep the positive changes in those relationships. It can also give the other person permission to continue to go deeper in conversations with us.

It may take us years to name some of the good things we've discovered through our grief, so don't feel bad if you can't identify anything good at first.

Recognizing Our Identity as Separate from Any of Our Life Roles

When I first started actively trying for children, I felt my life would become meaningless if I wasn't a mother. My identity had become wrapped up in the role of motherhood. I saw motherhood as my life's purpose and my destiny. Struggling with infertility helped me separate my identity from the different roles I might have in life, such as motherhood.

Our identities never change— each of us is first and foremost, a beloved child of God, made to love and be loved by him. We will probably have many roles in our lives that will change depending on the season though. Our identity, our core connection to God, will never change. Though circumstances may still shake our lives, no circumstances and no one, (or lack of anyone), can touch the truth that our lives have meaning since God created us with worth. Because of God's connection and acceptance, we can make life decisions from a new place of strength and security in our relationship with him.

Discovering New Purpose and Goals

Even when we're not ready to decide to stop trying for a child, we can open ourselves up to additional goals when we stop pinning *all* our hopes on having a biological child. We can ask ourselves:

- What are some sacrifices I've made, things I valued but gave up, or dreams I've put on hold while trying to have a child?
- Do I want to continue putting the same emotional, physical, and financial resources toward having a baby?
- Would I like to take a different direction in my career?
- Are the sacrifices I'm making still worthwhile to me?
- What new dreams might I want to incorporate into my future plans?

God knows what we yearn for deep down within our hearts whether we reveal it to him in words or not. When we ignore deep longings inside us, we may be the one who misses out. God may have planted those very yearnings to motivate us, though sometimes we need to stay open to them being fulfilled in new ways.

I used to think if I found any fulfillment outside of motherhood, God might see I was happy and would think I no longer wanted or needed a baby. (What a twisted view of God I had back then.) Once I realized God's love for me, I knew he was for me, wanted what was best for me, and wouldn't base decisions for my future on a manipulative game.

When I became open to other longings that might also be part of who God made me to be, he began to open doors for me to write. Writing became something I loved. It fulfilled me in a different way than mothering could. It became another way to nurture others and give deeper meaning to my life.

Everyone has gifts to help touch hurting people, to show God's love, or to bring encouragement to those who struggle. When we realize we're valuable to God and the world, we can begin to look for the gifts God has placed in each of us. God didn't make a mistake. Like Esther, perhaps we were created for such a time as this (Esther 4:14).

Your Personal Journey

1. How has infertility changed you?
2. Do you feel you've begun to regain your balance or are you still in the depths of struggling? If you've lost your joy during this struggle, what signs have you noticed or will you look for that your joy might be returning?
3. What important goals have you put on hold while pursuing a pregnancy? Are there any you'd like to pursue again?
4. Are you glimpsing some life beyond your infertility or loss? Do you still want to pursue a pregnancy? Or are you beginning to lean toward some other possibilities such as adoption or moving on as a family of two?

19

Embracing a Family of Two— Choosing to Lay Down the Burden

> *God saw all that he had made, and it was very good.*
> *Genesis 1:31 NIV*

> *When God created Adam and Eve,*
> *he called this family of two "very good"*
> *long before they became parents.*
> *—Jennifer Saake[90]*

> *Love is like a beautiful flower which I may not touch,*
> *but whose fragrance makes the garden a place of delight just the same.*
> *—Helen Keller[91]*

You may come to the point sooner or later when you've had enough of living in limbo or you've run into a firmly closed door to parenting. You may decide that continuing to pursue having a baby has become too draining with its distractions, expenses, emotional and physical pain of invasive medical procedures, and monthly cycles of grieving.

Perhaps you've tried unsuccessfully to adopt and concluded that adoption isn't for you whether because of the cost, your age, health problems, family dynamics, or other personal factors. Or you may have encountered too many closed doors, so have accepted that the door to children just isn't going to open for you. Whether you're confronted by the reality that you'll never have children or you decide to put an end to your time spent waiting, you find the freedom to accept or even embrace life without raising children. Whatever the reason, you've begun to feel a readiness to move on.

Hopefully, you've come to understand that in the bigger picture, having children is a part of life, not life itself. Along with this, you're also recognizing that you are deeply loved by God regardless of your parenting status. Your life with or without children still has incredible worth and meaning. So, you choose to lay down the burden of infertility and choose to refocus your energy. You wonder about a life without children. What would that look like? What meaningful life opportunities and goals might a life without children hold?

The decision to choose to be a *childfree* family of two is often made over time. Through prayer and circumstances, you feel drawn to remain a family of two. So you investigate what that might look like and try the thought on to see how it fits.

Grieving Clears the Way to Something New

You may need to start anew at this point, looking at yourself, what you value, and other longings stirring in your heart. This may seem a daunting task, but it will be worthwhile. Begin to notice how doing different activities make you feel. What gives you joy or a sense of *this is what I was created for*. What makes you tick? What do you find fulfilling?

The process of grieving often helps you begin to clarify who you are and what really matters to you. Maybe through processing your infertility grief, you've already started examining and becoming more deeply aware of your other values and longings besides parenthood. If so, you may not need to start from scratch now. You may have gotten clues to other life goals you want to pursue.

If you choose to close the door to having children, you can trust God is calling you to something equally valuable instead.

Redefining Our Family

Couples who choose to remain without children after infertility often use the term *childfree*. This term isn't used to demean children, but to emphasize that couples aren't lacking if they don't have children. They are free to choose a different route than parenthood and should also be free from criticism for making this choice.

Sandra Glahn writes about this option to redefine our sense of family in *When Empty Arms Become a Heavy Burden*:

> Having the freedom to make a choice affects our viewpoint. That's why it's important, at some point, to make a conscious decision to live without children rather than to passively feel victimized for the rest of your life. If you want a child, there are usually ways around the obstacles. If you don't plan to adopt after ending medical treatment, consider making an active point-in-time choice to be childless rather than coasting along in indecision and uncertainty forever....
>
> Most couples who have actively chosen this option prefer to call themselves *childfree* rather than *childless*. Childfree emphasizes wholeness, fulfillment, and completeness rather than the absence of something. Viewing one's self as

having moved from the first label to the latter is actually a moment of resolution.[92]

If someone asks, "When are you going to start a family?" your new answer can be, "We are a family." Identifying yourselves as a family of two also builds a sense of camaraderie rather than separatism between couples with children and those without. Whatever term you use, your value to God and society doesn't depend on whether or not you have children.

In my long journey with infertility, I've found that infertile women are some of the most loving, compassionate people I know. They have so much love to share and want to express that love in a fulfilling way. If at some point, they choose to stop trying for children, that doesn't suddenly change them into self-centered or uncaring people.

God values you regardless of whether or not you conceive or raise a family. Just as some didn't understand your struggle to have children, some may not understand a decision to give up the pursuit of children. The key is to keep in close communication with God. When you understand your worth as an individual to him and listen for his loving voice of truth above all others, it will be easier to gently educate those who don't understand your choice.

Freeing Our Hands for the New Thing God Wants to Place in Them

Even though the pain may have lessened and you've found some peace and contentment in quitting the struggle, you may still experience moments of longing. After five years on the infertility journey, Sara chose to stop pursuing a baby. She shared:

> I feel as if I've graduated from my support group. I didn't have a hoped-for pregnancy, but I've moved on. I knew I

was finally getting past the pain when we recently had a baby dedication at church. When I heard it was going to happen, I automatically started putting up the usual defenses. Then I realized I didn't need them. It doesn't hurt like that anymore.

Giving up the pursuit of a baby has been like giving up a boyfriend who I realized isn't right for me. At times, parts of him are still appealing, but the whole is not. At first, I found it hard to change my focus because my pursuit of that goal had been so intense. When I chose to stop all medical treatment though, that was a real relief. It's taken more processing for me to give up the big idea of having children at all, but I can see a great future.

What About Motherhood Being the Highest Calling for a Christian Woman?

It took me a while to look past the Bible stories that ended in miraculous children to see many other biblical stories of God-honoring lives that didn't include children. The Bible doesn't teach that the role of motherhood is a woman's highest calling. That's a cultural teaching. Motherhood is one role women take on, but our highest calling as women lies solely in our relationship with God. We're called to allow ourselves to be loved by God, love God fully in return, then allow that love to overflow to others. This can play out in many different roles.

Sandra Glahn writes in *When Empty Arms Become a Heavy Burden* about some of the misperceptions of childlessness in our culture:

> Is a childfree choice a selfish one? Some would say so, and the answer here is that it can be. So can a life of parenting. Selfishness is revealed not in the number or lack of children

but in the lifestyle.... Is childfree a valid option? Of course. Is it biblical? Certainly. The Bible is filled with people who lived full lives without biological children—Jesus being one of them.[93]

I hope this offers a sense of freedom to choose other biblical characters as role models when figuring out new life plans after infertility. For instance, Vicky Love points to some of these great life role models in her book, *Childless Is Not Less*. These individuals had the freedom without children to participate in many fulfilling adventures, including building the early church. She writes:

> What a glad relief came to my own heart to realize that I had been patterning my longing for life after the wrong model. For years everyone tried to encourage us…, commenting: "Remember Sarah. Don't ever give up hope." or "Why don't you adopt?"
> There never were any adequate answers. I now realize that those of us who are childfree do not have to become Abrahams and Sarahs. There are Pauls, Johns, and Annas, Mary-Martha-and-Lazaruses, and there are Priscillas and Aquilas in God's ample and varied pattern book.[94]

Watching for Benefits

There are benefits to living without children. A friend whose beloved husband died told me that part of her grieving process has been learning to focus on some good things in her life in this new season as a widow. Sometimes, she's had to think hard to find a positive to her situation because the negatives come much more easily. So, she's started keeping a written list. She listed that she doesn't need to buy toilet paper as often, she has the freedom to sleep and wake when she wants, and she can now cook more of what she prefers to eat, etc. The purpose of her list is not to take away the sadness of losing her husband but it's helping her to remember to look for positive things she currently has in this season of her life.

Some benefits those who decide to live as a family of two after infertility have mentioned:

- the need to examine their lives to find their God-given purpose can lead to pursuing that purpose wholeheartedly,
- more freedom to go back to school or make a highly satisfying career move,
- more time to spend on fulfilling causes, such as volunteering for community or church roles,
- more creativity to invest in artistic expressions, such as exploring writing, painting, or music,
- more energy to pursue a meaningful career without guilt,
- more ability to act spontaneously,
- more freedom to make less money, and
- more time and energy to invest in relationships with their spouse, extended family, and friends.

Focusing on how you're fertile in other areas
Closing the door on having children may prompt you to question what you'll fill your time with that will be meaningful and lasting. Or the transition may feel similar to a transition from working to retiring (especially if the medical treatments you're stopping took as many hours as a part-time job).

It can be hard to give up your infertile identity and stop trying to become parents because the pursuit can be so intense. After making the decision, you may need to find new goals to fill that hole and redirect your life. Prayer is an important part of this as well as discovering your gifts. Talk to your mate, good friends, counselor, women's ministry leader, or pastor. Ask what gifts they see in you.

Set a goal and outline specific steps to develop one or more of those gifts.

Part of Sara's decision to stop pursuing a baby was combined with the desire for a new goal. She said:

> I've started setting long-range goals and other plans that don't involve children but include parenting qualities like nurturing, creativity, etc. That sort of evolved. I decided I want to become a teacher. I'm going to go back to school to get a teaching credential.

Make an inventory of everything you like to do. List some farfetched and realistic dreams too. Put a star next to the activities for which you have gifts or skills. From these lists, develop some specific goals that sound possible. Start small to experiment. Instead of deciding to sign up for a new full-time degree program, start with a single class. This can allow you to try out something new before fully committing to it.

Spend some time remembering what used to make you happy before you started trying for a baby. What did you dream of doing? What made life worthwhile? What made it fun? What first attracted you to your mate? What did you like to do together? You may decide you can fulfill some of these interests in your life by means other than having children.

Embracing Your Nurturing Heart

Choosing not to parent doesn't mean you need to give up your desire to nurture. You can mentor others in business, arts, Bible study, or any other area. Many vocations are nurturing, such as the medical profession, teaching, counseling, chaplaincy, or coaching. Because of your struggles through infertility or loss, you may be uniquely suited to assist with your church's care ministry, such as Soul Care or Stephen Ministry.

Or you may be ready to nurture children, allowing them back into your life in a new, purposeful way. This can be a meaningful path to influence the next generation. You can choose to mentor college students or provide respite care for foster parents. You might teach children, run a daycare center, or embrace the role of an important aunt, uncle, or godparent. You can choose to impact a child's life by becoming a Big Brother/Big Sister or a CASA (Court Appointed Special Advocate) to help children in foster care navigate the court system.

Deciding to find fulfillment in new areas other than your own children can transform events that have always been painful. Caring for all of God's children and investing in the next generation can become a step to honor the way you still value children.

You can also nurture a child on a formal or informal basis, finding a child who is interested in something you do well, then passing on your knowledge or talents. You can mentor or tutor a child in learning another language, playing a musical instrument, coaching sports, or cooking. One of my friends is using the internet to teach a new generation how to cook.

During the years we weren't able to have a child, our desire to nurture motivated us to sponsor a young boy named Pau from Burma through Compassion International. Writing letters to Pau, continuing to get pictures as he grew, and nurture him in small ways like buying him glasses when he needed them, helped fill our yearning to nurture a child and pour into the next generation.

When Kayla was able to look away from her infertility toward a new direction, she wanted to honor her value of nurturing others. She said:

> I learned I wasn't going to die if I didn't have kids. It wouldn't be what I wanted, but God was in it. Having a ministry to other women has made me realize I could do some good and have a good future. It's been important to

me that I found something nurturing to do because that was a big part of what drew me toward wanting to be a parent.

A Future with Meaning and Purpose

At some point, almost everyone will need to refocus their lives from a season with children as the focal point. Having and raising young children is the focus of only one of life's seasons. You may simply experience this transition away from child-centeredness earlier than others. It can help to look for role models you admire who are living full lives without children. Also, consider talking to older women who've successfully transitioned to a new life focus after their children grew up and left home.

It takes time to develop new patterns of thinking and behaviors. You can learn to nurture yourself and others as you look for the joy God has planned for you. You will find the unique and good purpose he crafted for you before you were born. Because your life has been planned by a loving God, you can be certain you will find hope and meaning beyond children, and that God's good plan will be something that fits you.

God cares about your future and promises he has good plans for you, plans for delight, fulfillment, and productivity, plans for your highest calling. Here are two promises to hold onto while watching with anticipation for how God will lovingly lead each of you toward a new life of abundance and fulfillment:

> *You satisfy my every desire with good things.*
> *Psalm 103:5 TPT*

> *Watch closely: I am preparing something new;*
> *it's happening now, even as I speak,*
> *and you're about to see it.*

I am preparing a way through the desert;
Waters will flow where there had been none.
Isaiah 43:19 VOICE

Your Personal Journey

1. What gifts do you feel God has given you? This is key, so if you don't know, start to investigate this. Your identity in Christ and your value as an individual are so much more important than your role as a parent. Take a spiritual gifts, personality, or occupational assessment. Ask others who know you about gifts they see in you.
2. List five activities that were meaningful to you before you started trying to have a child. What brought you joy? Would you like to pursue some of those again?
3. Did you have any adults in your life, besides your parents, who positively influenced you? What role did they play in your life? Would you find it fulfilling to play that role in a child's or an adult's life? What concrete steps would you need to take to pursue that?
4. Can you think of other ways to fulfill some of your goals beyond having children?
5. What are three practical steps you can take to begin to develop your gifts?

Epilogue

When I finished the first version of this book years ago, I didn't know if we'd ever be able to have a second biological child, if God would allow us to adopt a child, or if something else would fulfill this desire for another child. At that point, we'd been told our chance of getting pregnant again was about .05 percent per cycle. While I knew God could perform a miracle, I also knew statistics often reflect how God generally chooses to work. What I chose to trust is that God would walk me through whatever the future held and that he was acting out of his love for me.

The promise I chose to hold onto and found great comfort in wasn't a promise for a baby, but a promise that God would not let me live a barren, empty life if I followed him:

> Jesus said,
> "I came to give life with joy and abundance."
> —John 10:10 VOICE

Second Edition Update

As the 2nd edition of this book goes to print, I'll share a bit more of the story. The journey to complete our hoped-for family of three children took seventeen long years. But it did finally happen. The arduous struggle included a total of seven unique and loved babies who I miscarried. It also included five adoption commitments to babies that came with deep heart and financial investments, but each was thwarted at different stages.

Meanwhile, the desire for the children we felt were missing from our family wouldn't go away.

As I wrote in chapter 13, our journey through primary infertility ended after almost seven years with the birth of our first biological child. Little did we know it would take ten more years after that for us to complete our family.

It wasn't until our first child was ten years old that we were able to complete the adoption of our baby girl from China. I believe God knew we were supposed to adopt our particular daughter from China, so he kept the longing alive and strong until we were able to complete the process of bringing her home that year in June.

Two months later, in August, I gave birth to our second birth son, who survived a difficult and miraculous pregnancy.

It was the summer of long-awaited and adored babies! The children who were meant to be in our family had finally arrived, and we were so grateful.

But spending seventeen years in this infertility journey has made a permanent impact on my life. My long and arduous years on this path make me feel instantly connected to others going through infertility or loss during pregnancy. It also fills me with compassion for those still trying to create their family.

I have been praying specifically that God would bless each of you reading this book with the child or children you desire. And I pray your journey won't be as long as mine! Even more, I'll continue to pray you'll feel the hand of God supporting you, loving you, and drawing you to him in comfort as you work through your journey to create a family.

I leave you with this prayer Paul prayed for his fellow Christians. No matter what the future brings, know God's intense love for you as a beloved child in his family will make the journey more bearable. I pray this for each of you readers:

> When I think of the wisdom and scope of his plan I fall down on my knees and pray to the Father of all the great

family of God—some of them already in heaven and some down here on earth—that out of his glorious, unlimited resources he will give you the mighty inner strengthening of his Holy Spirit. And I pray that Christ will be more and more at home in your hearts, living within you as you trust in him. May your roots go down deep into the soil of God's marvelous love; and may you be able to feel and understand, as all God's children should, how long, how wide, how deep, and how high his love really is; and to experience this love for yourselves, though it is so great that you will never see the end of it or fully know or understand it. And so at last you will be filled up with God himself (Ephesians 3:14–19).

More information is available at: AchingforaChild.com:

- Printable List of ART Questions to Ask Your Doctor
- Printable List of Embryo Questions to Ask Your Doctor
- Resources for Further Reading, Viewing, Listening, and Connecting
- Information on Starting or Joining a Care Group
- Glossary of Terms

To contact Deb for speaking engagements, email: speaking@achingforachild.com.

Connect with Deb here:
Website: AchingforaChild.com
Facebook: facebook.com/AchingforaChild
Instagram: instagram.com/AchingforaChild
Twitter: twitter.com/AchingforaChild

GLOSSARY

abortion—The medical term for the loss of a baby during pregnancy, whether by a spontaneous miscarriage or a deliberately induced termination of the pregnancy before the fetus can survive outside the uterus.

    complete—A pregnancy loss in which the fetus, placenta, etc. are completely expelled from the uterus.

    habitual—Spontaneous miscarriages occurring in three or more successive pregnancies.

    incomplete—a pregnancy loss in which part of the fetus or placenta, etc. remain in the uterus.

    induced—the intentional termination of a pregnancy.

    inevitable—A potential pregnancy loss that can no longer be prevented.

    missed—an embryo or fetus who has died, but remains in the uterus.

    spontaneous—a miscarriage before the twentieth week of gestation.

    threatened—Vaginal spotting and bleeding during pregnancy that may or may not result in a miscarriage.

AID, AIH—See artificial insemination.

anovulation—The absence of ovulation. This can occur even when menstrual periods are regular.

artificial insemination—A process in which sperm is placed into a woman's vagina or uterus by a medical procedure at the time of ovulation. Either the husband's sperm, Artificial Insemination by Husband (AIH), or a donor's sperm, Artificial Insemination by Donor (AID), or Donor Insemination (DI) may be used. When the washed sperm is placed into the woman's uterus, the process is called intrauterine insemination (IUI).

Assisted Reproductive Technology (ART)—A variety of high-tech procedures used to assist reproduction, such as In Vitro Fertilization (IVF), Gamete Intrafallopian Transfer (GIFT), and Zygote Intrafallopian Transfer (ZIFT).

basal body temperature (BBT) chart—A chart for graphing a woman's temperature throughout her menstrual cycle to verify and estimate the time of ovulation. (Search *basal fertility chart* or *basal fertility app* for sample charts or apps to track your BBT.)

Bromocriptine (Parlodel)—A drug used to suppress elevated prolactin hormone levels.

cervical mucus—Secretions of the cervix that aid in transporting and filtering sperm.

cervix—The narrow neck of the uterus that protrudes from the uterus into the vagina.

chemical (or biochemical) pregnancy—An early pregnancy only confirmed by a blood or urine test.

cilia—The minute, hair-like projections lining the insides of the fallopian tubes that propel the egg from the ovary toward the uterus.

clinical pregnancy—A pregnancy that has been confirmed by seeing evidence of the fetus in the uterus during an ultrasound exam.

clomiphene citrate (Clomid or Serophene)—A synthetic hormone drug often prescribed to induce ovulation.

conception—See fertilization.

corpus luteum—The collapsed follicle on the ovary that produces progesterone and estrogen after ovulation.

cryopreservation—The process of freezing and storing sperm, eggs, and embryos in liquid nitrogen in a frozen state.

Danazol (Danocrine)—A synthetic drug used to treat endometriosis.

diethylstilbestrol (DES)— A synthetic estrogen compound that was given to some pregnant women to prevent miscarriage. When the children of these women grew up, several were found to have abnormalities of the reproductive organs.

dilation and curettage (D&C)—Stretching open the cervix to scrape the interior walls of the uterus.

donor insemination (DI)—See artificial insemination.

ectopic pregnancy—A pregnancy that implants outside the uterus, usually in the fallopian tubes.

egg donor—A woman who donates her egg(s) (ova) to an infertile couple.

ejaculate—Seminal fluid (usually containing sperm) discharged through the urethra during male climax.

embryo—The developing baby from fertilization through the eighth week of pregnancy.

embryo donation—The transfer of an embryo (created through IVF) into a woman who has no biological connection to the embryo.

embryo transfer—The placing of an embryo that was fertilized in the laboratory into a woman's uterus.

endometrial biopsy—A procedure in which a physician scrapes or suctions a small portion of the lining of the uterus, then evaluates the ability of the lining to hold and nurture a fertilized egg.

endometriosis—A condition in which the endometrial tissue spreads outside of the uterus and implants in various locations in the pelvic cavity, where it can cause scarring, pain, damage to the reproductive organs, and is thought to contribute to infertility.

endometrium—The mucus membrane lining of the uterus that changes through the menstrual cycle to nurture an embryo if fertilization occurs.

epididymis—The duct behind the testes that stores sperm before it passes from the testes to the penis through the vas deferens.

fallopian tubes—The tubes attached to the upper ends of the uterus that serve as a passageway for the egg to travel from the ovary to the uterus.

fertilization—The union of egg and sperm, also called conception.

fetus—The developing baby, from nine weeks after fertilization until birth.

fimbriae—The fringelike endings of the fallopian tubes close to the ovaries that capture the egg as it is released from the ovary.

follicle-stimulating hormone (FSH)—A hormone released by the pituitary gland that stimulates the growth of follicles in the ovary or stimulates sperm production in the testes. Used alone in drug form (Metrodin) or in combination with LH (Pergonal) to induce ovulation.

gametes—Eggs or sperm.

gamete intrafallopian transfer (GIFT)—A procedure in which eggs are retrieved, then placed with washed sperm in a syringe and immediately transferred into one or both of the fallopian tubes in the hope that fertilization will occur in the tubes.

gonadotropins—The hormones FSH and LH that stimulate the ovaries to produce eggs or the testicles to produce sperm.

GnRH analogs (Lupron or Synarel)—A synthetic drug used to block the body's production of FSH and LH. They can be used to enhance a woman's response to fertility drugs or to treat fibroids or endometriosis.

hCG—See human chorionic gonadotropin.

hMG—See human menopausal gonadotropin.

HSG—See hysterosalpingogram.

human chorionic gonadotropin (hCG)—A hormone produced by the implanting embryo or placenta during pregnancy. It is also a drug used in combination with hMG or clomiphene to trigger ovulation.

human menopausal gonadotropin (hMG) (Pergonal)—A natural hormone drug used to induce ovulation, derived from the urine of postmenopausal women.

hysterosalpingogram (HSG)—A test in which dye is injected into the uterus and the fallopian tubes, then x-rays are taken to check the shape of the uterus and that the tubes are patent (open).

hysteroscopy—A direct visual examination of the cervix and the interior of the uterus using an endoscope (a narrow telescope).

immunologic infertility—The decreased ability of sperm to fertilize an egg due to antibodies (produced by a husband or wife) that attach themselves to the sperm.

infertility—The inability to conceive within one year of unprotected intercourse, or the inability to carry a child to live birth.

intrauterine insemination (IUI)—See artificial insemination.

in vitro fertilization (IVF)—A procedure in which eggs that are removed from the wife's ovaries and sperm that are collected from the husband are placed together in a petri dish and incubated to await fertilization. If the eggs are fertilized, the developing embryos are placed back into the mother's uterus two to three days after fertilization.

IUI—See artificial insemination.

laparoscopy—A minor surgery using a laparoscope (a narrow telescope) to view the outside of a woman's reproductive organs through a small incision in her abdomen. It may also be used to place sperm and eggs into a woman's fallopian tubes during a GIFT procedure.

laparotomy—A major surgery in which the abdomen is opened with an incision. The operation is performed under direct vision.

LH—See luteinizing hormone.

luteal phase defect—A shortened second half of the menstrual cycle (the time between ovulation and the beginning of menstruation) or an inadequate progesterone production during this time.

luteinizing hormone (LH)—A hormone produced by the pituitary gland that stimulates the ovary to release the mature egg, stimulates the secretion of estrogen, and the formation of the corpus luteum. It also stimulates testosterone production in males.

micromanipulation—A procedure (that is used to assist with severe sperm dysfunction) that creates a tiny opening in the outer covering of the egg to assist sperm penetration.

miscarriage—The spontaneous death of a baby, most often in the first trimester. (Also see *abortion*.)

morphology—The shape of sperm cells.

motility—The sperm's ability to move forward.

mycoplasma—A microorganism found in the female cervix or male urethra that may contribute to infertility or miscarriage problems.

oligospermia—A persistently low sperm count.

oligo-ovulation—Infrequent ovulation.

oocyte—An egg or ovum.

oocyte retrieval—A procedure to collect egg(s) from a woman's ovaries, usually done by inserting a long needle through the vagina.

ovaries—The female reproductive organs in which eggs are formed, then released. These also produce estrogen and progesterone.

ovulation—The discharge of one or more eggs from an ovary.

ovulation induction—The use of hormones to stimulate the ovaries to develop and release eggs.

ovum—A mature egg cell.

pelvic inflammatory disease (PID)—An infection that can cause scarring in the reproductive organs, particularly in the fallopian tubes. PIDs can contribute to infertility.

pregnancy reduction (selective termination)—An intentional abortion of one or more fetuses in cases of multiple pregnancy, by injecting a chemical substance into the fetus.

secondary infertility—The inability to conceive or give birth to a child after having carried at least one pregnancy to term.

semen—The fluid discharged at ejaculation that contains sperm and seminal fluids.

semen analysis—An analysis of a sample of semen under a microscope to estimate sperm count, motility, morphology, and other characteristics.

sonogram—See ultrasound.

sperm—The male germ cell that enters an egg in sexual reproduction to produce a new individual.

sperm antibodies—A protective substance produced by a man or woman's immune system that is directed against sperm.

sperm bank—A facility that stores frozen donor sperm.

sperm count—An estimate of the total number of sperm in an ejaculate.

sperm donor—A man who donates sperm to an infertile couple.

sperm washing—A technique that separates sperm from seminal fluid and concentrates the sperm best able to fertilize an egg.

Spinnbarkheit test—A test to estimate when ovulation is occurring by analyzing the *stretchability* of cervical mucus.

sterility—Permanent inability to produce the genetic material required to conceive a child.

stillbirth—The death of a baby in utero or during delivery during the third trimester of pregnancy.

superovulation—The stimulation of the ovary with fertility drugs to develop more than one egg.

surrogate mother—A woman who offers to carry a child for an infertile couple. She may have no genetic contribution to the child (gestational surrogate) or she may contribute the egg.

tubal patency—An open (fallopian) tube.

ultrasound—A procedure that bounces sound waves off the body to produce an image on a screen, often used to evaluate ovarian activity or pregnancy.

unexplained infertility (also idiopathic infertility)—A term used for infertile couples when no organic problem can be detected in either partner.

uterus—The hollow muscular organ in a woman's pelvis in which fertilized eggs normally embed that nourishes the fetus until birth.

varicocele—A varicose vein of the testicle that raises the temperature of the scrotum and has been associated with lowered sperm count and motility.

zygote—A single-cell embryo before it first begins to divide.

zygote intrafallopian transfer (ZIFT)—A procedure that transfers a zygote to the fallopian tube before it divides.

otes

1. National Institutes of Health. 2/8/18. How Common is Infertility? Accessed March 23, 2020. https://www.nichd.nih.gov/health/topics/infertility/conditioninfo/common.
2. World Health Organization. Infertility definitions and terminology. Accessed Sept. 6, 2021. https://www.who.int/health-topics/infertility#tab=tab_1.
3. "God's Greatest Gift": © Gibson Greetings, Inc. Reprinted with permission of Gibson Greetings, Inc. Cincinnati Ohio 45237. All Rights Reserved.
4. Ibid.
5. Resolve National Fertility Organization. "Tracking My Fertile Time." Accessed March 29, 2020. https://resolve.org/infertility-101/the-female-body/tracking-my-fertile-time/.
6. Jeffrey Ecker, MD. 9/24/15 "Treating unexplained infertility: Answers still needed." *Harvard Health Publishing*. Harvard Medical School. Accessed March 29, 2020. https://www.health.harvard.edu/blog/treating-unexplained-infertility-answers-still-needed-201509248340.
7. Resolve National Fertility Organization. Professional Services Directory. Accessed March 29, 2020. https://resolve.org/support/professional-services-directory/.
8. "World Health Organization reference values for human semen characteristics." 2010. *Human Reproduction Update*. 16:3, 231-245. Accessed March 29, 2020. https://www.who.int/reproductivehealth/topics/infertility/cooper_et_al_hru.pdf.
9. Thomas Stowitski, et al. 2006. "The human endometrium as a fertility-determining factor." *Human Reproduction Update*. Volume

12:5: 617-630. Accessed April 13, 2020. https://academic.oup.com/humupd/article/12/5/617/781305.
10. Aniket Kulkarni, et al. 2013. "Fertility Treatments and Multiple Births in the United States." *New England Journal of Medicine.* 369:2218-2225. https://www.nejm.org/doi/full/10.1056/NEJMoa1301467.
11. "Progesterone and Pregnancy: A Vital Connection." Resolve: The National Infertility Association. Accessed April 13, 2020. https://resolve.org/infertility-101/the-female-body/progesterone-pregnancy-vital-connection/.
12. Guan, Hai-Yun, et. al. 2018. "Induction of ovulation with clomiphene citrate combined with bromocriptine in polycystic ovary syndrome patients with infertility: A prospective, randomized, and controlled clinical trial." *Reproductive and Developmental Medicine.* Accessed Sept. 6, 2021. https://doaj.org/article/b83370ec6a6b4ac69f1fda0457b3da21.
13. C.J. Glueck, N. Goldberg, et. al. 2004. "Height, weight, and motor—social development during the first 19 months of life in 126 infants born to 109 mothers with polycystic ovary syndrome who conceived on and continued metformin through pregnancy." *Human Reproduction.* Vol. 19:6. June:1323-1330. Accessed Apr. 10, 2020. https://academic.oup.com/humrep/article/19/6/1323/2356628
14. Marmar, Joel. 2019. Varicocele and Male Infertility. *Springer.* Cham. 3-16.
15. Clark NA, et. al. 2013. A systematic review of the evidence for complementary and alternative medicine in infertility. *Int J Gynaecol Obstet.*;122(3):202-206. Accessed Jun. 8, 2020. https://obgyn.onlinelibrary.wiley.com/doi/abs/10.1016/j.ijgo.2013.03.032
16. Peterson, Andrew. 2019. *Adorning the Dark.* B&H Publishing Group. 14. Kindle Edition.
17. Manuel Velazquez. 1994. *Philosophy: A Text with Readings.* 5th ed. Belmont, California: Wadsworth Publishing Co. 427.
18. Tomlinson, M.J., et. al. 2012. "Assessment and Validation of Nonspermicidal Condoms as Specimen Collection Sheaths for Semen Analysis and Assisted Conception." *Human Fertility.* Vol. 15. https://www.tandfonline.com/doi/full/10.3109/14647273.2012.718100 .
19. Zavos, PM. 1985. "Characteristics of Human Ejaculates Collected via Masturbation and a New Silastic Seminal Collection Device (SDC)." *Fertility and Sterility.* Vol. 43: 491. https://doi.org/10.1016/S0015-0282(16)48457-8.

20 Amann, Rupert. 2009. "Considerations in Evaluating Human Spermatogenesis on the Basis of Total Sperm per Ejaculate." *Journal of Andrology.* 30:6, 626-641. https://doi.org/10.2164/jandrol.108.006817.
21 Zavos, PM, and J.C. Goodpasture. 1989. "Clinical Improvements of Specific Seminal Deficiencies via Intercourse with a Seminal Collection Device versus Masturbation." *Fertility and Sterility.* Vol. 51: 190–193. https://doi.org/10.1016/s0015-0282(16)60455-7.
22 To find special condoms to use for sperm testing or ART treatments, search online for "semen collection condom for fertility."
23 "Brain activity in sex addiction mirrors that of drug addiction." July 11, 2014. *University of Cambridge Research News.* https://www.cam.ac.uk/research/news/brain-activity-in-sex-addiction-mirrors-that-of-drug-addiction.
24 "Your Brain on Porn" *End Sexual Exploitation.* Accessed Jun. 8, 2020. https://www.yourbrainonporn.com/relevant-research-and-articles-about-the-studies/porn-use-sex-addiction-studies/cambridge-university-brain-scans-find-evidence-consistent-with-addiction/experiment-that-convinced-me-online-porn-is-the-most-pernicious-threat-facing-children-today-by-ex-lads-mag-editor-martin-daubney/
25 "How Porn Damages Consumers' Sex Lives." *Fight the New Drug.* Accessed June 8, 2020. https://fightthenewdrug.org/how-porn-damages-consumers-sex-lives/#c7.
26 Ibid.
27 Park, B.Y., et. al. 2016. "Is Internet Pornography Causing Sexual Dysfunctions? A Review with Clinical Reports." *Behav. Sci.* 6, 17. Accessed June 9, 2020. https://www.mdpi.com/2076-328X/6/3/17#cite.
28 "How Porn Damages Consumers' Sex Lives." iME Movement. Accessed 6/22/2021: https://www.imemovement.co.za/wp-content/uploads/2018/09/PORN-THE-HARMFULL-EFFECTS-ON-THE-HEART.pdf
29 Wooding, Dan. 2016. "Josh McDowell says porn epidemic sweeping the church." *God Reports.* Accessed June 8, 2020. https://www.godreports.com/2016/01/josh-mcdowell-says-porn-epidemic-sweeping-the-church/.
30 Layden, Mary Anne, Ph.D. "Talking Points: Pornography and Relationship damage Research." *National Center on Sexual Exploitation.*

Accessed June 9, 2020. https://pornharmsresearch.com/2013/12/talking-points-pornography-and-relationship-damage-research/.
31 Ibid.
32 Layden, Mary Anne, Ph.D. "Talking Points: Porn & Sexual Violence Research." *National Center on Sexual Exploitation*. Accessed June 9, 2020. https://pornharmsresearch.com/2013/12/talking-points-porn-sexual-violence-research/.
33 Donald L. Hilton Jr. 2013. "Pornography addiction – a supranormal stimulus considered in the context of neuroplasticity." *Socioaffective Neuroscience & Psychology*. 3:1. Accessed Sept. 6, 2021. https://www.tandfonline.com/doi/full/10.3402/snp.v3i0.20767.
34 Wolf, Naomi. 10/9/2003. "The Porn Myth." *New York*. https://nymag.com/nymetro/news/trends/n_9437/.
35 "Talking Points: Porn & Trafficking." *National Center on Sexual Exploitation*. Accessed Jun. 8, 2020. https://pornharmsresearch.com/2011/04/trafficking/.
36 McDowell, Josh. 2019. "The Porn Epidemic." *Josh McDowell Ministry*. https://www.josh.org/resources/apologetics/research/.
37 Zsolt Peter Nagy, Daniel Shapiro, Ching-Chien Chang. 2020. "Vitrification of the human embryo: a more efficient and safer in vitro fertilization treatment." *Fertility and Sterility*. Vol. 113, Iss. 2, 241-247. https://doi.org/10.1016/j.fertnstert.2019.12.009.
38 John Jefferson Davis. 1985. *Evangelical Ethics*. Phillipsburg, New Jersey: Presbyterian and Reformed Publishing Co. 73. Used by permission.
39 Annette Baran and Reuben Pannor. 1989. *Lethal Secrets*. New York: Warner Books. 37. Used by permission.
40 "George Moore: The Bending of the Bough IV." 1968. *Dictionary of Quotations*. ed. Bergen Evans. New York: Delacorte Press. 103.
41 Aniket Kulkarni. et al. 2013. "Fertility Treatments and Multiple Births in the United States." *New England Journal of Medicine*; 369:2218-2225. https://www.nejm.org/doi/full/10.1056/NEJMoa1301467
42 Personal correspondence with Dr. Tolonoy. 2016.
43 Several couples/families have documented their decision-making journey with extra frozen embryos on blogs. Search for "leftover frozen embryos." See also: https://beautifulpiecesofus.com/our-story/.

44 Lawrenz, Barbara. 2020. "The ART of frozen embryo transfer: back to nature." *Gynecological Endocrinology*. Mar. https://doi.org/10.1080/09513590.2020.1740918.
45 Abha Maheshwari, et. al. 2018. Is frozen embryo transfer better for mothers and babies? Can cumulative meta-analysis provide a definitive answer? *Human Reproduction Update*. Vol. 24, Iss. 1, January-February 35–58. https://doi.org/10.1093/humupd/dmx031
46 Wyatte Grantham-Philips. 2020. "'Changed our lives': Tennessee baby born from 27-year-old frozen embryo breaks record" *USA Today*. https://www.usatoday.com/story/news/nation/2020/12/01/tn-family-grows-embryo-adoption-baby-born-27-year-old-embryo/3784459001/.
47 John Stott. 1985. *Involvement: Social and Sexual Relationships in the Modern World*. Old Tappan, New Jersey: Fleming H. Revell. 194.
48 Search online for "embryo adoption clinics." Or the Embryo Adoption Awareness Center had a good list at: https://embryoadoption.org/embryo-adoption/where-to-find-embryos/embryo-adoption-agencies.
49 Strege, John. 2020. *A Snowflake Named Hannah: Ethics, Faith, and the first Adoption of a Frozen Embryo*. Grand Rapids, MI: Kregel Publications.
50 Ruth Harmes Calkin. 1974. "Ten to One." *Tell Me Again, Lord, I Forget*. Wheaton, IL: Tyndale House Publishers. ©. 84. Used by permission of Tyndale House Publishers. All rights reserved.
51 Philip Yancey. 1988. *Disappointment with God*. Grand Rapids: Zondervan Publishing House. 34, 37. Used by permission.
52 Dr. James Dobson. 11/21/91. Excerpt from "Focus on the Family" radio program. Colorado Springs, Colorado: Focus on the Family. Used by permission of Focus on the Family.
53 Glahn, Sandra and William R Cutrer, M.D. 2004. *The Infertility Companion: Hope and Help for Couples Facing Infertility*. Grand Rapids, MI: Zondervan. 13. Used by permission.
54 Ray S. Anderson. 1987. "God Bless the Children—and the Childless." *Christianity Today*. Aug 7. 28. Used by permission of *Christianity Today*.
55 Gary Vanderet. 1990. "Dealing with Discontent." Palo Alto, California: *Discovery Publishing*. #794. Used by permission.
56 Author unknown. 1991. *Stepping Stones*. Feb.-March.

57 Robert Nachtigall, MD, and Elizabeth Mehren. 1991. *Overcoming Infertility.* New York: Doubleday. 172.
58 Deborah Tannen. 1990. *You Just Don't Understand: Women and Men in Conversation.* New York: William Morrow and Company. 24–25.
59 Billett, Paulina & Anne-Maree Sawyer. 2019. "Infertility and Intimacy in an Online Community." *Partnering the Infertile: The Impact of Infertility on Women's Spousal Relationships.* New York: Macmillan.
60 Greil, Arthur, et. al. 3/22/17. "Relationship Satisfaction Among Infertile Couples: Implications of Gender and Self-Identification." *Journal of Family Issues.* https://doi.org/10.1177%2F0192513X17699027.
61 Peter Fagan, PhD, et al. 1986. "Sexual Functioning and Psychologic Evaluation of In Vitro Fertilization Couples." *Fertility and Sterility.* 46:4:668. Oct.
62 John Snarey. 1988. "Men Without Children." *Psychology Today.* March: 61–62.
63 Gary Vanderet. 1990. "Cultivating Intimacy in Marriage." Palo Alto, California: *Discovery Papers.* Used by permission.
64 Jack Hayford. 2003. *I'll Hold You in Heaven.* Hollywood, California: Hayford, Jack. 11.
65 Lamb and Leurgans. 1979. "Does Adoption Affect Subsequent Fertility?" *American Journal of Obstetrics and Gynecology* Vol.. 134:138–144.
66 Used by permission.
67 Philip Yancey. 11/20/91. Excerpt from "Focus on the Family" radio program. Colorado Springs, Colorado: Focus on the Family. Used by permission.
68 Ray S. Anderson. 1987. "God Bless the Children—and the Childless." *Christianity Today.* Aug 7. 28. Used by permission of *Christianity Today.*
69 Ellen Sarasohn Glazer. 1990. *The Long-Awaited Stork: A Guide to Parenting after Infertility* Lexington, Mass.: Lexington Books. 13. Used by permission.
70 Boz, Ilkay, et al. 2018. "Becoming a Mother after Infertility: A Theoretical Analysis." *ProQuest.* 2, 10:4:496-511. Accessed Sept. 6, 2021. http://www.cappsy.org/archives/vol10/no4/cap_10_04_08_en.pdf.
71 Palomba, S. Homburg, *et al.* 2016. "Risk of adverse pregnancy and perinatal outcomes after high technology infertility treatment: a

comprehensive systematic review." *Reprod Biol Endocrinol.* 14, 76. https://doi.org/10.1186/s12958-016-0211-8.
72 Margaret B. Spiess. 1991. "Teddy Bears." *Cries from the Heart.* Grand Rapids: Baker Book House. 34.
73 "Multiple Miscarriage." RESOLVE: National Fertility Organization. Accessed May 15, 2020. https://resolve.org/infertility-101/medical-conditions/multiple-miscarriage/.
74 Stefan Semchyshyn, MD, and Carol Coleman. 1990. *How to Prevent Miscarriage.* New York: Collier Books. 1990. 40–41.
75 Abdelazim, Ibrahim, et. al. 2017. "Miscarriage Definitions, Causes and Management: Review of Literature." *ARC Journal of Gynecology and Obstetrics.* 2, No. 3, 20-31. http://dx.doi.org/10.20431/2456-0561.0203005.
76 Ibid.
77 Freidenfelds, Lara. 2020. *The Myth of the Perfect Pregnancy: A History of Miscarriage in America.* New York: Oxford University Press. 2.
78 Bob Deits. 1992. *Life after Loss,* rev. ed. Tucson, Arizona: Fisher Books. 6. Used by permission.
79 Wayne Watson. 1990. "Home Free." Waco, Texas: Word Music. All rights reserved. Used by permission.
80 One organization that takes professional remembrance photos of the baby and gives the portraits to the family for free is based in Denver, but accepts applications from the United States of America, Canada, Ireland, United Kingdom, Germany, Switzerland, South Africa, Singapore, Australia, and New Zealand. Find them at https://www.nowilaymedowntosleep.org/ .
81 Rana Limbo and Sara Wheeler. 1998. *When a Baby Dies: A Handbook for Healing and Helping.* La Crosse, WI: Bereavement Services.
82 Helen Keller. 1992. *The Last Word: A Treasury of Women's Quotes* by Carolyn Warner. Englewood Cliffs, NJ: Prentice-Hall. 39.
83 Tim Malcolm. 1993. "Real Women." *Stepping Stones.* 4.
84 *Your Next Baby.* Centering Corp. https://centering.org/your-next-baby/.
85 Marty Heiberg. 1992. "Another Christmas Morning." *Loving Arms.* Winter. 4.
86 Gay Becker. 1990. *Healing the Infertile Family.* New York: Bantam Books. 13. Used by permission.
87 Cohain, J.S., Buxbaum, R.E. & Mankuta, D. 2017. Spontaneous first trimester miscarriage rates per woman among parous women with 1

or more pregnancies of 24 weeks or more. *BMC Pregnancy Childbirth.* 17, 437. https://doi.org/10.1186/s12884-017-1620-1.
88 Bob Deits, *Life after Loss*, rev. ed. 65–66.
89 Ibid. 261.
90 Jennifer Saake. 2005. *Hannah's Hope: Seeking God's Heart in the Midst of Infertility.* NavPress. Kindle Edition.
91 Helen Keller. 1992. *The Last Word: A Treasury of Women's Quotes.* Englewood Cliffs, NJ: Prentice-Hall Direct. 204.
92 Glahn, Sandra. 2016. *When Empty Arms Become a Heavy Burden.* Kregel Publications. 218-220. Kindle Edition. Used by permission.
93 Ibid. 221-222. Used by permission.
94 Vicky Love. 1984. *Childless Is Not Less*. Minneapolis, MN: Bethany House. 180.

www.ingramcontent.com/pod-product-compliance
Lightning Source LLC
Chambersburg PA
CBHW032146080426
42735CB00008B/600